BJ1251.C65 1985

0 0068 08092367 9

Clouse, Bonnie/Moral development :pers
Whitworth College Library

W9-CSQ-781

Moral Development

DISCARD

Moral
Development

Perspectives in Psychology and Christian Belief

Bonnidell Clouse

BAKER BOOK HOUSE
Grand Rapids, Michigan 49506

Copyright 1985 by
Baker Book House Company

ISBN: 0-8010-2506-0

Library of Congress
Catalog Card Number: 85-71174

Unless otherwise indicated, Scripture references are taken from New
International Version © 1978 by New York International Bible Society;
those marked TEV are taken from Today's English Version © 1966, 1971,
1976 by American Bible Society.

Printed in the United States of America

To **Robert**
for his love and encouragement
and
to our sons, **Gary** and **Ken**

Psalm 1

Blessed is the man
    who does not walk in the counsel of the wicked
or stand in the way of sinners
    or sit in the seat of mockers.
But his delight is in the law of the Lord,
    and on his law he meditates day and night.
He is like a tree planted by streams of water,
    which yields its fruit in season
and whose leaf does not wither.
    Whatsoever he does prospers.

Not so the wicked!
    They are like chaff
    that the wind blows away.
Therefore the wicked will not stand in the judgment,
    nor sinners in the assembly of the righteous.

For the Lord watches over the way of the righteous,
    but the way of the wicked will perish. (NIV)

Contents

6. A Theological Approach: *Morality as
   Godliness*   299

1

Introduction

The argument has been made that there is more good in the world than evil. We misunderstand the human condition because we fasten on the worst rather than the best in others. We are more interested in the bizarre than in the beautiful, in violence than in peace, in calamity than in tranquility. Few people would read a newspaper that featured meekness, temperance, love, and brotherhood. Nor would they watch a newscast that centered on nations at peace, organizations that help the needy, and communities with sound schools and intact families. The media caters to our interest in the unusual by reporting the murders, the rapes, and the robberies; by picturing a nasty confrontation between labor and management; and by featuring wars and other acts of aggression throughout the world.

To be sure, the human fascination with evil that appears normative in peoples everywhere may keep us from giving the proper weight to the good. Greater attention could be given to the many individuals and groups that make the world a better place in which to live; and our lives would be enriched if we followed the scriptural injunction to think on those things that are pure and lovely and admi-

rable (Phil. 4:8). Nevertheless, we know that a little evil
goes a long way. Even as "a little leaven leaveneth the
whole lump" (1 Cor. 5:6 kjv), one murder or one rape or
one robbery may adversely affect an entire community.
One unresolved confrontation between labor and management may result in hundreds losing their jobs. One war
may mean that thousands will lose their lives. The news
media serves as a constant reminder that all is not well
in our world; there are social cancers eating into the very
heart of the culture and threatening its survival. We live
in a world that needs to be changed, a world that needs
to be turned upside down, a world that desperately needs
to be moral. The good may or may not outweigh the bad,
but the bad permeates the whole society and must not be
left unchallenged.

The problem of evil is not unique to our times. In every
culture and in every age, societies have had to cope with
selfishness and hate, avarice and greed, deception and
wanton destruction. And in every culture concerned citizens have spoken out against the immorality of their day,
calling for repentance or for punishment or for the training
of the young or for whatever they thought would make a
difference. The questions we grapple with today have been
asked by parents and teachers and religious leaders and
philosophers for centuries, each generation having to cope
with them anew. Morality is so closely tied to the very
fabric of the social order that if society is to remain all in
one piece there must be ways of dealing with the problem
of evil.

The social difficulties, however, are indicative of a more
deep-seated problem, namely that of what people are like
within themselves. C. S. Lewis (1960) developed this
thought in *Mere Christianity* when he wrote that morality is concerned with three things: "Firstly, with fair play
and harmony between individuals. Secondly, with what
might be called tidying up or harmonising the things inside each individual. Thirdly, with the general purpose of

human life as a whole: what man was made for" (p. 71). The first has to do with relations between one person and another, the second with what a person is like within the self, and the third with how the person relates to the Power that made him. Lewis noted that most people think of morality as encompassing only the first of these, that of interpersonal relationships. They say that as long as no one else is hurt it does not matter what they do. But the first cannot be separated from the second, nor the second from the third. Fair play and harmony between individuals is not possible unless individuals are right within themselves and unless they understand who they are in relation to the One who created them.

Lewis likened morality to a fleet of ships sailing in formation. First, all ships must be in the proper position. It simply will not do for one ship to go off on its own or to turn into another ship, crippling them both. Second, each ship must be in good operating condition; all parts must be functional. Third, the purpose of the voyage must be known. Why are the ships sailing? What is their destination? Lewis graphically illustrates how the first condition is dependent on the second:

> What is the good of telling the ships how to steer so as to avoid collisions if, in fact, they are such crazy old tubs that they cannot be steered at all? What is the good of drawing up, on paper, rules for social behavior, if we know that, in fact, our greed, cowardice, ill temper, and self-conceit are going to prevent us from keeping them? . . . Without good men you cannot have a good society. (p. 72)

But how do we get "good men"? This second condition is dependent on the third. Unless people understand the purpose of life, unless they are aware of their destination, they will not know when the parts within them (mind and will and emotions) are in good working order. This third aspect of morality is considered even less by secular writers than is the second. "It is in dealing with the third that the main differences between Christian and non-Christian morality come out" (Lewis, 1960, p. 73). It is only the believer in Christ who understands the true reason for humanity's existence. It is only the Christian who is aware of the destination of the human race. The written Word of God provides a guide for how one is to relate to others, and the living Word provides the power to keep the parts within oneself in good working order.

The Imperative for Involvement

Within the past twenty years there has been a considerable increase in both theoretical statements and research investigations on the subject of morality. Events in recent history have undoubtedly contributed to this interest. The disgrace of Watergate, the horror of Jonestown, and the terror of assassinations have shocked the nation into wondering what can be done to prevent such tragedies in the future. We see progress being made in medicine and technology, but little advance in moral sensitivity. Shoddy workmanship, domestic violence, people afraid to leave their homes after dark, and the ever-present possibility of nuclear annihilation compounds the problem and makes us wonder if, in fact, we may be going backward rather than forward in our striving for moral development.

The approach some people take to this gloomy picture is to say that little can be done. Methods have been tried before and programs developed with scant return for the effort expended. The best we can do is to protect ourselves and those closest to us. We will look to the interests of our family, our friends, our church, and the immediate community. We will teach our children right from wrong, attend the church of our choice, and live in a neighborhood where safety is assured and where our children will develop friendships with other children who come from similar types of homes. If these areas of life are beyond our influence, we will attend a different church, put our children in a private school, put another lock on our door, or move to a better neighborhood.

Although the primary responsibility of parents is to their own children—primary in the sense that it provides the children with their first contact with others and primary also in the sense that the influence occurs during the most important, or critical years,—it is important that the imperative for involvement extend beyond one's own family and even beyond one's own church or school or community. This is not to imply that we put ourselves or our children needlessly in danger, but it does mean that we should concern ourselves with people we may not know and may never meet. There are good reasons for helping them as well as ourselves. In the first place, we cannot isolate ourselves from the rest of the society. We may buy some time by changing schools or neighborhoods, but we cannot separate our lives from others indefinitely. Their misery becomes our misery, their frustrations and needs, our frustrations and needs. We will have to pay for their care if they are unemployed, their incarceration if they run afoul of the law; and if they steal from us or hurt us in other ways, we will become less trusting and less psychologically healthy than before the encounter. A second reason, less self-centered than the first, is that we should realize that all people are made in the image of God and are loved by him. As such they have value whether rich or poor, attractive or unattractive, intelligent or dull, moral or immoral. We may have more advantages, more integrity, more ability to organize our lives, but we are not better in the sense of having greater worth (Acts 10:34). Our advantage translates, not to pride or even to benevolence, but to a genuine caring for other people. Our integrity means being decent and fair even with those who are not decent and fair with us, and our ability mandates greater responsibility to help those who cannot manage their own lives.

This does not mean, of course, that we can do it all. The task is great, and perhaps none of us will make more than a dent in the cause for goodness. But that is a start and definitely to be preferred to making no impression at all, and together we can do a great deal. We can review methods that have been used in the past to see how effective or ineffective they appear to be. We can study programs currently being used and note the results. We can become involved socially, politically, and educationally to help wherever we see a need.

Churches have had an enviable record of helping people develop morally. Furthermore, the teachings of Christian churches include all three aspects of morality: how one should relate to others, what one should be like within the self, and how one is to relate to the Power who made him. Many churches have followed the Great Commission to go into all the world and preach the gospel, a gospel that will equip a person "for every good work" (2 Tm. 3:17). They have begun in "Jerusalem" with church buses fanning out into surrounding neighborhoods, continued into "Judea" and "Samaria" with the establishment of new congregations, and extended their influence "to the ends of the earth" (Acts 1:8) by sending missionaries abroad.

Few would disagree that the major responsibility for moral training lies with the home and with the church. But some children are not taught by their parents, and some children do not attend church. Although parents today may be as desirous for their children to develop morally as were their parents before them, many have less time with their children because both parents may work outside the home. Even when everyone is home, the television often usurps the time that otherwise would be spent in conversation. Churches continue to teach right from wrong, but even those children who attend regularly, spend only a small fraction of their time in the place of worship compared to the time spent with other influences. It is obvious that another source of instruction must be found, and the logical choice is the school. All children attend school regardless of the type of home from which they come and regardless of whether they frequent church services. Thus, the school has added to other responsibilities formerly assumed by parents—that of the moral education of the young.

The extent to which the school has accepted the challenge is indicated by the fact that the *Moral Education Forum*, a journal devoted to information about experimental programs and curricula in moral education, each year lists dozens of new books and hundreds of new articles on the topic. A wealth of ideas is available for educators who wish to pursue either a unit on morality or to incorporate exercises and discussions on moral issues as an integral part of other aspects of the curriculum.

The imperative for involvement is to each of us—as parents, as church leaders, and as teachers. We must look for ways in the home, the church, and the school to enhance moral development, and we must extend our influence to an ever-expanding segment of the population.

The Question

It is generally recognized that young children are unable on their own to understand what is right and what is wrong and therefore are in need of instruction or encouragement in order to become moral persons. The agreement as to the amoral condition of the infant is in contrast to the variety of views as to humankind's original state. Some people accept the Lockean idea of the *tabula rasa*, or blank slate, which holds that children are born neither good nor bad but become whatever the environment engraves upon them. Others take a view much like that of Rousseau who believed that children are inherently good and, like the "noble savage," must have the opportunity to realize their potential in an unrestrictive environment. Still others adopt a position similar to that of Christian theology, maintaining that children are born in sin and therefore are in need of salvation. But whatever the view taken, all agree that infants are unaware of their state and consequently are amoral, knowing neither good nor evil.

The question, then, facing parents, educators, and church leaders is *How does the amoral infant become capable of morality?* What is the process by which the child proceeds from the amoral to the moral? What methods or techniques may be used by parents, teachers, and pastors to foster moral development? Are some methods better than others? If so, which ones? The questions may be stated in a number of ways, but they are components, nevertheless, of a basic inquiry into the developmental process by which children go from the age of innocence to the age of accountability, from a time when they know neither good nor evil to a time when they understand what is right and what is wrong and choose to take the right way. Seeking answers to these questions has prompted numerous conversations, curricular changes within the schools, workshops for teachers, counseling sessions for parents, sermons by ministers, and a myriad of articles by those wishing to share their research and disseminate their views.

The Answer

Traditional Approaches

The most widely used approach to the question of how the amoral infant becomes capable of morality is that of *character education.* Character education is a direct method in which adults tell children what they should and should not do, and children are taught to behave accordingly. There are rules to be learned, and obedience is important. Character education goes with the common sense idea that training in such habits as cleanliness, obedience, care of property, truthfulness, and dependability is important to a child's development. Children are instructed in these virtues and given rewards for compliance and punishment for infractions. Children at school, for example, are not to run in the halls, hit other children, or play in the restroom. They are to do the assigned work, tell the truth, and be moderately quiet. This monitoring of the child's actions as a way of teaching morality is used daily by both parents and teachers and is based on the universally accepted premise that adults know better than children what is proper. Directions and guidelines are essential for both the development of the young person and for the smooth functioning of the home or the school.

The term *character education* has been used by some writers to include not only the overt or behavioral components of morality, but also the internalized desire on the part of the child for what is right and good. Nevertheless, the method chosen is almost always didactic in nature, and the child's behavior is directly supervised. Dubbed a "bag of virtues" by some psychologists who say that morality cannot be learned at the "facts" level as one would learn the ABCs, character education still remains a popular technique (Goble & Brooks, 1983). A perusal of the literature shows that educational programs adopted by Christian day schools are heavily weighted in favor of the character education approach.

Another answer to the question is that of *social adjustment.* The social adjustment approach became popular after the First World War when the mood of America began to change and opposition arose to using a direct method to teach moral principles. Part of this was a healthful criticism of some techniques used, such as frightening a child into being good or administering harsh physical discipline. Part came as a result of studies showing that children who were enrolled in character education classes, Boy Scouts, or Sunday school were not more likely to be honest in the classroom than those without these advantages (Hartshorne & May, 1928–1930). Also, the thirties, forties, and early fifties were a time of optimism, based on a philosophy of social evolution that perceived people as getting better and better; so it seemed that specific training was not needed to promote moral growth. During this period the main thrust in education, other than teaching the necessary skills of reading, writing, and ciphering, was to promote social adjustment. If children could get along with peers, teachers, and family, they would develop into adults who would be good neighbors and respected citizens, and they would be a credit to themselves and to their country. A preponderance of such well-adjusted adults would assure the kind of democratic living so highly prized.

The social adjustment approach is still highly regarded, and most individuals in our society if asked what morality is would include getting along with others as a principal element. Almost all programs in moral development included social adjustment, and parents today, as parents have done in the past, encourage their children to get along with siblings, peers, and adults as a necessary condition for being a good person.

Respect for authority is yet another answer to the question. Deferring to those who have jurisdiction over us and doing what they tell us to do has long been considered a moral trait. "Honor your father and your mother" (Ex. 20:12) is the first commandment with promise, the promise being the continuance of life itself. Respect for one's Maker (Is. 17:7), payment of tribute to Caesar (Mt. 22:21), and submission to the governing authorities (Rom. 13:1) and to those who are older (1 Pt. 5:5) are commanded in Holy Scripture. One cannot have a more firm basis for behavior than the Word of God. A society in which people do not respect those in authority would not be the kind of society in which any of us would care to live.

Both the social adjustment approach and the respect for authority approach have been seriously questioned, especially since the Second World War. "The barbarities of the socially conforming members of the Nazi system and the other-directed hollow men growing up in our own affluent society have made us acutely aware of the fact that adjustment to the group is no substitute for moral maturity (Kohlberg, 1976, p. 5). We are reminded that whether we should adjust and whether we should obey depends on *which* society and *which* authority. Conformity to a society that advocates violence, whether it be a street gang in Chicago or a nation that prepares for nuclear destruction of the enemy, is not in keeping with a recognition of humanity as being made in the image of God; and to obey an authority whose wishes are contrary to the authority of God (Acts 4:19) is also not in God's plan for his followers.

Other traditional approaches are, for the most part, varying combinations of the three mentioned: character education, social adjustment, and respect for authority. The fact that these methods still are used shows that they have stood the test of time. But there are newer approaches as well that have their foundation not so much in tradition as in the major psychological theories prominent today. The psychological answers to the problem are more clearly spelled out both in theory and in method and are based on empirical investigation. Although they include some elements of the traditional, they are, nonetheless, more sophisticated in design and go beyond the thinking of the traditionalists.

Psychological Approaches

Each of the four major psychologies that comprise the main body of this book gives a different answer to the question of how the amoral infant becomes capable of morality. A brief preview of these psychologies will be given at this point with details reserved for later chapters.

The Learning Approach: Morality as Moral Behavior. Learning psychologists say that children are born neither good nor bad but will grow to be whatever they are made to be by the environment. What the person *does* is considered the most important aspect of morality. The focus of the learning position is on publicly observable responses and on the environment that instigates or reinforces those responses. If the child has a good environment, he or she will learn to be good; if the child has a bad environment, he or she will learn to be bad. Adults also respond to environmental contingencies and are more apt to perform those tasks for which they are rewarded and eliminate those behaviors that are followed by pain or punishment. Thus, people *learn* to act as they do. Morality and immorality are learned behaviors. The method used by learning psychologists is to arrange environmental events in such a way as to produce behaviors that are best for the individual and for the society. Numerous studies have been conducted that show optimal ways for conditioning the child to act morally. Some learning theorists also emphasize the importance of the model and say that children will learn to be moral or immoral by imitating the behaviors of other people.

The Cognitive Approach: Morality as Moral Reasoning. Cognitive psychologists emphasize the judgmental and thinking processes involved in making moral decisions. They believe that people are born with the capacity to construct their own experiences and knowledge of themselves and the world, and as children grow older they become more adept in this ability. Moral reasoning or judgment involves the standards one has about what is right and what is wrong and the way one reasons from these standards to determine what to do in a given situation. Although what one does is recognized as important, the cognitive psychologist listens to what one *says* as the basis for determining the level of morality. The process of moral reasoning is stressed more than the behavioral outcome. Each person proceeds through a series of stages in

Melanie Barr
4/11/87

moral reasoning, each stage involving a higher level of cognitive organization and based on the stage preceding it. Higher stages are to be preferred to lower stages in terms of both the impact on the individual and on the society. The philosophical concept of justice provides the basis for determining the hierarchy, and the method used is to encourage discussion of moral dilemmas so that the person can listen to the reasoning of someone at the next higher stage and thus to be drawn to that higher stage.

The Humanistic Approach: Morality as Moral Potential. Humanistic psychologists see children as naturally good and as having the potential for self-development. As unique and free persons children are deserving of dignity and respect. What they need from others is encouragement and affirmation to become all that they can be. Humanists stress the significance of emotions, feelings, personal fulfillment, and relationships. They are dedicated to an understanding of what makes the individual distinctly human and are committed to promoting personal welfare in every way possible. The *force-for-growth* postulated as inherent within each person includes the propensity to achieve moral maturity as well as to become mature in other areas of life. Moral development thus is seen as one of the many consequences of a total striving for self-direction and creative potential. Made in the image and likeness of God, there is something almost sacred about people in contrast to all other forms of life. The method used by humanists is to encourage the child's natural striving to develop morally. Emphasis is given to techniques that will enable persons to clarify their values and to act upon them.

The Psychoanalytic Approach: Morality as Moral Conflict. Freudian psychologists see the newborn as an *id* or an "it" with irrational passions and instincts. As such the infant has a depraved nature that is oriented to gratification and pleasure. As the child grows older, the *ego* or "I" emerges which is oriented to reality, and later a *superego* or "conscience" develops which is oriented to issues of right and wrong. Development from infancy to adulthood is seen as bringing about a more goodly or moral creature, goodly in the sense of the person's being able to live in a society with others and also in the sense of developing a conscience that will monitor his or her behavior. Conflict arises between the id which says, "I want," and the superego that says, "Thou shalt," or, "Thou shalt not." The ego must look to the real world in making the decisions of "I will" or "I won't." The psychoanalytic method encourages a favorable combination of ego and superego characteristics so that the person will be able to cope both with a world of reality and with the realm of the moral.

We see, then, that each of the four psychological approaches emphasizes a different expression of morality, begins with a different assumption as to the nature of humankind, and employs a different method for enhancing moral development. Learning psychologists stress the behavioral component of morality, say that the child is born neither good nor bad, and advocate a control of the environment in order to produce responses that are moral. Cognitive psychologists emphasize the rational or thinking processes in moral development, say that the child is born with the ability to construct his or her own experiences and knowledge of self and the world, and make use of moral dilemma stories to encourage moral reasoning. Humanistic psychologists underscore the emotional and motivational aspects of morality, say that the child is born a goodly individual with the capacity to become morally mature, and favor the encouragement of the child's natural propensity to be moral by the use of values clarification strategies. Psychoanalytic psychologists stress the conflicts brought about by the advent of the ego and the superego, see the child as born depraved, and maintain that identification with the parents during the child's early years is the natural way for conscience development to take place.

For each psychological approach we will look in greater depth at the basic assumptions; the techniques employed; the answer to the question of how the amoral infant becomes capable of morality; the problems associated with the basic assumptions or techniques; some practical applications to the home, the school, and the church; and theological support or refutation of the theory. Each psychology will be presented in a separate chapter: learning psychology in chapter 2, cognitive psychology in chapter 3, humanistic psychology in chapter 4, and psychoanalysis in chapter 5.

A Theological Approach

In the last chapter (chap. 6) the focus will be on a theological answer as to how moral development takes place. Those of us who call ourselves Christians hold to the basic tenet that the Holy Bible is the inspired Word of God, the only unerring guide to faith and morals. It is to be expected that parents, church leaders, psychologists, and others who hold to the historic Christian position will look to Scripture as the most advanced thinking possible in the realm of moral discernment.

In the Bible, to be moral means to be "good." But Jesus said that "no one is good—except God alone" (Mk. 10:18). Goodness, then, means godliness. Yet in our natural state we are far from God (Is. 55:9). So God in his infinite mercy provided a way that we could be like him, "holy and blameless in his sight" (Eph. 1:4). The account of how this was made possible is the most beautiful story ever written. It is a story of salvation and of hope for each one who believes.

In Christian theology there is an emphasis on all four psychological expressions of morality—the behavioral, the reasoning, the potential, and the conflict. Godliness is manifested not only in what we do and in how we think but also in what we can be through Christ and in the struggles we face along the way. Only in the Word of God do we have an adequate and complete basis for determining what is right and what is wrong (2 Tm. 3:16-17). Morality as godliness is the ultimate expression of what it means to be moral.

In an address presented at the American Psychological Association in Toronto in 1984, Noël Mailloux spoke to Division 36 members (Psychologists Interested in Religious Issues) about the growing interest in the subject of moral development. "It will suffice to give a quick look at most recent issues of many professional journals to realize the magnitude of the contribution that our discipline will be expected to offer in an area of obviously renewed interest." Father Mailloux's stated purpose for the presentation "was to suggest that a long neglected area of research might soon be found to be a most promising and rewarding one in this frontier zone where psychologists can rest assured that their collaboration will be most welcome and eagerly appreciated by representatives of moral science" (Mailloux, 1984, p. 4).

In a similar vein, psychiatrist Mansell Pattison (1972) wrote in an essay on psychology in *Christ and the Modern Mind:* "This issue of morality may prove to be the most vital of all in the dialogue between psychology and theology. ... The contemporary concern over morality in both psychology and theology may open the doors to collaboration in the most vital enterprise of our society" (pp. 200-201).

The present volume is an attempt to contribute to that dialogue. An effort has been made to present the ideas in as clear a way as possible, especially for the reader unfamiliar with psychological theory. However, one need not understand every aspect of a theory to apply the methods and techniques. Some ideas will appeal to some readers, other ideas to others. It is hoped that each one who picks up this book will find something of value.

References

Goble, F. G., & Brooks, B. D. (1983). *The case for character education.* Ottawa, IL: Green Hill.

Hartshorne, H., & May, M. A. (1928–1930). *Studies in the nature of character: Studies in deceit* (Vol. 1); *Studies in self-control* (Vol. 2); *Studies in the organization of character* (Vol. 3). New York: Macmillan.

Kohlberg, L. (1976). The quest for justice in 200 years of American history and in contemporary American education. *Contemporary Education, 48,* 5-16.

Lewis, C. S. (1960). *Mere Christianity.* New York: Macmillan.

Mailloux, N. (1984). Emotional basis of moral attitudes. In R. D. Kahoe (Ed.), *Psychologists Interested in Religious Issues Newsletter, 9*(4), 3-4.

Pattison, E. M. (1972). Psychology. In R. W. Smith (Ed.), *Christ and the modern mind.* Downers Grove, IL: Inter-Varsity.

2

The Learning Approach
Morality as Moral Behavior

Blessed is the man
  who does not walk in the counsel of the wicked
or stand in the way of sinners
  or sit in the seat of mockers. (Ps. 1:1)

People have been interested in psychology for hundreds of years, but it was not until Wilhelm Wundt, son of a Lutheran pastor, founded the first psychological laboratory in Germany in 1879 that psychology could be said to have become a science. Later, around the turn of the century, a Russian physiologist by the name of Ivan Pavlov, using methods similar to Wundt's, made an interesting discovery. Pavlov noticed that dogs in the laboratory would salivate to the sound of a bell if they associated the bell with getting food. Pavlov called salivating to the bell a psychic secretion to differentiate it from the unlearned physical reaction of salivating to food. Pavlov did not consider himself a psychologist, but the word "psychic" used in the experiment seemed to stick, and today "psychology" is often used to mean the study of animal and

31

human behavior and seldom to mean the study of the "psyche," or soul, as its literal interpretation would imply.

That the time was ripe for psychology as a science was apparent. In America especially it was thought that because all people are created equal, one needed only an opportunity and success was assured. The environment was all important to what a person became. By studying environmental events (called stimuli) and overt behaviors (called responses), researchers could note cause-effect relationships and supply information that would help make for a better life. Although not totally denying the realm of emotions or the life of the mind, or even the existence of their own souls, early learning psychologists insisted that it was only as psychology became a science, linking environmental events with observable behaviors, that humankind would be in a position to control its world and understand its conduct.

Psychologists who look at behavior as having been learned from the environment go by a variety of names including those of "behaviorists" because they emphasize overt behaviors, "associationists" because they show the relationship of one stimulus to another, "S-R psychologists" because they link stimuli and responses, and "learning psychologists" because they believe that people learn to be whatever they become. But whatever the name, these men and women comprise one of the largest groups of American psychologists, and their record over the years is impressive. Beginning with salivating dogs and proceeding to cats in puzzle boxes and rats running mazes, learning theorists have extended their studies upward along the phylogenetic scale to show that many of the laws operative in animal learning are applicable to complex kinds of human behaviors as well.

The learning approach, then, adopts the position that people start out neutral and learn to be whatever they are made to be by the environment. Our personalities, our interests, our temperaments, and our motivations are the result of our experiences. We learn to be pleasant or disagreeable, happy or sad, aggressive or helpful, capable or ineffective. And we learn to be moral—or immoral, as the case may be. If we grow up in a good environment we learn to be good. If we grow up in a bad environment we learn to be bad. Most of us are both good and bad, good when we are with good people and bad when we are with bad people. And whether we are good or bad depends on what we *do,* on how we behave. A look at the basic concepts of learning theory as applied to morality will enable us to understand better how moral behavior occurs.

Basic Assumptions

The learning psychologist believes that the society determines what is right and what is wrong, what is good and what is evil. Society takes as its highest priority its own survival, and for this reason the preservation of the social order becomes the greatest good and the destruction of the social order becomes the greatest evil. A good person is a good citizen, complying with the mandates of the social group to which he or she belongs. *To be moral is to act in ways that benefit the society; to be immoral is to act in ways that harm the society.* If people conform to the behavioral standards of the group, they are moral for they are responding to the environment in a way that will enhance the well-being of others. If people reject the behavioral standards of the group, they are immoral for they are responding in a way that will have a deleterious effect on others. The emphasis of learning psychology is on overt behavior not on what a person says or thinks, for what one does more directly affects others than any other type of response. People who are immoral need to change their behavior not their temperament or their motives or their thought processes. Once the behavior is changed, the problem is solved. A child who tells lies, for example, needs to learn to tell the truth for lying is harmful to others. When the child stops lying and speaks truth, the problem no longer exists and the child is conforming to the expectation of the group. Rather than trying to find some hidden reason for the lies, such as innate depravity or a weak will or a devious mind, learning theorists would say that lying *is* the problem. Lying is an external problem with external consequences. Deal with the problem and you deal with the consequences.

Moral (or immoral) behavior does not just happen; it is a product of environmental conditioning. None of us starts out moral or immoral, nor do we happen to become one way or the other. Rather, moral behavior like all behavior is learned. Learning is defined as a change in behavior as the result of experience. Experience comes from living in an environment composed of thousands of stimuli that act upon the learner in such a way as to produce a variety of responses. B. F. Skinner (1974), a leading spokesman for learning psychology wrote:

> A behavioristic analysis rests on the following assumptions: A person is first of all an organism, a member of a species and a subspecies. . . . The organism becomes a person as it acquires a repertoire of behavior under the contingencies of reinforcement to which it is exposed during its lifetime. . . . It is able to acquire such a repertoire under such control because of processes of conditioning. (p. 207)

The relationship between "contingencies of reinforcement" and "processes of conditioning," to use Skinner's words, results in moral or immoral behavior, even as it results in other kinds of behavior. Furthermore, this relationship is not capricious but is the very stuff of which science is made. A basic tenet of scientific research is that there is order in the world, that certain events bring about certain responses, that future behavior can be predicted on the basis of past behavior, and that there are commonalities between members of a particular species so that information gathered from some members may be generalized to other members. Learning theorists do not need to observe every child to know what most children will do in a given set of circumstances. Psychologists who are interested in the area of morality and hold to the learning approach look for correlations between environmental events and overt behaviors to understand better the nature of the relationship between them.

Moral (or immoral) behavior may be learned by a process of classical conditioning. The term *classical* comes from Pavlov's classic experiment in which he found that dogs learned to respond to the neutral (conditioned) stimulus of a bell if the bell previously had been paired or associated with the natural (unconditioned) stimulus of food. The sound of a bell does not ordinarily produce activity of the salivary glands, but food in the mouth does. By pairing the bell with the food, the dogs would salivate to the bell in the same way that they would salivate to the food. Although it is a giant step from salivating dogs to moral behavior in humans, some studies indicate that moral or immoral behavior may be learned by pairing a stimulus that would not naturally produce the behavior with a stimulus that does produce the behavior. For example, a child who comes when called engages in the moral act of obedience. The word *come*, like all words, is a conditioned stimulus, for it has no meaning apart from its association with natural events. As a toddler the child may have associated the word "come" with outstretched arms, smiles, and good food. It is because of this association that the child will come when called even though the natural unconditioned stimuli of favorable attention and good food may not be present. The child has been conditioned to obey.

Moral (or immoral) behavior may be learned by a process of instrumental conditioning. Unlike classical conditioning in which two or more stimuli are associated *prior* to the response, instrumental conditioning looks at what happens *after* the response. It is the consequence of the response that determines whether the response is strengthened or weakened. If something pleasant (called a reinforcer) happens after a response, the response is more apt to occur again. The response is instrumental or useful to the one making the response. If something painful (called a punisher) happens after a response, the response is not instrumental and is less apt to occur again. Also, if nothing happens after a response, it is not useful to the organism to have made the response, and the response is less apt to be repeated. Moral or immoral behavior is strengthened when reinforced and weakened when punished or ignored. If a moral act like telling the truth is praised or an immoral act like stealing means more money, these acts have been reinforced and are more apt to occur again. If, however, telling the truth means a spanking or stealing means getting caught and jailed, these acts have been punished and are less apt to reoccur. When "good" behavior like playing quietly is disregarded or "naughty" behavior like throwing a temper tantrum is ignored, these behaviors are not instrumental or useful and are less apt to be repeated. Moral behavior, then, is learned when the child associates socially acceptable responses with rewards and socially unacceptable responses with punishment.

Behaviors may be followed by both immediate and long-range consequences. When this occurs, immediate reinforcers and punishers take precedence over the long-range reinforcers and punishers. "The behavior [the organism] exhibits at any moment is under the control of a current setting" (Skinner 1974, p. 207). A person who overeats does so because the immediate reinforcers of good taste in the mouth and pleasant fullness in the stomach take priority over the more remote punishers of poor health, less energy, and a less attractive appearance. A student who finds studying to be unpleasant probably will do very little of it. The punishers accompanying studying behavior take precedence over the more distant reinforcers of good grades and the promise of a better income. In the same way, *moral (or immoral) behavior is more apt to be learned if reinforcers and punishers occur immediately following the behavior than if they occur at a later time.* A young child may need reinforcers every few minutes, whereas an older child may need reinforcers every hour. The learning psychologist believes that if reinforcers are delivered immediately following the behavior and if they occur with sufficient frequency, the learning of the behavior is assured. The same applies to the learning of moral behavior. But unfortunately, we underestimate the number of reinforcers necessary for optimal functioning, and our timing in providing punishers and reinforcers is so far removed from the behavior exhibited as to lose maximal effectiveness. We ignore behaviors that should be reinforced (e.g., the child is supposed to be good), and extend the punishers (e.g., "You'll get a spanking when your dad gets home") and the reinforcers (e.g., "If you don't get a grade less than a C you'll get a bicycle for Christmas") past the time of their greatest usefulness. We would do well to analyze how we respond so that we and others will learn to be moral.

Moral (or immoral) behavior may be learned by imitating the behavior of another person. Learning to be good or learning to be bad by imitating a model is called social learning. Social learning theorists emphasize the importance of incidental learning, that is, learning that takes place incidentally, or without instruction. The child learns more by percept than by precept, more by watching and imitating the behaviors of others than by following their directions and rules. The parent who says, "Do what I say, not what I do," is not reckoning with the way learning takes place. The principal who tells the student while paddling him, "This will teach you not to hit people," is providing a model of aggression that may have more effect on the child than the pain inflicted. Good habits are formed by imitating the good behaviors of others. Bad habits are formed by imitating those behaviors that are detrimental to the society.

Classical Conditioning

The conditioning method used by Pavlov was adopted by an American psychologist named John B. Watson, who, with his assistant, Rosalie Rayner, conditioned an eleven-month-old child to fear a white rat. "Little Albert" liked to play with furry creatures such as rats and rabbits, but he did not like loud noises. Earlier studies made Watson believe that infants have a fundamental or unlearned fear of loud noises, so when Albert reached for the white rat, Watson sounded a loud noise behind him. After several pairings of the rat (the conditioned stimulus) with the noise (the unconditioned stimulus), Albert reacted to the rat in the same way that he did to the noise. Just seeing the rat made Albert cry and try to crawl away (Watson & Rayner, 1920).

Pavlov had found that dogs would salivate not only to the original conditioned stimulus of the bell but to other bells as well. How much salivation occurred depended on how close in tone a second bell was to the original bell. This phenomenon is known as *stimulus generalization,* which means that the learner will generalize from the original conditioned stimulus to other stimuli similar to it. Watson saw this with Little Albert as well. Not only did Albert learn to fear the rat but he also learned to fear objects resembling a rat. Albert became afraid of a white rabbit, a sealskin coat, a Santa Claus mask, and Watson's hair. Albert even showed a reaction to cotton, although cotton was too far removed in similarity to the rat to produce much of a response. Albert showed no fear of blocks and other objects that did not resemble a rat (Harris, 1979).

The significance of Watson's study is apparent. He had

shown that the emotions people experience may be learned by pairing one stimulus with another. No longer need one look for mentalistic explanations or internal forces to account for human responses. What was needed was to identify the observable conditions that influence behavior. In order to control behavior one had only to supply the proper stimuli at the proper time. Here was a science of psychology unhampered by introspective techniques and deductive assumptions. Here was a cause-effect relationship between stimuli and responses, between the environment and what one does (Watson 1931).

Watson was so pleased with the results that he stated that by taking any healthy infant and controlling the environment he could make the child into any kind of specialist he might select—a doctor or a lawyer, a merchant or a chief, and even a beggar-man or a thief. It was the environment that made people what they are, not their ancestry or temperament or any special innate abilities. To Watson the environment and the behaviors resulting from the environment were the proper subjects for psychology. However, Watson did not have the opportunity to continue his studies. He became involved in a divorce scandal and was dismissed from his post. Unable to find another position in the academic world because of the incident, Watson left the field of psychology and became a businessman. Nevertheless, his influence continued and still is being felt today. Known as a behaviorist because he emphasized overt behaviors and the environment that produced those behaviors, Watson's ideas were received readily by Americans who wanted to believe that heredity means little and environment means a great deal.

The effects of classical conditioning are all around us. We see it in animals as well as in our own behavior. The family cat comes running and meowing when she hears the electric can opener. The sound of the can opener (a conditioned stimulus) has been associated with getting food (an unconditioned stimulus). Her meowing awakens the dog who comes running to see if there is food for him. The cat's conditioned response of meowing becomes the dog's conditioned stimulus to come, the dog previously having associated a meowing cat in the kitchen with getting food. Horses also are trained by the process of classical conditioning. Both "giddap" and "whoa" (conditioned stimuli) have been associated with natural stimuli that unconditionally produce the response of going or the response of stopping. At the human level, as well, all of us have experienced seeing someone we have never seen before and having an immediate emotional reaction. Stimulus generalization has occurred, for the person reminds us of someone we already know. Even if we cannot remember who the original person (conditioned stimulus) is, we know immediately whether our reaction to the original person was favorable or unfavorable by our reaction to the one just seen. The emotion remains even though our knowledge of the original conditioning may not.

Over the years conditioning studies have become more sophisticated so that now very complex kinds of human behaviors may be attributed to classical conditioning. As was mentioned, words are conditioned stimuli that have been paired with concrete referents. These words, in turn, may be associated with other words, resulting in "verbal habit-families" (Staats, 1961) and bringing about higher mental processes, such as language acquisition, concept formation, and problem-solving ability. Both the emotions generated by words and the meaning of words have been explained by classical conditioning. When people react in different ways to the same words, it is because they have learned the words in different settings. Words like *communism, humanism, Christianity,* and *Buddhism* evoke varying reactions. One man's meat is another man's poison. The learning psychologist would say that if we were raised in the same environment and had the same experience as the people we disagree with, and if they had been raised as we had been, we would have their attitudes and they, ours.

Classical conditioning also may be used to explain moral and immoral behaviors. Hans Eysenck (1960) took the position that children will learn to fear situations in which aggressive or cheating behaviors, for example, have been associated with slaps, withdrawal of privileges, or shamings. The pain (unconditioned stimulus) associated with the punishment produces a natural (unconditioned) response of avoidance. When the pain is paired with a situation (conditioned stimulus) in which the child wants to aggress or wants to cheat, the child will associate the desire with the pain and will tend to avoid that situation. In other words, if aggressive or cheating behavior is associated with punishment, the child will learn to avoid situations in which he or she is likely to aggress or likely to cheat. Many learning psychologists play down individual differences, but Eysenck takes exception to a strict environmentalism and says that differences in the ease with which children are acculturated into the society may be accounted for by differences in their nervous systems. Extroverts are harder to condition than introverts. At the extrovert extreme is the psychopath, who, in spite of adequate intelligence and a good upbringing, is devoid of moral sense. At the introvert extreme are neurotics who make themselves miserable by suffering feelings of guilt over behaviors few people would consider wrong. Eysenck (1960) has demonstrated that psychopaths, compared with normal people, need many more pairings of conditioned and unconditioned stimuli before any effect is seen. Neurotics, with "a conscience much more tender than the average person" are "particularly easy to condition" (p. 15).

Instrumental Conditioning

All learning does not take place by a process of classical conditioning. Some learning occurs because the consequence of behavior results in the behavior being repeated. This is known as instrumental conditioning. It differs from classical conditioning in that instrumental conditioning is based on what follows the response rather than on what has preceded it. A dog lopes down the road, turning left at the intersection. A baby lies in a crib making baby noises. A man whistles while he works. A student types a term report. Unlike the reflexive act of salivation or the emotion felt when seeing someone who reminds us of someone else, these behaviors occur because the organism is capable of making the response and has found the response to be useful or instrumental. The dog finds food to the left rather than to the right or straight ahead. The baby receives attention from the mother. The man enjoys the sound of his whistling. The student gets a better grade with a typed report. In each case, it is the consequence of the behavior rather than a prior stimulus that determines its continuance.

Instrumental conditioning, unlike classical, usually involves responses that are spontaneous. The responses seem to emanate from the learner and are said to be emitted. Emitted behaviors are called operants because they operate on the environment to produce results. Often when we say we have learned something we are talking about a change in behavior that has occurred due to instrumental conditioning. Motor skills such as walking or writing a letter, intellectual skills such as saying the Gettysburg Address or memorizing the multiplication tables, and moral behaviors such as telling the truth or helping another person would be examples of learning by a process of instrumental conditioning.

The fact that living beings, both animal and human, respond to the consequences of their behavior has been known for centuries, but it was not until B. F. Skinner of Harvard University wrote *The Behavior of Organisms* in 1938 that the position now known as instrumental (operant) conditioning was formalized. His later works (1953, 1971) clarify and expand the position. Skinner does not deny the existence of mental processes, but he takes the view that if psychology is to explain behavior it must of necessity look at overt responses and at the environment that produced those responses. Skinner further believes that it is truly the environment with its reinforcers and punishers that determines human behavior, not mentalistic desire or choice. People are not free agents governing their own lives but are rather the products of environmental contingencies. A person may speak of will-power or of self-control, but these terms are misnomers. No one is free; all are controlled by the environment. We may say we are free, usually when we are fortunate in having a favorable environment, but we are only fooling ourselves, making it more difficult to understand why we act as we do. We feel not-free when our lives are filled with noxious or painful events, yet we are no more free when we feel free than when we do not. Reinforcers are as important as punishers in determining behavior, and our awareness of environmental effects or lack thereof in no way changes the facts.

In *Beyond Freedom and Dignity* (1971), Skinner explained his position. "The feeling of freedom becomes an unreliable guide to action. . . . Non-aversive measures are not as conspicuous as aversive" (p. 32).

> Man's struggle for freedom is not due to a will to be free.
> . . . The literature of freedom . . . has been successful in
> reducing the aversive stimuli used in intentional control,
> but it has made the mistake of defining freedom in terms
> of states of mind or feelings, and it has therefore not been
> able to deal effectively with techniques of control. . . . It
> is unprepared for the next step, which is not to free men
> from control but to analyze and change the kinds of control
> to which they are exposed. (pp. 41-42)

In instrumental conditioning the controls are called reinforcers and punishers. There are two types of reinforcers and two types of punishers. Reinforcers are said to be positive or negative, and punishers are said to be Type I or Type II. Both positive and negative reinforcers *increase* the probability that a response will occur, and both Type I and Type II punishers *decrease* the probability that a response will occur. Reinforcers (negative as well as positive) are desirable or rewarding to the learner; punishers of both types are undesirable or noxious to the learner.

A positive reinforcer is any stimulus which, when *added* to the situation, increases the probability of the response. Positive reinforcers for a child would be consumables, such as candy or pop; manipulatables, such as trinkets or toys; social, such as a smile or a compliment; or the use of the Premack method. The Premack method was named after David Premack (1965) who wrote that high probability behavior may be used to reinforce low probability behavior. High probability behavior for teenagers may be listening to the stereo, and low probability behavior may be studying. If listening to the stereo means they do not get their studying done, then listening to the stereo may be contingent upon their having completed a specified amount of studying first. The idea, of course, is not new. Mothers for years have told their children, "Take out the garbage and then you can go play." But being aware of the seemingly endless possibilities of the Premack method increases the alternatives for dealing effectively with ourselves and with others.

A negative reinforcer is any stimulus which, when *removed* from the situation, increases the probability of the response. The stimulus removed should be negative, or undesirable, in order for its removal to be reinforcing. For instance, we tend to avoid people who constantly complain about how they feel. Listening to them talk about their aches and pains is irritating. We also put on sunglasses to remove the sun's glare, and we dodge chuckholes in the street when we are driving. All these behaviors we find reinforcing because they remove unpleasant events. Negative reinforcement is also exemplified in the old saying that we like to sit on a hot stove because it feels so good when we get off. Getting off the hot stove is reinforcing because it removes a painful stimulus. Having been negatively reinforced for such behaviors, we will continue to avoid complainers, put on sunglasses, dodge chuckholes, and jump off hot stoves.

A Type I punisher is any stimulus which, when *added* to the situation, decreases the probability of the response. Type I punishers include being spanked, scolded, and threatened. Any stimulus that is noxious or aversive may be used as a punisher. A Type II punisher is any stimulus which, when *removed* from the situation, decreases the probability of the response. The stimulus removed should be desirable or rewarding in order for its removal to be punishing. Not letting children watch their favorite television program or taking away their allowance when they have done something wrong are examples of Type II punishers. Losing one's job would be punishing to many adults.

We tend to like people who provide reinforcers and dislike people who administer punishers. Policemen are usually thought of as meting out punishers. They are more likely to apprehend offenders than to help small children and elderly women across the street. For this reason policemen get more than their share of criticism. Rather than giving us a positive reinforcer such as a package of M&Ms or a twenty-dollar bill when they see us driving in a safe manner or providing a negative reinforcer such as recommending that the chuckholes in the street in front of our house be filled, they wait until we break the driving code and give us a ticket (a Type I punisher) and remove our money (a Type II punisher).

Whether a stimulus is reinforcing or punishing depends on whether it increases or decreases the response, not on whether the one providing the stimulus considers it to be reinforcing or punishing. A teacher may think Johnny is being rewarded when his writing paper is put up on the board. But if Johnny begins to write poorly, he has been punished instead. A closer look may reveal that Johnny's best friend does not write well or that Johnny is teased on the playground for being "teacher's pet." The teacher may scold Suzie for being out of her seat and threaten to send her to the principal's office. If Suzie continues out-of-seat behavior, it may be that the attention she receives from the teacher and the grins and looks she gets from her peers is reinforcing. To the teacher the scolding and threat are punishers, but to Suzie they provide an environment in which she receives the attention she wants. A stimulus may be reinforcing to one child and punishing to another. Jimmy, in kindergarten, likes a gold star on his picture. Jerry, in eighth grade, would find the gold star demeaning. Michelle is pleased when the teacher puts her writing paper on the board even though Johnny is not. Michelle does not care when the kids call her teacher's pet. She does not like those children anyway, and besides, Michelle's best friend writes well and her paper is also displayed.

Whereas Watson leaned heavily on the studies of Pavlov, Skinner was influenced by the writings of an American researcher named Edward Lee Thorndike. Thorndike, appropriately called the father of educational psychology, observed both animals and people in problem-solving situations and concluded that whenever a response is followed by a satisfying state of affairs, the connection between the stimulus and the response is strengthened (a cat in a puzzle box will get out sooner the second time in the box). If, however, a response is followed by an annoying state of affairs, the connection between the stimulus and the response is weakened. Before 1930, Thorndike held that the effects of satisfiers and annoyers were equal and opposite, but after 1930, with continued experimentation, he changed his mind and concluded that satisfiers (rewards) are more powerful than annoyers (punishment).

For example, he found that students learned Spanish words more quickly if told when they were right than if told when they were wrong. Although it may be questioned whether being told you are wrong constitutes a punishment, if Thorndike's conclusions are correct, the social implications of his work are immense.

Skinner and others who have built upon Thorndike's truncated "law of effect" and have conducted their own research on this issue say that even though punishment is very effective at the time the learner is being punished, there are side effects that must be considered, and in the long run the results of punishment may be worse than the original inappropriate behavior for which the learner was punished. Whenever we are in a situation that we associate with punishment, we become anxious and fearful. We try to escape physically, to leave the scene. If this is not possible, we try to escape mentally by daydreaming or sleeping. If mental diversion is not allowed, a whole complex of aggressive behaviors comes into play. We become belligerent and strike out verbally or physically. If we cannot turn our anger against the one who perpetrated our discomfort, and usually we cannot, we will lash out at anything or anyone around us. Sometimes we turn the aggression inward against ourselves, deprecating our abilities and our personalities. In extreme cases, people have taken their own lives. This means that it is better to reinforce desirable behavior than to punish undesirable behavior. Although punishment is necessary at times, it has been used in many situations in which it was not needed. Parents and teachers and others in power use punishment because the press of the moment seems to demand it, and they cannot separate immediate results from long-range effects. Rewarding a competing, socially acceptable behavior may be as effective as punishment and has the further advantage of not being detrimental to personal happiness or hindering interpersonal relationships.

The effects of instrumental conditioning are constantly

with us. We know what will produce pleasure and what will produce pain, what will work and what will not, what will bring attention and what will be ignored. Teaching pets and circus animals to do tricks is accomplished by instrumental techniques. Much of human behavior, as well, has been acquired by operant means. Learning to talk is a case in point. Even as the meaning of words is learned by classical conditioning, the pronunciation of words is learned by instrumental conditioning. The baby lies in the crib making babbling noises which sound something like "ma-ma-ma-ma" or "da-da-da-da." As these sounds approximate the words "mama" and "daddy," the infant receives favorable attention, and the parents gradually shape the infant's speech by reinforcing closer and closer approximations to saying the sound "ma" or "da" just twice rather than several times. As the child matures, he or she will learn to say "mommy" and "daddy," or whatever the parents wish to be called, only to change to "mom" and "dad" after the child starts to school and is told by peers that "mommy" and "daddy" are only for "kindergarten babies."

The learning approach holds that moral and immoral behaviors are learned in the same way as other behaviors. This means that morality and immorality may be learned by the process of instrumental conditioning. If a behavior that is moral (or immoral) is reinforced, it is strengthened and more apt to occur again. If a behavior that is moral (or immoral) is punished or ignored, it is weakened and less apt to occur again. In every society there are people who engage in behaviors that are immoral and do not engage in behaviors that are moral. It is obvious that for them vice does not carry its own punishment nor virtue its own reward. Punishments and rewards come from without, not from within.

But who is to decide what is moral and what is immoral? How is a determination to be made as to what is right and what is wrong, what is good and what is bad?

The learning psychologist has an immediate answer. It is the society that makes the decision. It is the society that determines which behaviors are acceptable and which cannot be tolerated. The society must protect itself and will endorse those actions that make for its continuance and condemn those actions that make for its demise. The reason that stealing, lying, and murder are condemned in all cultures is because these behaviors have been found to bring about the destruction of the social order. Slothfulness, as well, cannot be tolerated except for the few who are unable physically or mentally to be productive. "People are not ethical or moral by nature, nor do they simply grow ethical or moral. It is the ethical and moral sanctions maintained by other members of a group which induce them to behave in ethical and moral ways. . . . A culture imposes its ethical and moral standards upon its members. It can do nothing else" (Skinner, 1978, p. 158).

As a society becomes more civilized, it reduces its use of aversive controls and replaces physical means with verbal means.

> The group classifies behavior as good, bad, right, and wrong and uses these terms as conditioned reinforcers in strengthening or suppressing behavior. It describes some of the more important contingencies in the form of rules, and by following rules its members conform more quickly and avoid direct exposure to punitive consequences. Individuals may act to maintain the very contingencies to which they conform and when they do so without supervision, they are said to show self-control or the possession of an ethical or moral sense. (Skinner, 1978, p. 8)

It is in this manner that society transmits the rules from one generation to the next, but always it is with the understanding that physical means will be used if necessary to keep in line anyone who does not adhere to its stated demands. The more advanced the society, the more advanced the judicial system that deals with offenders. When the individual and the society are at variance, it is the society that wins. It has no choice but to impose its norms upon its members.

Social Learning

A third way that learning takes place is by imitating the behavior of other people. We learn to talk like the people around us, to adopt their dress styles, and even to rise to our feet at a concert when we see others doing so. Studies show that we are more apt to copy the behaviors of people we perceive as being similar to ourselves, those of the same socio-economic class, race, sex, and occupation. Advertisers make use of this fact by featuring models with whom we can readily identify. We also take into consideration the place and the occasion, and even the time of day. From early childhood we have been taught that appropriate behavior is often specific to the situation. Had we lived in another age or in another culture our mannerisms and appearance would be quite different. Pictures of our parents when they were young strike us as quaint, and a visit to a foreign country shows us that customs vary from place to place. In some parts of the world men wear dresses, and in other parts of the world one is expected to give a loud belch after a meal as a compliment to the hostess.

Learning psychologists have different names for imitative behavior including observational learning, matching behavior, incidental learning, and vicarious learning. But the term usually given is "social learning."[1] Social learning is so much a part of our lives that it would seem to be almost contagious. It begins early in life with the toddler cocking his head to one side just like dad, sitting in a rocker with a book in his lap just like grandmother, and saying "uh-oh" with the same tone of voice as older brother. Peer influence begins early, as parents know who have observed their own fairly well-behaved youngster acting like a regular hellion when visiting relatives or friends whose children are allowed to do whatever they please. By the age of three, most children copy what they perceive to be sex-appropriate behavior; for example, boys will play with toy cars, and girls will serve tea to their dollies. Even in homes where parents disdain sex-role differences and model this by both working outside the home and both taking physical care of the children, the influence of the larger society is evident. A four-year-old boy in nursery school will not continue to play with dolls if he is teased by the other children for doing so. He finds he must restrict his activities or be punished by his peers.

In order for social learning to be put within the framework of learning psychology, three elements must be present. There must be a stimulus, a learner, and a response. The stimulus acts upon the learner, and the learner makes the response. The response is then linked to a reinforcer that assures the continuance of the response until a habit pattern is formed. In social learning the stimulus is the model, the learner is the person who copies the behavior of the model, and the response is the behavior imitated. Any event within the environment following the response that makes the learner more apt to respond in the same way is called a reinforcer. A person will not copy the behavior of another person unless he or she feels rewarded or reinforced in some way for doing so. The reinforcer may come directly from the model, as in the case where dad thinks it is cute when his young son cocks his head, and grandmother says he is "such a good boy" when he sits in a rocker with a book in his lap. The attention they give the child makes him eager to engage in these behaviors again. Or, the reinforcer may be built into the behavior itself. If the child says uh-oh after spilling his milk, his mother thinks he feels badly about the incident and is less apt to scold; and when he asks for more milk (a verbalization he learned by copying the speech of others) he is more apt to be given the milk and is reinforced by its good taste. A third type of reinforcer is vicarious in nature, that is, the imitator sees the self as receiving the same rewards as the model. For young children, models include not only parents and peers but community helpers, sports figures, detectives, cowboys, and cartoon characters seen on television. When the child imitates these personages the child imagines that he or she is being given all the attention and praise and recognition that they receive.

It matters not to children whether the model is real or imaginary, for in their minds they become whatever they pretend to be. If they are garbage collectors they will do with toy garbage trucks exactly what they see real garbage collectors do with their truck. If they are cowboys they will dress like cowboys, practice roping, and their pets become "dogies" out on the range. If they are Mighty Mouse, a cartoon figure some readers will remember from the sixties, they will put a cape over their shoulders (a pinned towel will do), jump from the highest perch their mother will allow (the step stool they climb on to reach the bathroom faucet), and sing loudly, "Here I come to save the day. Mighty Mouse is on the way." They are at that moment the hero, the one who will get the villain Oil Can Harry and save the beautiful maiden Pearl Pureheart. They accept as their own all the glory and prestige befitting one who is so brave and daring as to fight "the bad guy" and rescue the lovely lady.

Teenagers are notorious for copying the behavior of friends. Witness junior-high students on their way to school—all wearing the same kind of sneakers, the same style of jeans, the same type of T-shirt. Even socks must be a certain color and length. And verbal expressions must be up-to-date, "outasight" and "funky" being replaced with "beautiful" and "keep it cool, man." Senior-highs get up early to shampoo and blow-dry their hair. If the hair does not look just right, back it goes in the water for another try. Hair must be styled like everyone else's. And then they are off to school (hair style gone with the first gust of wind) in a car equipped with stereo, speakers, an equalizer booster, and the right cassette "jammin" in high volume. When asked by the parent why this is necessary, the answer is, "Because that's the way it is." Young people wonder that their parents are so naive as not to understand that to be different is to be ostracized by the group. Parents, in turn, wonder why their children talk about being free and doing their own thing when "doing your own thing" turns out to be just like everyone else's "thing."

Research in social learning abounds. In a typical study, a group of subjects will be exposed to models who act one way while another group of subjects will be exposed to models who act another way. The subjects are then watched to see if their behaviors differ depending on which models they observed. For example, a child may be told not to touch the candy in the room where he or she is playing. A second child is sent into the room having been told there is some special candy waiting there for him. Does the presence of the candy-eating peer mean the first child is more apt to eat the candy than would be the case if the second child had not come into the room or if the second child were instructed not to touch the candy and did not do so? Albert Bandura, well known for his work in the area of social learning, showed children a film in which an adult was seen hitting and punching an inflated Bobo doll. When these children were placed in a room with Bobo (and observed through a one-way mirror) they were more apt to hit and punch the doll than were children who had not seen the film (Bandura, Ross, & Ross 1963). Bandura (1965) also found that children who see an adult model praised after engaging in an aggressive act are more apt to imitate the aggressive act than are children who see the adult model scolded for the behavior. However, if children think they will be reinforced for acting

aggressively, they will do so regardless of the consequences of the same action to the model.

There are occasional instances of animals imitating
people and of people imitating animals, but this is relatively rare. For this reason social learning is generally
thought of as a human phenomenon. Social learning also
has the distinction of accounting for a larger repertoire of
behaviors than does either classical conditioning or instrumental conditioning. Language acquisition is a case in
point. Whereas the meaning of words may come about by
classical conditioning and the pronunciation of words may
take place by instrumental conditioning, social learning
provides for a complete behavioral sequence of verbal
expression. A person may reproduce a sentence or even
several sentences by imitating the speech of others and in
this way eliminate the need for the pairing of each word
(conditioned stimulus) with its concrete referent (unconditioned stimulus) as in the case of classical conditioning,
or the reinforcement of each word in a chain of words that
makes up a sentence as in the case of instrumental conditioning. With imitative behavior, meaning is given to
the sentence as a whole, and reinforcers accompany the
total unit of speech.

Moral and immoral behaviors are learned by observing
and imitating others. If a person imitates behaviors that
are sanctioned by the society, the person is said to be
moral. If a person imitates behaviors that are condemned
by the society, the person is said to be immoral. Some
expectations of conduct are universal, being found in all
cultures, whereas other expectations vary from culture to
culture or from place to place. All societies mandate some
standard of honesty and dependability to assure the survival of the group. Yet immigrants to a new land, for example, must make many adjustments before they feel at
home in their new surroundings. Even if one moves from
one social class to another, as in the case of prolonged
unemployment or unexpected affluence, changes in behavior will accompany the move. Middle-class norms, in-

cluding moral strictures, are predominant in our Western society, but they differ, nonetheless, from both lower-class and upper-class expectations. Even within a social class, children may find that their parents have one view of right and wrong while their peers have another. When this occurs, children will act one way when with their parents and another way when with their friends. *Flexibility* and *adjustment* are terms used to connote the positive aspect of this capacity to change, whereas instability and opportunism are the negative counterparts of this phenomenon.

Learning psychologists would say, then, that morality is not a fixed entity to be applied to all situations and to all people. Nothing is good in and of itself to be accepted and uniformly applied to every situation. Rather, morality changes as the occasion changes. A behavior may be moral in one situation but not in another. When in Rome, one does as the Romans; when not in Rome, one does something else. Each culture, each society, each group must determine what is good and what is bad, what is moral and what is immoral. The moral person is the one who picks up on the cues (stimuli) within the environment and responds in such a way that his or her behavior is supportive of the goals and aspirations of the group.

This does not mean there are no criteria by which to judge what has value and what is of little worth. One has only to compare the consequences of some standards with the consequences of others to see that some behaviors promote optimal functioning of the group whereas other behaviors destroy the very fabric of the society, and even result in its demise. Brotherhood and kindness promote the health of any group; divisiveness and aggression eat into the society like a cancer. Learning to be moral means that children will acquire through imitation behaviors that profit others, and they will inhibit those behaviors that are detrimental to those around them. Each individual is a member of the groups to which he or she belongs, and in this sense each one is part of one's own destiny, a part of whether one lives in a moral or an immoral world.

Techniques Employed

The techniques employed will depend on whether learning takes place by a process of classical conditioning, by instrumental conditioning, or by social learning. As has been said, classical conditioning occurs when a neutral (conditioned) stimulus is paired with a natural (unconditioned) stimulus so that an association is formed between the two stimuli and the organism responds in the same way to the neutral stimulus as it would to the natural stimulus. Associations of this kind happen to all of us on a regular basis, but usually we are unaware as to how or when they occur. Researchers trained in classical conditioning techniques will use these methods in the laboratory to obtain desired responses, and parents and teachers also may use the method, even though they will lack the precision and refinement of the trained psychologist. For instance, a mother who wants her child not to be afraid of electrical storms will take the child to the window when she sees a storm approaching, and while holding the child close, will talk about the beauty of the lightning and the deep tones of the thunder. By associating the storm with her warmth and pleasure, the child will come to appreciate one of the wonders of nature.

In the same way, the parent who wants the child to have positive feelings about helping others or about hearing God's Word or about going to church will endeavor to link these events (conditioned stimuli) with natural occasions (unconditioned stimuli) that are pleasant. For the very young child, eating graham crackers, knowing that mother is near, and not being restricted in moving around is pleasant; being hungry, lacking contact comfort[2] and being made to sit still is unpleasant. As the child grows older the specific conditions that bring pleasure will change, and these too will be linked from time to time with the desired events. But the tone has been set in the child's life, and the child's responses to the conditioned stimuli will continue even though the original unconditioned stimuli are no longer present. The child will learn to help others, to enjoy Bible stories, to look forward to going to church because from his or her earliest recollections these events have been associated with warmth and love and positive sensations.

Behavior modification, in the broadest sense of the term, is a modification of behavior regardless of the technique used, but its usual meaning in psychological literature is an application of instrumental (operant) conditioning procedures to changing one's behavior. Rather than pairing two stimuli prior to the response as in the case of classical conditioning, instrumental conditioning focuses on what happens after the response. If good things happen after a response is made, the response is reinforced and is more apt to occur again; if bad things happen after a response is made, the response is punished and is less apt to be repeated. Behavior modification strategies demand the manipulation of environmental conditions so that good things happen after socially acceptable behaviors and bad things happen after socially unacceptable behaviors. By arranging the consequences of a person's acts, desirable behavior is strengthened and undesirable behavior is weakened or extinguished.

There are a series of steps one follows to assure that behavior modification will occur, and although it is not essential that every step be taken, doing so provides order and direction to the procedure. The first step is to decide who the subject will be. The subject is the person whose behavior will be modified. It may be oneself, a friend, or a child in the home. The next step is to note a specific undesirable behavior of the subject, done on a fairly regular basis. This is not hard to do. Eating too much, eating the wrong foods, cracking knuckles, swearing, complaining, making excuses for not doing assigned tasks, hitting, plus a thousand more, are all possibilities. Third, the baserate is taken. Baserate is the number of times within a specific period that the undesirable behavior occurs naturally before behavior modification begins. In obtaining baserate, the behavior must be broken into overt responses that can be observed and tallied. If the undesirable behavior is eating too much, baserate would be the amount of food consumed in a typical twenty-four-hour period. If the undesirable behavior is smoking, one has only to count the number of cigarettes smoked each day or each week. If the undesirable behavior is swearing, one must tally the number of times swearing occurs in a typical day. If overeating or smoking or swearing differs from one situation to another, baserate should be taken in each situation. Although it is not always essential to take baserate, without it one would not know how much improvement had taken place after behavior modification has begun.

The fourth step is to determine the reinforcer for the undesirable behavior. Learning psychologists say that there is always a reason for people to do what they do. One of the tenets of operant conditioning is that an organism will not continue a behavior that is not instrumental or useful, and behavior is useful when the organism gets something it wants by engaging in that behavior. The reinforcer for eating too much may be the good taste of food or the alleviation of feelings of anxiety when the stomach is full. The reinforcer for smoking may be that one's friends smoke and the subject wants to be like one's friends, or it may be that smoking reduces the physical tension produced by a craving for nicotine. The reinforcer for swearing may be the attention the subject receives while swearing or the good feeling one has when hostility is released in this way. After the reinforcer is determined, the next step (step five) is to set up a program so the reinforcer does not follow the behavior. The subject who eats too much may pretend that the spaghetti is worms and the meatloaf is dung, or the subject may imagine that the stomach is getting so full it will explode. The smoker sees each cigarette as another nail in the coffin, but rather than saying this glibly as some smokers do, he or she pictures the self in a coffin suffocating and gasping for breath as each "nail" is pounded in. The person who swears turns from others so as not to receive their attention or tells the self how wrong it is to swear, thus removing the good feeling one normally would have after swearing.

Whenever a reinforcer is removed, as in the examples given, either nothing happens after the response, or a Type II punisher follows the response. Either way, the response will not continue under these circumstances. But some people are unwilling to use this method, or sometimes it is impossible to remove the reinforcer as in the case where smoking a cigarette satisfies the craving for nicotine. When this occurs, the undesirable behavior must be followed by an aversive or painful event, known as a Type I punisher. A Type I punisher for overeating might be "looking at a picture of a girl in a string bikini who weighs 260 pounds" or "doing twenty sit-ups" or "running the stairwell." For smoking, the aversive stimulus might be "having friends tell you how bad it is for you" or "telling yourself it stinks" or "trying a different brand that has an unpleasant taste." For swearing, it might be "putting a quarter in a jar each time you swear" "pinching yourself hard."[3] One student carried a surgical mask that he wore for five minutes each time he swore. The punisher, either Type II or Type I, must have sufficient intensity for the undesirable behavior to be weakened or extinguished. For obvious reasons, punishers are best applied to oneself. Care should be taken in using punishers with someone else.

At the same time the undesirable behavior is being punished, a desirable competing behavior is selected. A desirable competing behavior is any socially acceptable behavior that cannot occur at the same time as the undesirable behavior. One does not eat modestly and overeat at the same time, nor does one refrain from smoking and smoke at the same time, nor can one be silent and swear at the same time. A person may substitute celery for pastries, sugarless gum for cigarettes, and kind words for swear words. This sixth step of selecting a desirable competing behavior is followed by the seventh step of using either the original reinforcer or another reinforcer to strengthen the desirable behavior. A reinforcer for not overeating may be feeling better physically or shopping for new clothes. The reinforcer for not smoking may be using the money formerly spent on cigarettes to buy cassettes for the car stereo. The reinforcer for not swearing may be getting the attention of others one likes, as in the case of the student who wore the surgical mask so that a girl he wanted to date who did not like swearing would go out with him.

Sometimes a person will decide to skip the fifth stage of punishment, go directly to the sixth and last stages of selecting a desirable competing behavior and reinforcing that. It is undoubtedly more pleasant for all concerned if punishment is not used, and in some cases it is best not to punish. However, research and observation tell us that combining both a punisher for the undesirable behavior and a reinforcer for the desirable behavior increases the effectiveness of the technique and shortens the length of time needed for conditioning to take place. Behavior modification procedures work. They are efficient, and the steps are easy to understand and to implement. Anyone who says the method does not work either has not proceeded through all the steps or has not found adequate punishers for undesirable behaviors or adequate reinforcers for desirable behaviors. Even those with a bias against operant techniques, if trained in their use, have to admit that they do work.

Social learning includes both classical conditioning and instrumental conditioning, but the presence of the model is all important. The model may be a parent, a teacher, peers, or anyone else the child imitates. Exemplary models are needed for the child to observe and copy. The research method used by social learning psychologists is to provide a variety of models in a variety of settings to subjects differing in a variety of ways and then to note the results. In this way the most effective means by which observational learning takes place can be ascertained. In a less structured manner, parents will be aware of their own behavior, knowing that small eyes watch what they do and small ears listen to what they say. Teachers will videotape their performance in the classroom to be analyzed later in terms of how the child would see them, or they may observe other teachers who are successful and model their behavior after them. Recognizing the importance of adults as models, some parents are careful to exhibit the kinds of behavior they would like to see in their children; and school administrators, knowing the need for exemplary models, have instituted such practices as setting aside fifteen minutes each day for silent reading in which everyone in the school reads. Whomever the child chooses as a model—teacher, peer, principal, secretary, or janitor—that person is reading.

Morality and immorality, like other behaviors, are learned by observation and imitation. Both good habits and bad habits are formed when we copy the actions of the people around us. We learn to be good when we imitate people who are good; we learn to be bad when we imitate people who are bad. And good and bad depend on what we do, not on internal states of thinking or feeling. The learning psychologist would say that none of us is good or bad in and of ourselves. Rather, we become what we are made to be by the environment. Faulty behavior reflects a faulty environment, not a faulty person. We should not think of ourselves and others as moral or immoral in the sense of some inherent quality. Instead, we should look to our actions to see if we are exhibiting the kinds of behavior that will make for the continuance of the society rather than the kinds of behavior that will bring about the destruction of the social order.

Whether the technique employed by the learning theorists is that of classical conditioning, instrumental conditioning, social learning, or some combination of the three, the emphasis is on control. If one can control the environment by rearranging external events, one can control one's own behavior and the behavior of others. The control may be by pairing a neutral stimulus with a natural stimulus as in classical conditioning; ignoring, reinforcing, or punishing responses as in instrumental conditioning; or providing appropriate models as in social learning. But whatever the method, the focus is on manipulating the environment in such a way that overt behaviors are altered from socially undesirable to socially desirable forms. We know that behavior changes as circumstances change and an understanding of how this takes place puts us in an advantageous position for modifying our own behavior and the behavior of those entrusted to our care.

The Learning Theory Answer

The question asked in chapter 1 was how the amoral infant becomes capable of morality. What is the process whereby the child goes from a state in which he or she knows neither right nor wrong to a state in which he or she knows the difference and follows the right way? Learning psychology takes the position that what is moral is what society says is moral. To be a good person one must conform to the standards and norms of the social system.

Learning theory has its roots in the philosophy of British associationist John Locke, who held that the child is born as a *tabula rasa,* or blank tablet. Nothing is written on the tablet until the child interacts with an external world. It is the child's circumstances, not heredity or temperament or choice, that determine what is inscribed upon him. John B. Watson picked up this view when he said he could take any healthy infant and make him the kind of specialist he might select—doctor or lawyer, merchant or chief, and even beggar-man or thief. It is the child's experiences that determine the kind of person he or she will be. Control the experience, and you control whether the child will be moral or immoral.

Moral behaviors, then, are learned responses, and the learning does not differ in kind from the learning of all other behaviors. Moral behaviors are learned when the child is in a good environment; a good environment being one in which the child has adequate models of moral behavior and in which the child is reinforced for socially desirable conduct and punished for socially undesirable conduct. The learning theory answer to the question is that *the amoral infant becomes capable of morality by training, example, reward, and punishment. By imitating the actions of appropriate models and by being reinforced for behaviors deemed good by the society and punished for behaviors deemed bad by the society, the child learns to be a moral person.* Consistent and extensive training in good behaviors will result in good habits that persist into adulthood.

The advantage of the learning position is that those in charge of dependent children need not shrug their shoulders and say that nothing can be done to help the child who has already learned socially undesirable conduct. The idea of a critical period beyond which there is little hope has no place in the learning framework. To be sure, older children are less apt to change their behaviors than younger children due to years of previously conditioned responses. Nevertheless, age is not the important variable. As long as there is an environment surrounding the person—and always there is that—the person can change. Parents and teachers and ministers not only are invited to control but are obligated to control. They are to provide good modeling as well as appropriate reinforcers and punishers. The learning theory answer is encouraging to those who work with people of all ages.

Problems

Learning psychology has been presented up to this point in a relatively uncritical way, but the reader probably is aware that there are a number of problems inherent in the position and has thought of several of these already. We will look at some of the objections given in the literature to see what the critics have to say.

One problem is that the learning approach provides no theoretical basis for deciding what is right and what is wrong. As such, it gives little direction as to which of many behaviors one should choose in order to be a moral person. Without a philosophy or theology that transcends the present culture, one can never be sure of what is the right thing or how to choose the good over the evil. There are so many opinions, so many models, so many views of what is right and what is wrong. How does one know which opinion to listen to, which model to imitate, which view is best? If the only guideline for what is good and what is bad is what benefits the society or harms the society, and if societies change from time to time or do not agree among themselves as to what is beneficial or harmful, the result is confusion. Truth becomes relative to the occasion, and one is left with what is often referred to as "situation ethics." Each of us is a member of several groups or subgroups at the same time, and without guiding principles we are hard pressed to know to which of these groups we should give our allegiance. Suppose, for example, that a child and several friends have devised a method for cheating on a test. At test time the child is a member of the group composed of cheaters, a member of the class as a whole, a member of the entire school, and also a member of the community. Which of these groups has the right to say whether cheating is right or cheating is wrong? The child's friends say it is right if it means a higher grade. Other children in the class say it is wrong because the child may get caught or because it violates a rule. The teacher may say that children who cheat are only cheating themselves. People in the larger community may not care, but some will say that cheating is at cross-purposes with what we are trying to teach our children. Who is to decide? To which of these groups of people does the child listen? Some adults who would criticize a child for cheating on a test will misrepresent their earnings for income tax purposes and feel justified in doing so because their friends approve of the action and it will mean a more comfortable life for their families. So, who is to determine whether falsification of records is good or bad? Does it depend on who is doing the lying? Should the extent of the misrepresentation be considered? Does it matter who is being lied to? Does one's motive make a difference? Is every situation different, each occasion to be determined on its own merits? Without anchorage in a philosophy that supersedes the event, one is hard pressed to answer these questions.

A second problem is that moral behavior is a superficial way of looking at morality. It is superficial in that the emphasis is on overt behavior rather than on internal qualities that produce the behavior. One is not moral because one acts in moral ways. Rather, one acts in moral ways because one is moral. Good deeds are a manifestation of goodness, not goodness itself. This is made abundantly clear when we see that people are good for a variety of reasons. Some possess integrity and strength of character, and the goodness is a natural consequent of an inward condition. Others are good because they perceive it to be in their best interests to be that way, but given another time or a different situation, the good behavior no longer is present. Unless a view of morality includes other components of the moral process, such as reasoning that sees beyond the benefits of the moment, emotional states of empathy and love that enable a person to put self in the place of others and be concerned with their well-being as well as with one's own, or a religious commitment that holds that all humankind is made in the image of God and therefore befitting of dignity and respect, morality as moral behavior is shallow and unfeeling. By focusing on the external, the development of internal controls is lost sight of. By limiting morality to the study of stimulus-response connections, much of the significance of what it means to be a good person is forfeited. Moral behavior is only a part of what it means to be moral, a surface manifestation of an inward state, which in some people is a reflection of a true sensitivity to moral concerns and in others, nothing more than the opportune response at the moment.

Another problem or criticism is that the uniqueness of the human race as thinking, feeling, creative beings is not recognized. Humans are seen as an extension of the phylogenetic scale, and, like other animals, seek only to avoid pain and increase pleasure. They become mere pawns or puppets of environmental contingencies, passive organisms to be manipulated by others, the objects rather than the subjects of psychological study. People have no choice, no free will, no autonomy. Consequently, they have nothing to say about their behavior, including their moral behavior. Nor are they in a position to construct a value system based on their interests and tastes. As infants they were like all other infants. It was the environment—not heredity or maturational processes, not temperamental predisposition or cognitive potential, not decision-making or any desire on their part—that made them what they are today. Not even their enthusiasm, plans, aspirations, and hard work played a role except as these were programmed by an external world. All the characteristics that give human beings a special place in the universe and elevate them to a position superior to other life forms have been largely ignored in learning theory. Even religious views come from external sources, the joys of heaven and the sufferings of hell being used as reinforcers and punishers to encourage appropriate behaviors and discourage actions society does not want.

If people have no say in what they become, it is most unfair to hold them responsible for the kind of persons they are. How can they be praised or blamed for their interests, their personalities, their motivation—or lack thereof? They did not make themselves intelligent or unintelligent, fascinating or dull, moral or immoral. Nor can people be held accountable if they lack appropriate models to imitate. It also follows that we should not hold ourselves responsible. We did not get ourselves into the mess we are in, nor can we get ourselves out. How can we rise above our environment and be anything other than what we have learned to be? If we are mean or abusive toward others or alcoholic or homosexual, we are in no way to blame. We did not make ourselves this way, nor can we change. If others want us to be different, it is up to them to make it worth our while. They can provide reinforcers and punishers to get us to comply with their way of doing things, or they can provide socially acceptable models for us to emulate.

This stance of not holding others or ourselves responsible is understandably attractive to some people. It marks us as nice people not to judge others whose circumstances differ from our own, and it certainly is more pleasant to blame someone else for our difficulties than to take the blame ourselves. But an unwillingness to assume any role in the kind of people we are lets us off the hook, so to speak, much too easily. It is generally understood that all of us have something to say about who we are and what we do. We make decisions all day, every day. It begins with mind over mattress first thing in the morning and continues with what we wear and what we eat and what we say to our spouse and to our children. And many of the decisions we make are moral in nature because they directly affect others. To say we are not accountable for what we do or what we are militates against the common understanding of what it means to be a member of the human race, a good or a bad person. A morality without personal responsibility is a morality lacking an important ingredient.

Still another criticism is that learning psychology confuses means and ends. Reinforcing a child for appropriate behavior today may or may not result in desirable behavior tomorrow. If the only reason for not swearing is to avoid punishment, the child will not swear when in the presence of the punishing adult but will swear when out of earshot. Short-term control does not always mean long-term results. Behaviorists say that if consistently reinforced for acceptable behavior and punished for unacceptable behavior, the child will develop good habits that persist into adulthood; as the twig is bent, so grows the tree. Obviously, there is an element of truth to this, but the problem comes when we see that though some individuals continue the behaviors they were taught as children, other individuals go in very different directions. Siblings are usually treated in much the same way in the home, yet they turn out differently. Granted, no two people have exactly the same environment, and siblings will choose different friends and have different school situations; even so, it does not appear that the environment alone accounts for such discrepancies in their lives. There is reason to believe that all the variables that relate to moral behavior are not external; some components must come from within. Even as external and internal are not to be confused, means and ends are not to be confused. Process and product relate to each other, but one is not the same as the other. Means must be appropriate to the valued ends, but each remains separate from the other, to be considered together and individually for an understanding of how moral development occurs.

Adults may not be suitable models. Learning psychologists are aware of this, but it remains, nevertheless, a problem in their approach. As parents we say one thing but do another. We say we want quiet and yell at our children. We say we want honesty but do not always deal honestly with them. We say we want industry but lie on the davenport watching television while they are to do their homework. We may even expect our children to be more emotionally mature than we are. They are not to fuss or cry, but we feel justified when we complain about what happened at work or give an accounting of our latest aches and pains. The inconsistency between what we expect of our children and our own behavior is often glaring, and it seems to be greatest in homes where the parent takes the attitude that by virtue of being a parent one can do no wrong. Whatever the parent decides is right, and whatever the parent does should be accepted without question. The reason is not that the parent's decision or performance is necessarily best for the child, or even for the household in general, but rather that as the one in charge the parent has the authority to make the decision and therefore should be given respect. Even if we agree that parents do indeed have the right to demand performance from their children that differs from their own, the fact remains that children learn more by what they see than what they are told. Copying another's behavior comes naturally, obeying authority does not. Yelling calls for yelling, dishonesty brings dishonesty, and laziness results in laziness. And if punitive measures are such that children cannot exhibit these behaviors when with the parent, they will exhibit them in nonpunitive environments or when they are old enough that the parent no longer can control them physically. There are always exceptions, of course, but usually a child will take on the characteristics of the parents. It is sobering to see ourselves reflected in the behavior of our children. If we truly care for them we will be willing to change our own actions in an effort to become more suitable models.

The last problem we will consider has to do with the ethics of control. Some learning psychologists speak to this issue while others show little concern. Whenever the desire to control others and the satisfaction of one's own need for power becomes more important than the best interests of the one being controlled, there is reason to believe that the one in charge is not acting in a moral or ethical way. The controller should be as concerned with the ethics of his own behavior and the reason for wanting to be in charge as he is with the ethics of the behavior of the one being controlled. This is especially important when those controlled are in a dependent position—children, students, employees, or prisoners—and are either unaware of the ways in which they are being manipulated or are unable to leave the scene in which they find themselves. It is not unusual for persons in charge to begin their leadership with the best interests of those in their care in mind, but as time goes by and they are reinforced by increasing adulation, they change from ethical administrators to vindictive tyrants interested only in making life easier and more glorious for themselves. The adage "power corrupts" is no better illustrated than in the horror of Jonestown. Yet it is seen on a small scale all around us, making us aware that we need checks along the way to be sure that, whether we are controlling or being controlled, we do not fall into the trap of exalting authority for the sake of authority alone. Those in power must recognize that they are not somehow a different breed of humankind or better than those they command. Compassion, accountability, and humility are necessary ingredients for ethical leadership.

It would be inaccurate to say that these problems apply to the ideas of every learning psychologist. There are many variations on the learning theme that have not been touched on. Only the major ideas of classical conditioning, instrumental conditioning, and social learning have been dealt with, and there are varieties within each of these. Also, care must be exercised not to take a theory to its extreme conclusions, thereby creating a caricature rather than an accurate portrayal. But in the realm of morality there appears to be a deficit in the learning position. By fastening attention only on observable responses and on the external events that strengthen or weaken those responses, much of what is generally thought of as morality is excluded. Behavioral conformity is an important component of the moral condition and affects other people more directly than any other aspect, but it is, nevertheless, only one part of the total picture and by itself stands bare and incomplete. Morality as moral behavior finds its greatest expression in relationship with other components of morality so that together a totality is formed that imposes upon the parts a certain organization and yet is above or distinct from the parts.

Whether we accept or reject learning psychology as a philosophy, the fact remains that we are constantly modifying the behavior of those around us, even as they are modifying our behavior. We can do it unconsciously with unknown and often unhappy results, or we can do it consciously and deliberately, programming our actions so as to develop desirable qualities in others. Learning techniques work. Furthermore, they are easily understood and readily applied. By knowing the problems we are in a better position to avoid the pitfalls. Now we will consider ways in which learning psychology may be applied to the home, the school, and the church.

Practical Applications

No formal training is needed to apply learning psychology to our everyday lives. Perhaps this is because we already engage in learning practices, and by becoming familiar with the principles of the learning approach we can understand better what is taking place when we interact with others. A knowledge of behaviorism clarifies what we are doing and shows ways we may have erred in the past and how we can do a better job in the future. Both direct intervention, as seen in behavior modification and indirect mediation that comes with imitation and modeling are included in the learning approach. We will turn our attention first to ways in which parents may use learning psychology to foster moral behaviors in their children.

Application to the Home

Infants have a need for nutrients and contact comfort. These needs are met when they are given the breast or the bottle and held close in their mothers' arms. The tension that arises from hunger or being alone is reduced by the food and by body contact with another human being. In classical conditioning terminology, the food and body contact are unconditioned or natural stimuli that result in the unconditioned or natural responses of sucking the nipple and of fingering the mother's breast or hair. As the child is fed, other stimuli also present are associated with these unconditioned stimuli and take on importance for the child. The sound of the mother's voice as she talks or sings to her baby, her facial expressions, the way she holds the baby, and even odors and colors, are associated with the meeting of the child's basic needs. These conditioned stimuli (so called because they have significance only as they relate to or are conditioned on unconditioned stimuli) take on importance in their own right, and infants will come to desire the presence of the mother even when she is not directly meeting their needs for sustenance and contact comfort. They will make sounds to bring her to them, and when they are old enough to get around they will follow her, making sure she is close by. Her gestures and words begin to take on special significance, a nod or a yes telling them what they are doing is all right and a shake of the head or a no telling them to stop whatever they are doing and to go no further. In the classical conditioning paradigm all words are conditioned stimuli for they have no meaning apart from their concrete referents. So a mother who takes good care of her little ones, staying close by to meet their needs will have a profound effect upon their behavior as she communicates with them.

Further stimulus generalization, often referred to as higher order conditioning, occurs when the conditioned stimuli of the mother's presence and her words are linked to other conditioned stimuli. For example, she may tell her children of a heavenly Parent who loves and cares for them. Even as earthly parents approve or disapprove of their actions, a heavenly Father approves or disapproves of their behavior, and even as they are to listen to and obey mother and father, they are to listen to and obey God. There are times when these higher order conditioned stimuli may be linked directly with unconditioned stimuli, thereby strengthening the bond between the fulfilling of spiritual needs and the meeting of primary drives. Bible stories may be read to the small child when the child is sitting on the parent's lap, or the whole family may read the Scriptures together while enjoying a good meal or while sharing interesting experiences. As the child grows older and influences outside the home play a larger part in his or her behavior, it becomes increasingly difficult for parents to stamp in associative bonds, so it is important that this be done on a regular basis during the first few formative years of the child's life. A cohesive family in which members continue to engage in activities together will sustain the early influences of classical conditioning for a longer period of time.

Not only does stimulus generalization occur, but response generalization also takes place. Children who learn to act properly at home are more apt to act properly away from home. If they cooperate with parents, they will probably cooperate with others. Response generalization, also called habit generalization or response tendencies, means a person acquires behaviors that become so automatic he or she engages in these practices even without thinking about them. Saying please and thank you and sharing possessions and interests are examples of desirable response tendencies. Often we do not have time to think through what we should do in a given situation, so it becomes important that these reflexive responses considered to be good and right by the society become part of our automatic response repertoire. Classical conditioning also reveals how emotions develop, and even though the focus of learning psychology is on overt behaviors rather than on affective responses, the two cannot be separated entirely. Emotional generalization is as relevant to an understanding of how moral behaviors are learned as is stimulus generalization and response generalization. The feelings of children toward their parents and their pride in being members of the family relate directly to their behavior. Conditioning children to act morally thus should be done in the atmosphere of the home. It is the most natural and effective place for the development of dependable and responsible actions.

Relatively little has been written about the application of classical conditioning in comparison with a myriad of articles and books on instrumental (operant) techniques. Even so, most of the information on instrumental methods applies to the school rather than to the home. An exception to this is Gerald Patterson's *Living with Children* (1976), written in a style most parents will find easy to understand and to use. The ideas presented were pretested with over one hundred families, and thousands more have profited from their use. The down-to-earth language and programed approach of the book make it an informative guide to handling problems adults often have with their children. All parents would do well to be familiar with steps to take to deal with such behaviors as disobedience, whining, not wanting to go to bed at night, bedwetting, and temper tantrums. Changing unacceptable responses to acceptable responses is what behavior modification is about. There is also a section in this small volume on children who steal or lie. As stealing and lying are categorized in all societies as immoral behaviors, it is interesting to note ways parents may weaken or extinguish these unacceptable acts by rearranging environmental events. Another source of information is Rodger Bufford's *The Human Reflex* (1981). In a chapter entitled "Application of Behavioral Approaches to Child Rearing" he has given a detailed account of how parents can systematically shape the behavior of the child in areas such as getting dressed, toileting, table manners, and body hygiene.

Criticisms may be leveled against any form of control, but behavior modification seems to have received more than its share. Opponents say that the child is supposed to be good and therefore should not be bribed to behave. Yet the question may be asked, How many adults would continue to go to work each day and do a good job if they knew they would never receive another pay check? Is getting paid bribery? Or the charge is made that no one has the right to exercise that much control over another human being. But the fact remains that all of us are controlling each other all the time anyway. Parents control their children and children control their parents. It is a two-way street. Is it unethical to know what we are doing so we can do a better job? When we think of the many people who are unhappy because they have unconsciously trained family members to complain or be rude or be lazy, it would seem that they owe it to themselves and to each other to be aware of what they are doing and program their behaviors to produce more optimal results. The objection is often raised that children will learn to play the game and will act badly unless they are externally reinforced for every task completed. Again, this is a misunderstanding of the technique. One of the guidelines of contingency management is that the one in charge will reinforce children in such a way that in time they will learn to provide their own reinforcers. Children who find reading frustrating and painful, for example, may do a great deal of it if they are given a tangible reward contingent upon the amount read. The parent will pair the tangible reinforcer with the social reinforcer of praise so that the child will receive both reinforcers at the same time. When the tangible reinforcer is dropped, the social reinforcer is paired with the child's pride in doing something that is hard to do. The child also is gaining favor in the eyes of the teacher and classmates. The object is to get the child to read well enough that reading no longer is frustrating and painful and the child can enjoy the story for itself. But some children will never get to that place unless they first are given a tangible reward. By contrast, one would not tell a child who loves to read that a reward will be given when the book is finished. That is going the wrong direction and is at cross-purposes with behavior modification principles.

Parents not only condition the child to act as he does, they also are the child's first example of how people are supposed to behave. Parents should not be held completely responsible for what the child becomes, but they are, nonetheless, the salient influence during the early years when habits are formed. Imitating parental behavior is usually indirect inasmuch as neither parent nor child is aware of the extent to which it occurs. Studies indicate that children see the parent as having more privileges and greater power, so they are reinforced by the thought that they, too, will have these advantages if they act in the same way. Modeling also may have a direct or didactic function when used to teach a specific skill. "Watch what I do and then you do it the same way" is a familiar phrase. Learning to tie shoelaces, prepare a meal, swim, or drive a car may be acquired by consciously imitating a model. Language acquisition involves both indirect and direct forms of modeling. The child imitates the speech of the adult and also puts words together in grammatically correct patterns when instructed to do so. In a similar fashion, parents who talk about the things of the Lord and spend time reading the Scriptures may observe the same behaviors in their children, and if they direct their children to engage in Bible reading and prayer, the results are even more visible.

The indirect approach may not be sufficient in and of itself to obtain the desired results. When this occurs, the direct approach also must be used. We all have seen parents who were kind and considerate of their children and who assumed that their children would automatically treat them in the same way. When this did not happen, they wondered what went wrong. The direct approach of giving specific instructions as to the behavior expected along with reinforcers for appropriate actions and punishers for inappropriate actions is needed as well. But parents should keep in mind when reinforcing or punishing not to exhibit behaviors they do not wish to see in their children. This is not always possible, but at least an effort should be made. Sears, Maccoby, and Levin (1957) interviewed 379 mothers of kindergarten age children asking them how they had raised their children from birth. Mothers who reported the least amount of aggression in their children were mothers who did not allow the child to act aggressively, and when the child did begin an aggressive act, the mother would stop the child in a nonaggressive way. For example, if the child tried to hit her (as all small children do from time to time) she would catch the child's arm tightly, but without hurting the child, and would tell the child in a calm but firm voice that this was something he or she must *never, never* do. Mothers who reported considerable meanness or aggression in their children used a different pattern of control. Children were allowed to act aggressively after which they would be punished for the act. If they hit her, she would hit them back. They could be abusive to other members of the family and show their anger in other ways, but it was only when the quarreling or loud noise or door slamming or whatever made the mother sufficiently uncomfortable occurred that she would step in and stop them, often with loud scolding and slaps.

In this way, children developed patterns of aggressive behavior and also observed aggressive actions on the part of the parent.

We live in an aggressive society, and the home is one of the least safe places for many people to be. In a study of over twenty-five hundred male offenders, Glueck and Glueck (1974) found that most delinquents and criminals came from homes in which discipline was overstrict or erratic. By comparison, few offenders came from homes in which discipline was firm but kindly. Both overstrict and firm parents punish their children, but the difference lies in the severity of the punishment, the fairness with which it is administered, and the extent to which it is used in comparison with less aggressive ways of keeping the child in line.

Other influences in the home also play a part in whether the child will act in moral or immoral ways, and the parent would do well to exercise control in these areas. The books the child reads, the magazines looked at, the pictures and plaques hung on the walls, the programs watched on television, the records and tapes listened to—all are a part of the environment of the home. The effect of television alone is enormous. In a two-volume 1982 National Institute of Mental Health report summarizing twenty years of research and more than three thousand scientific studies, a major finding was that televised violence is linked to later aggressive behavior in children (Rubenstein, 1983). Lisa Kuhmerker (1976), editor of the *Moral Education Forum*, wrote:

> We have become very much aware of the potential harmful effects of violence on television, of the fragmentation of children's attention, of the lack of demand that the medium makes on children's attention span. But there are other potential effects of television whose influence have hardly begun to be explored. ... I think we should look long and hard to see what the effect on children may be when they repeatedly hear canned laughter in situations

where sympathy might be the appropriate reaction. . . . In real life children get many non-verbal cues from adults which correct the initial impression that another person's misfortune is funny. The stereotypes of situation comedies and the simplistics of cartoons carry no such corrective message. (p. 263)

The learning theory stress on the importance of the environment and the way in which the environment relates directly to overt behavior is one we all share. It *does* make a difference what type of home the child has, and the moral environment of the home is as important as any other aspect of the environment. A moral environment is present when parents are good models of moral behavior and when they condition their children to act in socially desirable ways.

Application to the School

The behavioral approach to morality is the one taken by school children when asked to determine what is proper. The following list (with spelling errors *un*corrected) was given by sixth-graders in response to their teacher's request to write "class standards."

Listen to the teacher when she is talking or yelling.
Keep your shoes on in school.
Don't say shut up if the teacher doesn't like it.
Don't stay in the restroom all day.
Don't go to the bathroom all the time.
The bathroom isn't a meeting place and classes aren't held
there.
Don't hide in the bathroom on hot days.
Don't play with thing.
Leave your treshures at home.
Stand when you walk into class.
Be ploite to all the teachers, not just yours.
Don't be a taital tail.

Don't lend back of your chair.
Don't scrap your chair.
Stay in your set.
Stay in your sit.
Try not to hit your classmates.
Be good to the little people.
Don't ride on another girl's back, you could get hurt.
No pooping bags at lunch.
Don't spit on the playground.
If the teacher says something funny, don't pound on your
   desk.
Don't bother the Princeble.
Youse are time wisley.
Four people don't have to take one hurt person to the office.
Don't fall out of your chairs.
Dont' crew gun or candy.
Don't crawl on floors.
Witch your mouth.
Wash your language. (Amory, 1971, p. 10)

Children are very serious about providing rules for conduct but think a separate rule must be given for each behavior. The list becomes so long that no one could
remember it all. Adults realize that only a few regulations
should be given at any one time and so will state a rule
in such a way that a number of behaviors will be included,
such as: "Follow directions." "Complete all assignments."
"Do not leave the classroom without permission." "Keep
hands, feet, objects to oneself." "Work independently."
Both classical and instrumental techniques are helpful in
conditioning the child to adjust to the stated demands.

Classical conditioning develops habits in the child that
make for the smooth functioning of the institution. Children learn that the bell means to put their books in their
desks and line up for recess or that recess is over and it is
time to get in line and go back in. The bell is a conditioned
stimulus that provides a cue for what the child is to do.
Classical conditioning also may be used by the school psy-

chologist to help the phobic child. The phobia probably developed by stimulus generalization, and the child shows a fear reaction to events that normally would not bring about such a response. The child needs to be reconditioned or desensitized to these events, and this is done by pairing a stimulus remotely resembling the original conditioned stimulus with a pleasant rather than an unpleasant unconditioned stimulus and gradually introducing conditioned stimuli that are closer and closer to the original conditioned stimulus on which the fear reaction took place. Suppose, for instance, that we were to recondition Watson's Little Albert. We would begin by showing Albert some white cotton while giving him good food or an interesting toy. When Albert no longer showed a fear of cotton, a Santa Claus mask would be paired with the food or the toy—then a stuffed Easter rabbit, a fur coat, and so on, until finally a live rat would be presented. The child would now associate the rat with the food or the toy rather than with the loud noise, and the fear reaction would be extinguished. School phobia is dealt with in the same way. If it has emerged full blown (not the occasional reluctance of the child to go to school, in which case the child is marched off to school anyway) the phobic child is gradually given more and more exposure to the school situation until he or she is able to go to school for a full day.

Desensitization methods are used by peers to change the child who does not conform to their way of behaving. The first-grader who has temper tantrums at home may not have them at school because such action is labeled as infantile by his or her classmates, and a junior-high student displaying normal behavior for one's age may be quickly acculturated into a delinquent group by being hardened, systematically, against actions the larger society considers to be decent and right. Delinquent teenagers link a concern for others and a respect for authority with weakness and effeminacy, whereas starting a fight or shoplifting is considered daring and clever. Parents and teachers are understandably concerned when they see a child from a good home spending time with peers who engage in antisocial acts, for they know it is only a matter of time before this child will talk and act in the same way. Stability of behavior tends to be maintained when a person remains in an environment that does not demand such change, and, realizing this, parents may seek a school for their child that will continue the expectations of behavior established in the home. Proponents of Christian day schools give this as a major reason for the establishment of church-supported educational institutions.

Instrumental conditioning is used in schools to modify the behavior of the "acting out" child, the child who does not seem to care, and the child who is emotionally disturbed, but its principal application is in the use of programed materials. Teaching machines, computer-assisted devices, and programed booklets are based on operant techniques and provide for a unit of study being presented in small steps with immediate feedback as to whether the student's answer is right or wrong. Not only is there the advantage of not having to wait for the teacher to grade the lesson, but each problem or frame is based on the one preceding so there is a sequence of steps in learning the lesson. Children progress at their own rate, and even the teacher who may lack formal training in the discipline can supervise a whole class at a time.

The greatest enthusiasm for teaching machines and other programed approaches came in the 1950s and early 1960s when a number of studies indicated that children learned more in a given period of time by using programed materials than when they were taught by traditional methods. But the excitement was short-lived. The materials were expensive and the machines often needed repair. Besides, good programs were difficult to write and seemed to be the exception rather than the rule; later studies showed that the rapid learning reported earlier did not continue over the long run, probably because the novelty had worn off and children became bored. Furthermore, the materials were appropriate only for certain subjects, like mathematics, in which there was one right answer. They did not lend themselves to other subjects, like social studies, in which class discussions were of value. Reasoning, creativity, insight, and the sharing of ideas cannot be programed into a machine or a book; yet, they play a vital role in the education of the child.

The heaviest use of programed materials at the present time appears to be in Christian day schools using Accelerated Christian Education (ACE) materials. Advertised by its founder and president, Donald Howard (1979) as "the most completely Christian curriculum on the market" (p. 10), ACE is in booklet form and each packet of material "quotes Scriptures and is carefully planned to glorify God and to teach and encourage Christian living" (Howard 1979, 10). Students set their own goals as to how many pages they will do that day and begin the next day where they left off. E. E. Wiggin (1981) wrote that "Christian day schools now are opening at the rate of one every seven hours. Two-thirds of these schools employ the new and innovative Accelerated Christian Education program." It was estimated in 1981 that "ACE has grown to more than 3,000 schools and 200,000 students." "Pupils work independently in their 'offices' (which have partitions high enough to discourage talking) throughout most of the day. . . . Incentives are offered by means of an elaborate, but effective, system of rewards and privileges, which include field trips and trophies" (pp. 40, 41, 44).

Public schools still make use of programed materials, but to a lesser degree than was true twenty or twenty-five years ago. At times the programed approach is appropriate for it adds interest and variety to the educational process, but it has been shown that its effectiveness diminishes when employed on a large scale. Programs need to be selected carefully and used only for certain types of materials. Nor should such lessons be used as a substitute for the well-trained teacher. Being educated is far more than knowing one correct answer to a question. Being educated means being creative, learning to get along with others, preparing for a career, appreciating the world in which we live, and acting in socially acceptable ways—skills that do not lend themselves to programed instruction.

Teachers also need to be reminded from time to time that many pairs of eyes see what they do and many pairs of ears hear what they say. Younger children are more apt to imitate the mannerisms and speech of the teacher, but older children are more aware of the teacher's lifestyle and feel it unfair to be criticized for engaging in the same behaviors they see exhibited in their instructors. A lesson on personal cleanliness or physical fitness is less effective when taught by someone with oily hair or obese proportions, and teenagers feel it most unjust to be penalized for an activity such as smoking when the one who punishes them slips off to the furnace room several times a day to have a smoke.

The content of basal readers and books on library shelves is receiving increased attention as concerned citizens find that many of the characters depicted in these books are unworthy role-models for the child. Children are influenced by exemplars in stories as well as by real people, and if they read of people who act and talk in dishonorable ways and yet no criticism or punishment is forthcoming for these behaviors, it only stands to reason that they, in turn, will be inclined to engage in similar activities if they perceive it to be in their best interests to do so. Lying may be condoned in a story as long as everything turns out all right at the end, and outwitting a younger or less intelligent child may be pictured as entrepreneurial and shrewd. The pros and cons of censorship of classroom materials have been hotly debated, but the fact remains that our major responsibility is to our children and to their moral and spiritual development. Counteracting worldly influences may be done to a degree, and we do not wish to shelter our sons and daughters more than is necessary, yet a steady diet of the literature found in some classrooms will not result in the kinds of behavior we wish to see in the next generation.

Some educators have advocated a return to the type of story read by children at the turn of the century. Interestingly, Graney (1977) found little difference in the overt behaviors of children depicted in McGuffey's Readers and the behaviors of children depicted in currently used readers. He did find, however, that the model of authority had changed from individual figures in McGuffey to a combination of individualistic and collectivistic authority figures in modern readers and that the characters in McGuffey's Readers were more inner-directed, whereas the exemplars in modern readers were more inclined toward being in harmony with the peer group. Parents and teachers who feel there are times when the child should not go along with the crowd have reason to be concerned with some of the messages given in textbooks today.

Application to the Church

What is the child's reaction when the words *church, God,* or *Bible* are heard? Is the response favorable? The answer lies in the experiences (unconditioned stimuli) the child associates with these words (conditioned stimuli). Learning about God relates both to the everyday activities in the home (Dt. 6:7) and to those special times when the people of God gather together to worship and praise their Redeemer. In the Old Testament we read that these special occasions meant a break from the regular duties of the week (Lv. 23:3-4) and an opportunity for feasting (Ex. 12:14) and for storytelling (Jos. 4:21-24)—events that all children enjoy, and in the New Testament we learn that Jesus himself at the age of twelve journeyed to Jerusalem to observe the Passover (Lk. 2:42).

But twentieth-century America is different. Times have

changed, and going to the place of worship may not be the high point of a person's week or traveling to another town to observe a religious holiday the principal reason for taking a vacation. How can the church of today compete with all the stimuli in a child's life—the television, the theater, and the ever-present video game? How can the Sunday school capture the interest of those who have no religious background and little encouragement from their families? Is there an answer? Some church leaders say that there is, and, interestingly, the answer lies in a full-scale implementation of instrumental techniques. The results are impressive and show that operant procedures are as effective when used in the church as when used anywhere else. If success can be measured by numbers of people, and many feel that it can, there are few success stories that rival those of churches that have gone all out for a program based on contingency management.

The First Baptist Church of Hammond, Indiana, boasted of an average weekly Sunday school attendance of 13,500, most of whom were children bused from the Chicago area. How did the church do it? Edgerton (1975) explains:

> There is fierce competition between the bus workers to increase attendance at the Sunday school. The children are offered everything from on-board entertainment (such as the man in the gorilla outfit) to food and gifts (rubber spiders and "flowers for mom"). Recently, children who brought in new members were told to dip into a bucket of "pennies from heaven," and next week they will be taken to McDonald's for "Egg McMuffin Sunday." (p. 1)

From candy to Kung Fu exhibitions to a trip to Jamaica as a prize for "soul-winning," the reinforcers were given, and all with the purpose of reaching boys and girls with the message of Jesus Christ.

Those who find the method intriguing will enjoy Bill Wilson's *Buses, Bibles, and Banana Splits: Promotional*

Ideas for Bus Ministry and Children's Church (1977).
Activities follow the yearly calendar, and pages in the
book are perforated so that individual sheets may be removed and copied or used for advertising purposes. Events
include breakfast on the bus, hotdog day, pumpkin Sunday, and haunted house, with a free boat ride or helicopter
ride for the boy or girl bringing the most visitors. Children
on the bus with the most passengers are treated to a giant
banana split. The ideas in the book are said to be passed
on to the reader "as a manual for evangelism, to be used
in your Jerusalem, Judea and to the uttermost parts of the
world" (Wilson, 1977, inside back cover).

Some people object to the use of tangible reinforcers to
increase church school attendance, and yet the method
probably is used to some extent in all churches.[4] Gold
stars are placed after children's names each time they come
or pictures of Bible story characters are colored and proudly
taken home. When children attend enough Sundays con-
secutively they are given pins to wear or certificates to
keep, and their names are printed in the church bulletin.
In one study (Captain, 1975) the tangible reinforcer of
money was found to be effective in getting high school
students to read the Bible and to have a positive attitude
toward themselves in relationship to Bible reading.

Instrumental conditioning is used to enhance the work
of the church in other ways as well, and several writers
have explained how it is done. Collins (1969) describes the
use of teaching machines and programed booklets to teach
Bible stories, and Ratcliff (1978) explains how lay persons
may be shaped into effective soul-winners by gradually
reinforcing closer and closer approximations to the desired
behavior seen in actual witnessing. Bufford (1981) shows
how memorizing Scripture verses, learning religious concepts, and planning the Sunday school curriculum are enhanced by the use of operant procedures, and George and
Dustin (1970) write that the pastor of the church should
function as a behavioral counselor pinpointing for the pa-

rishioner-client the actions that produced the problem and being "a potent source of reinforcement" (p. 18) when those actions change to more acceptable forms of behavior. It appears that a number of Christian authors would agree with Steckel (1979) when he says that "religious institutions will be enriched by behavior modification in their tasks of . . . social action, pastoral care and counseling, and religious education. . . . And church education programs may become far more successful in specifying the kinds of persons and institutions we want ourselves to be as religious people, by using behavioral analysis and behavior modification methods" (p. 166).

Despite numerous criticisms of the behavioral approach it will continue to be used in the church. It will be used by both the critic who is seemingly unaware of the ways in which he or she uses it and the supporter who may need to exercise greater caution and restraint. As additional research is conducted and more attention is given to methodology, our understanding of how to apply the principles of behavioral psychology to the ongoing work of the church will be increased.

One of the ways in which the pastor or Sunday school teacher encourages moral behavior is to live a moral life and to help others to do the same. As was mentioned, the reinforcer for imitating the behavior of another may come from the attention one receives when imitating, or it may come from the consequence of the behavior itself, or in some cases, it is vicarious in that the one imitating sees the self as having the experiences and characteristics of the one imitated. Coming to the place of worship, bowing one's head in prayer, and singing hymns of praise are learned by seeing others do these things, and if copying these behaviors meets with approval or if people feel better for having done them they will engage in these behaviors again and again. The young person who thrills to the stories told by missionaries and who pictures himself or herself as a missionary with all the adventure and risk involved is more apt some day to be a missionary than the young person who was never exposed to such a model.

The work of the church is served by those who are aware of their influence and are careful to live exemplary lives. The apostle Paul understood this when he said to the Corinthians, "Follow my example, as I follow the example of Christ" (1 Cor. 11:1). But exemplary models are not sufficient to assure similar behaviors in others. Paul wrote to Titus that an elder in the church must not only be "blameless" (Ti. 1:6) but "must hold firmly to the trustworthy message as it has been taught, so that he can encourage others by sound doctrine" (v. 9). Training programs or discipling arrangements will help future leaders understand the truths of God's Word both with regard to Christian doctrine and with regard to appropriate conduct. As Paul exhorted Timothy, "What you heard from me, keep as the pattern of sound teaching. . . . Flee the evil desires of youth, and pursue righteousness . . . so that the man of God may be thoroughly equipped for every good work" (2 Tm. 1:13; 2:22; 3:17).

Theology and the Learning Approach

In the Old Testament, signs were used to remind the people of God of those times when Jehovah had intervened on their behalf in some miraculous way. By pairing the sign (conditioned stimulus) with the event (unconditioned stimulus), the children of Israel were made aware of God's blessing long after the miracle had taken place. The sign also served as an object lesson by which the next generation would learn the story of deliverance. "When your descendants ask . . . 'What do these stones mean?' tell them. . . . The Lord your God did to the Jordan just what he had done to the Red Sea. . . . He did this so that all the people of the earth might know that the hand of the Lord is powerful and so that you might always fear the Lord your God" (Jos. 4:21-24).

In the New Testament, as well, signs and ordinances were instituted to remind believers of important events. The star seen by the wise men was a sign that the Messiah had come, and long after the Messiah had fulfilled his purpose on earth and had returned to the Father, Christians were admonished to come together to remind one another of Christ's death and coming again, even as Christ had met with his disciples on the day of the Passover. "The Lord Jesus, on the night he was betrayed, took bread, and when he had given thanks, he broke it and said, 'This is my body, which is for you: do this in remembrance of me.' . . . For whenever you eat this bread and drink this cup, you proclaim the Lord's death until he comes" (1 Cor. 11:23-24, 26).

In classical conditioning, the conditioned stimulus is not to be equated with the unconditioned stimulus but rather serves as a reminder of the unconditioned or original event. In the same way, the sign or ordinance in Scripture is not the event itself but is given to the people of God to refresh their memories of past deliverance and future blessing. Readily visible conditioned stimuli are needed to help us retain an image of God's workings in our lives and to keep before us the more remote, but nevertheless important, hallmarks of Christian experience. Without tangible reminders we soon forget, and without behavioral opportunities to respond to the reminders we often become neglectful.

Reinforcers also are needed so that we "never tire of doing what is right" (2 Thes. 3:13). God made us and knows what we are like. He knows that we will continue those behaviors for which we are rewarded and discontinue those behaviors for which we are punished; so, in his Word he offers blessings (reinforcers) dependent upon acts of obedience, and cursings (punishers) contingent upon acts of disobedience. In the Christian life, as with all of life, the reinforcers and punishers do not always occur at the moment of behavior, making it difficult for us to stay on course. We may look around and feel as did the psalmist that it is the wicked who prospers and the righteous who in vain keeps his heart pure (Ps. 73:13). To offset this confusion of the temporal with the eternal, David went to the sanctuary of God and after contemplation came to an understanding of one's final destiny (v. 17). We, too, are asked to go to the house of the Lord, to meet with other believers, and to look forward to the time when God's final blessing will be revealed—a time when we will receive "the crown of righteousness" (2 Tm. 4:8).

> We are told to pair the social reinforcement of praise, encouragement, and comfort with the rewards that await us in heaven to motivate us toward good deeds. ... The social reinforcement of speaking confidently, associated with the hope of eternal life, provides an incentive for desirable behavior. ... These reinforcers may also serve as discriminative stimuli for the primary reinforcement of Christ's return. (Bolin & Goldberg, 1979, pp. 171-172)

One of the ways in which we encourage one another to good works is to live a life that is pleasing to God. The Scriptures provide examples of such a life. We learn "endurance" from the prophets and "patience" from Job (Jas. 5:10-11), "sound speech" from the minister (Ti. 2:8), and the importance of hard work from the apostle Paul (2 Thes. 3:7-9). A whole roster of men and women who lived by faith is given for us in Hebrews 11. But it is only when we look to Jesus that we see the perfect model, for it is only in Jesus that we see a perfect life. In him alone we find forgiveness and healing, holiness and the promise of eternal life. And in him we find love—love that covers a multitude of sins. Paul told the believers at Ephesus to "live a life of love, just as Christ loved us" (Eph. 5:2).

In *The Jesus Model*, David McKenna explains why Jesus as our model is of prime importance.

Christian Faith pivots on a person—Jesus of Nazareth.
. . . As the Son of God, he claimed to be our Lord; as the
Son of Man, he claimed to be our Model; and as fully God
and fully man, he claimed to be our Redeemer.

When the case of Christianity is presented in the secular
world, the authority of Jesus as Lord and Redeemer carries
the weight of the argument. . . . In response, we cannot
forget that Jesus' claim to be the Son of Man holds equal
authority in the Christian portfolio. If Jesus was a real and
complete man who participated fully in the human experience, then he must be our Model and our hope. Anything
less and the case for Christianity is dismissed. (pp. 13-14)

The Christian hope is that someday "we shall be like him,
for we shall see him as he is" (1 Jn. 3:2), and even though
we presently fall short of exemplifying Christ in our lives,
we can look forward to that wonderful day when we will
indeed be like Him.

Psychologists and theologians interested in relating
learning theory and Christian belief have taken sides on
the issue of whether the philosophy underlying behaviorism and the technology practiced by behaviorists are so
inextricably linked that an acceptance (or rejection) of one
mandates an acceptance (or rejection) of the other. Mc-
Keown (1981) states that theory and methodology cannot
be divorced, for "to embrace 'methodological behaviorism'
implicitly means accepting theoretical behaviorism because one incorporates its language and its metaphysics"
(pp. 18-19). Vos (1978) likewise writes that "an application
of behavioral psychology cannot disown its commitment
to the thesis that the environment alone is a cause in
human affairs. This thesis contradicts what is both im-
plied in and asserted by biblical principles, namely, that
man is an agent, free and responsible" (p. 210).

The majority opinion (Bolin & Goldberg, 1979; Bufford,
1978; Collins, 1977; Cosgrove, 1982; Hammes, 1973;
Llewellyn, 1973; MacKay, 1979; Steckel, 1979), however,
is that philosophical behaviorism and technological be-

haviorism differ, and that when each is compared with Christian belief, the philosophy of behaviorism is incompatible with Christianity, whereas the technology of behaviorism is consistent with Scripture and reflects the way in which God created us. This view is expressed in a variety of ways. Donald MacKay (1979) uses the terms *negative behaviourism* and *positive behaviourism,* negative behaviorism being "behaviouristic *philosophy* as distinct from science" and "characterized by what it *denies.* . . . Religious values are downgraded to mere 'reinforcers.' . . . Freedom of choice is held to be an illusion." Positive behaviorism, by contrast, "is theologically neutral and not of itself at all inimical to human dignity" (p. 47). Gary Collins (1977) writes, "The scientist and the theologian might disagree over behaviorism, mechanistic determinism, or the irrelevance of religion, but this is a conflict not so much over empirical facts as over the presuppositions that guide one's data-gathering and interpretation of facts" (p. 109). Russell Llewellyn (1973) puts it succinctly when he says, "Skinner as science is great. Skinner as religion is terrible" (p. 7).[5]

That behavioral philosophy and Christian belief differ is readily apparent. One holds that children are born neither good nor bad but learn to be what they are made to be by the environment; the other holds that children come into the world with a natural propensity for wrongdoing, and even the best of environments will not bring an about-face. One says that morality is moral behavior; the other says that morality is an inward condition, and overt behaviors are a manifestation of that inward state (Mt. 23:25-26). One believes that people are moral if they advance the cause of the social order; the other believes that people are moral if they advance the cause of the kingdom of God (6:33). For one, goodness is submitting self-interests to the well-being of the group; for the other, goodness is submitting self-interests to the plan and will of God (Rom. 12:1-2). One has dispossessed autonomous man

(Skinner, 1971); the other has witnessed the fall of man because humans were given autonomy by God and made the wrong choice. Yet, it is the freedom of choice that offers hope, as once again through Christ's sacrificial death, we are offered "the gift of righteousness" (Rom. 5:17).

Ideological differences, as great as they may be, do not negate the fact that God created us as beings who respond to reinforcers and punishers in our environment and who have a natural inclination to imitate the behaviors of the people around us. The learning approach, although deficient in terms of *a priori* principles, is, nevertheless, an informative source to help us understand ourselves and others. By being knowledgeable of the techniques used and applying them appropriately as the occasion demands, we can enhance God's plan in the lives of those entrusted to our care and demonstrate by our actions that we belong to him (Jas. 2:18). Morality as moral behavior is an important ingredient of the Christian life.

Notes

1. Social learning includes within its perimeters, not only learning psychology but also psychoanalysis. The learning theory concept of imitation and the psychoanalytic concept of identification (presented in chap. 5) are closely related, the two developing simultaneously in the young child. Theoretically speaking, however, they are far apart. Imitation emphasizes overt responses learned when a person copies the behavior of another, whereas identification stresses the internalization of normative demands and the adoption of the ideas and attitudes of the model. Imitation results in the acquisition of good habits; identification brings about the development of a conscience or superego. For an in-depth discussion of the way in which social learning spans the distance between these two disparate psychologies and includes portions of both within its scope, see Hoffman, M. L., (1970) Moral development, in P. Mussen (Ed.), *Carmichael's manual of child psychology*, Vol. 2, New York: John Wiley & Sons; Kohlberg, L., (1963) Moral development and identification, in H. W. Stevenson (Ed.), *Child psychology: 62nd yearbook of the National Society*

for the Study of Education, Chicago: University of Chicago Press; and Woodward, W. R., (1982) The "discovery" of social behaviorism and social learning theory, 1870-1980, *American Psychologist, 37,* 396-410.

2. Contact comfort refers to the satisfaction an organism feels when in close physical contact with another being. A toddler cradled and rocked in her father's arms experiences contact comfort. Child psychologists believe that contact comfort is as important to psychological development as good food is to bodily growth.

3. The phrases in quotes are responses given by undergraduate students enrolled in the author's classes. Each student went through the steps of behavior modification using himself or herself as the subject.

4. The author and her husband became aware that church people differ in their ideas of what constitutes an acceptable prize (reinforcer) when they purchased a thoroughbred cocker spaniel puppy to be given to the child who brought the most visitors to Sunday school. Placing the pup in a box on top of the piano during the Sunday school hour for all to witness her cute antics did far more to inspire the children to bring their friends than it did to win the approval of some of the older and more staid members of the congregation. Since that time more Bibles have been purchased than puppies.

5. A number of other Christian authors have taken this same position. Examples include John Hammes (1973) who writes, "One cannot fault Skinner's experimental data, which stand on their own merit. It is his theoretical formulations, based on this data, that can seriously be questioned" (p. 8); Roger Bufford (1978) who states, "Metaphysical behaviorism is inherently in conflict with the biblical view; however, methodological behaviorism does not pose this problem. Practical application of behavior modification may make a significant contribution in helping us put biblical principles into practice" (p. 125); and Bolin and Goldberg (1979) who comment, "Behavioral psychology has been slow in being accepted as a viable source of theological integration because of the questions it raises concerning man's freedom, dignity, self-control, and responsibility. Although these are valid concerns of philosophical behaviorism, they are merely pseudo-issues regarding methodological behaviorism. Reflecting the natural laws of God's universe, methodological behaviorism integrates with Scripture on many points" (p. 167). Mark Cosgrove (1982) shares this view when he said, "The Christian has no quarrel with Skinner's data. Skinner has uncovered some of God's laws governing certain animal and human behaviors. The problem arises only when Skinner generalizes from his data and makes broad assumptions about the nature of real-

ity that are unsupportable by data and in conflict with biblical revelation" (p. 108).

References

Amory, C. (1971, February 27). Trade winds. *Saturday Review, 54,* 10.

Bandura, A. (1965). Influence of model's reinforcement contingencies on the acquisition of imitative responses. *Journal of Personality and Social Psychology, 1,* 589-95.

Bandura, A., Ross, D., & Ross, S. (1963). Imitation of film mediated aggressive models. *Journal of Abnormal and Social Psychology, 66,* 3-11.

Bolin, E. P., & Goldberg, G. M. (1979). Behavioral psychology and the Bible: General and specific considerations. *Journal of Psychology and Theology, 7,* 167-75.

Bufford, R. K. (1978). God and behavior mod II: Some reflections on Vos' response. *Journal of Psychology and Theology, 6,* 215-18.

_____. (1981) *The human reflex: Behavioral psychology in biblical perspective.* San Francisco: Harper & Row.

Captain, P. A. (1975). The effect of positive reinforcement on comprehension, attitudes, and rate of Bible reading in adolescents. *Journal of Psychology and Theology, 3,* 49-55.

Collins, G. R. (1969). *Search for reality: Psychology and the Christian.* Wheaton, IL: Key Publishers.

_____. (1977). *The rebuilding of psychology: An integration of psychology and Christianity.* Wheaton, IL: Tyndale House.

Cosgrove, M. P. (1982). *B. F. Skinner's behaviorism: An analysis.* Grand Rapids, MI: Zondervan.

Edgerton, M. (1975, November 3). Sunday school uses bus fleet and candy to win kids' souls. *The Wall Street Journal,* pp. 1, 24.

Eysenck, H. J. (1960). The development of moral values in children: The contribution of learning theory. *British Journal of Educational Psychology, 30,* 11-21.

George, R. L., & Dustin, E. R. (1970, December). The minister as a behavioral counselor. *Pastoral Psychology, 21,* 15-20.

Glueck, S., & Glueck, E. (1974). *Of delinquency and crime: A panorama of years of search and research.* Springfield, IL: C. C. Thomas.

Graney, M. (1977). Role models in children's readers. *School Review, 85,* 247-63.

Hammes, J. A. (1973). Beyond freedom and dignity: Behavioral fixated delusion? *Journal of Psychology and Theology, 1*(3), 8-14.

Harris, B. (1979) Whatever happened to Little Albert? *American Psychologist, 34,* 151-60.

Howard, D. R. (1979). *Facts about Accelerated Christian Education.* Lewisville, TX: Accelerated Christian Education.

Kuhmerker, L. (1976). Social interaction and the development of a sense of right and wrong in young children. *Journal of Moral Education, 5,* 257-64.

Llewellyn, R. C. (1973). A second look at B. F. Skinner. *Journal of Psychology and Theology, 1*(3), 3-7.

MacKay, D. M. (1979). *Human science & human dignity.* Downers Grove, IL: Inter-Varsity.

McKenna, D. L. (1977). *The Jesus model.* Waco, TX: Word Books.

McKeown, B. (1981). Myth and its denial in a secular age: The case of behaviorist psychology. *Journal of Psychology and Theology, 9,* 12-20.

Patterson, G. R. (1976). *Living with children: New methods for parents and teachers.* Champaign, IL: Research Press.

Premack, D. (1965). Reinforcement theory. In D. Levine (Ed), *Nebraska symposium on motivation, 1965* (pp. 123-80). Lincoln: University of Nebraska Press.

Ratcliff, D. E. (1978). Using behavioral psychology to encourage personal evangelism. *Journal of Psychology and Theology, 6,* 219-24.

Rubenstein, E. A. (1983). Television and behavior. *American Psychologist, 38,* 820-25.

Sears, R. R., Maccoby, E. E., & Levin, H. (1957). *Patterns of child rearing.* Evanston, IL: Row, Peterson.

Skinner, B. F. (1938). *The behavior of organisms: An experimental analysis.* New York: Appleton-Century-Crofts.

————. (1953). *Science and human behavior.* New York: Macmillan.

————. (1971). *Beyond freedom and dignity.* New York: Alfred A. Knopf.

————. (1974). *About behaviorism.* New York: Alfred A. Knopf.

————. (1978). *Reflections on behaviorism and society.* Englewood Cliffs, NJ: Prentice-Hall.

Staats, A. W. (1961). Verbal habit-families, concepts, and the operant conditioning of word classes. *Psychological Review, 68,* 190-204.

Steckel, C. J. (1979). *Theology and ethics of behavior modification.* Washington, DC: University of America Press.

Vos, A. (1978). A response to "God and behavior mod." *Journal of Psychology and Theology, 6,* 210-14.

Watson, J. B. (1931). *Behaviorism.* London: Routledge & Kegan Paul.

Watson, J. B., & Rayner, R. (1920). Conditioned emotional reactions. *Journal of Experimental Psychology, 3,* 1-14.

Wiggin, E. E. (1981, August). Should your grade schooler receive Accelerated Christian Education? *Christian Life, 43,* 40-4.

Wilson, B. (1977). *Buses, Bibles, and banana splits: Promotional ideas for bus ministry and children's church.* Grand Rapids: Baker.

3

The Cognitive Approach
Morality as Moral Reasoning

But his delight is in the law of the Lord;
and on his law he meditates day and night. (Ps. 1:2)

A number of psychologists have been dissatisfied with the learning theory position and its emphasis on environmental stimuli and overt responses and have turned to an explanation of human behavior known as cognitivism. The term *cognitive* comes from the Latin word *cognito*, which means "knowledge" and includes the higher mental processes of memory, attention, information-processing, decision-making, and understanding. Although some learning theorists, usually referred to as neo-behaviorists, provide classical and instrumental conditioning paradigms to explain mental functioning, the bulk of the writing in cognitive processing has been done by psychologists (appropriately called cognitive psychologists) who have a very different orientation as to the nature of the learning process.

Early work in cognitive psychology came from a group of German scholars known as Gestalt psychologists who were interested primarily in the nature of perception. The term *Gestalt* may be loosely translated to mean "form" or "pattern," and studies were conducted as to the way patterns are seen by the individual. It was noted that although the parts of a pattern may be analyzed, it is not the parts themselves but rather the relationship of the parts to each other that produces a particular Gestalt. For example, a whirlpool is made up of drops of water, but it is a whirlpool only because the drops are in a specific relationship to each other. Place a stopper in the sink and the whirlpool no longer is present even though drops of water remain. A melody is heard as the same tune regardless of the key in which it is played because the parts retain the same relationship or pattern even though the actual notes differ. Studies in Gestalt psychology showed that people come to understand their world not so much by the effect of the actual environment upon them as by their own inborn capacity to organize life into understandable patterns or wholes.

Today's cognitive theorists, borrowing from Gestalt psychology, focus on the person as a conscious, perceiving organism capable of acquiring meaning from the world. Each person plays a constructive role in his or her own learning and development. Rather than being a pawn of environmental contingencies, each of us is endowed with the ability to interact with the world in such a way as to make sense out of what goes on around us, to construct our own experiences, to understand ourselves and others. This does not mean that the nature of the environment is unimportant, but it does mean that the focus of attention is on the person rather than on external stimuli. The world has no meaning apart from the image of that world on the consciousness of the person. Thus, the most important topic in psychology, according to the cognitive theorist, is the study of individuals as persons capable of understanding the world around them, of putting it together in meaningful ways, and interacting with it so that future growth is ensured. Each of us generates our own development as we are shaped, in turn, by previously acquired cognitions.

Basic Assumptions

Cognitive psychologists view morality as developmental in nature and are interested in changes that occur as a person progresses from lower to higher levels of moral maturity. A concept basic to the cognitive position is that *moral development occurs within the individual.* Morality cannot be produced or generated by an outside source. By its very definition, morality must be rooted within the personality. People are not moral simply because they engage in moral acts; they are moral as they understand moral concepts and their subsequent behavior reflects a more mature level of cognitive organization. Although the environment may encourage morality or may produce conditions that impede it, the dynamic remains within the organism.

Cognitive theorists also hold that *moral development parallels intellectual development.* As children increase in mental ability, they also increase in the ability to reason at higher levels of moral judgment. There obviously is not a one-to-one correspondence between morality and intelligence. We all know capable people who do not show high levels of moral reasoning. But studies using groups of children or adults show positive correlations between these two factors. Although one may be intelligent but not moral, one cannot be moral in the cognitive sense of the term and not have reached a certain level of intellectual attainment.

Moral development occurs in a series of stages that are invariant, hierarchical, and universal. Each person passes through the same progression of stages, sequenced in a certain order because earlier stages are less differentiated and are attainable before later stages. Just as children sit before they walk and babble before they talk, they also exhibit less mature forms of moral thinking before going on to more comprehensive patterns of moral thought. Although any particular individual's development may cease at any given stage, there is no skipping those stages that precede the final attainment. For this reason, the sequence of stages of moral development is said to be invariant. The stages also constitute a hierarchy because each stage is the product of learning that occurred during the previous stage and becomes a preparation for the stage that follows. Although each stage or level is qualitatively different from the one preceding it, lower levels are prerequisite to higher ones, and the attainment of any particular level must include understandings from earlier ones. As each gradation in the hierarchy constitutes a greater integration of the individual's thinking and enables the individual to do a better job of analyzing problems and relating to the world, higher stages are preferable to lower ones. The hierarchy thus becomes not only an integrative model but also one that provides a framework for evaluating the merit or worth of any particular stage. Considerable cross-cultural research has shown that children in countries around the world go through the stages in the same order. The rate of progression may differ from one culture to another and the percentage of adults who attain to the higher levels of moral reasoning may also vary but the sequence remains universal.

Moral development comes by conflict. When cognitive conflict occurs, that is, when individuals become aware of discrepancies between their experiences and their perceptions, a kind of disequilibrium is created which motivates them to restructure their views and thus accommodate themselves to the world around them. "A fundamental reason why an individual moves from one stage to the next is because the later stages solve problems and inconsistencies unsolvable at the prior stage of development" (Kohlberg, 1973, p. 13). Cognitive conflict does not necessarily imply turmoil or distress, though these may be included, but rather it refers to conceptual contradictions that continuously occur as a person forms and reforms ideas about the world. Conflict speaks to the whole process of learning and understanding, a process which is for the most part an exciting and rewarding adventure.

Cognitive psychologists believe that *moral development is philosophically sound and is not contrary to any major religion.* Because conflict occurs by questioning, social dialogue, raising doubt, or being introduced to new ideas, it follows that cognitive theorists would claim their position "had its origins in Socrates' Athens . . . a universal conception of justice which was rational or cognitive" (Kohlberg, 1976b, p. 213). Plato wrote of a society where men would be educated for justice, and he envisioned a republic where just men or philosopher kings would rule. Descartes, Leibnitz, and Kant are considered to be forerunners of the cognitive position in that they were interested in the genesis of self-consciousness in the individual. John Dewey, with his "democratic reformulation of Plato's Republic," is historically important in moral development theory (Kohlberg, 1976a, p. 14). Dewey believed that the "greatest of all construction" is "the building of a free and powerful character," and this is accomplished by education "supplying the conditions" so that individuals can "mature and pass into higher functions" (Dewey, 1895, pp. 207-208). Each of the stages in the moral developmental process deals with one or more of the issues with which philosophers of ethics have traditionally been concerned—issues of authority, property, cooperation, social adjustment, conscience, equity, and the value of life. These are matters of concern to the major religions of the world as well, for they speak to basic human aspirations in this life and in the life to come. Studies have shown that religious values seem to go through the same stages of development as do other values, and members of a variety of religious groups (e.g., Catholics, Protestants, Jews, Buddhists, and Muslims) proceed through the stages of moral reasoning in the same invariant order (Kohlberg, 1981).

Cognitive psychologists also accept the premise that *moral development is a fully scientific claim about human nature and can be measured.* Science cannot say what morality is or what it should be, but science can test whether a philosopher's conception of morality fits the psychological facts. The cognitive position that morality proceeds in invariant universal stages with justice (concern for the equality of others) being the cornerstone, makes possible the construction of measuring instruments that will determine one's position in the hierarchy of moral stages. Differences in moral judgment that exist between individuals or between cultures are explained, not by ethical relativity, but by differences in the stage or level of moral development of the individuals and cultures being considered. An internal dynamic lying within all healthy people is to accept higher levels of moral reasoning when the next higher level is understood. As such, morality is transcultural, nonrelative, and rooted in reality. Assessment instruments based on this fixed standard may be openended, providing opportunity for an extended response to a story involving a moral dilemma; or the tests may offer a number of statements representative of different stages of moral judgment, and the person chooses those statements that are thought to be most relevant to the moral problem in question. Either way, determination of the level of moral judgment is made, not by what one does, but rather by what one *says.* Although one's behavior is recognized as being important, the cognitive theorist listens to one's verbal reasoning as the basis for the measurement of moral judgment. The cognitive approach measures, then, not so much the content of morality, but the process by which a moral position is formed.

Stages of Moral Reasoning

The Early Work of Jean Piaget

The outstanding pioneer in the field of moral reasoning was Jean Piaget, an eminent Swiss biologist and philosopher whose early work on cognition extended to an investigation of moral judgments in children (Piaget 1932). Piaget did not adhere to separate and discrete stages of moral development, but by observing children between the ages of four and twelve, he noted that older children gave more mature responses to questions than did younger children. Piaget saw moral development as proceeding from *heteronomy,* or the constraint of an external authority, to *autonomy,* or self-rule. Heteronomy occurs in early childhood between the ages of three and seven when the child is under the domination of the parent. Rules are thought by the child to be timeless and to emanate from God. Goodness lies in respecting those in authority, in obeying their commands, and in accepting whatever rewards and punishments are given. Justice is what the parent says is right. "Right is to obey the will of the adult. Wrong is to have a will of one's own" (Piaget, 1932, p. 193). This unequal relationship between children and parents, or "unilateral respect" as Piaget calls it, is accepted by children because they are *moral realists.* This means that young children structure their thinking to their own experiences, and the consequences of behavior determine what is good and what is bad.

Heteronomy is a vital process in moral development, necessary for the training and safety of the child, and a part of the legal system. But the child needs to move on from a morality that is imposed from without to one that is guided from within, from one that is determined by objective consequences to one that is judged by motives, from one based on authority to one based on equality and fairness.

Autonomy begins around seven or eight years of age and should be well formed by the age of eleven or twelve. Intellectual growth and opportunities for peer interaction are basic to the development of autonomy, which includes cooperation, reciprocity, and mutual consent. For a time, heteronomy and autonomy will "coexist at the same age and even in the same child. . . . Objective responsibility diminishes on the average as the child grows older, and subjective responsibility gains correlatively in importance. We have therefore two processes partially overlapping, but of which the second gradually succeeds in dominating the first" (Piaget, 1932, p. 129). Rules are still respected but are based on consensus rather than on authority. Rules may be altered "on the condition of enlisting general opinion on your side" (p. 18). Concern for the rights and welfare of others develops naturally through interaction with one's age-mates and leads the child to nonegocentric, reciprocal thought. "Autonomy therefore appears only with reciprocity, when mutual respect is strong enough to make the individual feel from within the desire to treat others as he himself would wish to be treated" (p. 194).

Beginning at age eleven or twelve, the child progresses to an even higher concept of justice called *equity*, which includes benevolence and an understanding of universal love and forgiveness. The older child has become a *moral relativist*, which means that the child now is aware of differing viewpoints regarding rules. Piaget mentions this final process only briefly, the bulk of his writing on moral judgment being a description of heteronomy and autonomy with examples of statements made by school-age children representative of the "two moralities of the child" (p. 326).

The Later Work of Lawrence Kohlberg

It was not until the early 1960s that Piaget's ideas gained in popularity. Part of the increased recognition was due to the writings of American psychologist Lawrence Kohlberg of Harvard University, who is considered by many to be the foremost authority on the development of moral judgment. Like Piaget, Kohlberg developed a distinction between moral realism and moral relativism, maintained that a person passes through earlier or lower stages of development before going on to later or higher stages, and emphasized the form of moral thought rather than the expression of moral behavior. Kohlberg's research, however, focused on the adolescent and young adult in contrast to Piaget's studies, which were conducted with children between the ages of four and twelve. By observing young people who are at a higher level of cognition, Kohlberg was able to expand Piaget's original two-process system to a six-stage sequence that extends from early childhood through adulthood.

Each of Kohlberg's six stages occurs in an invariant sequence, is qualitatively different from the one preceeding it, and represents a more comprehensive system of intellectual organization. A key term used by Kohlberg is *conventional,* which means that right and wrong is determined on the basis of convention or what society expects of its members. The conventional level is at the midpoint of moral development and includes the two middle stages (stages 3 and 4) in the hierarchy of moral reasoning. A child at the earlier *preconventional* level (stages 1 and 2) interprets a situation in terms of physical consequences rather than in terms of what society says is right or wrong. An adult at the *postconventional* level (stages 5 and 6), having progressed through the previous four stages is able to see beyond social norms and regulations and make decisions based on principles upon which any good society is established (Kohlberg, 1984).

It is not unusual for a person to make statements at more than one stage and sometimes at more than one level. If we say that a person is "at" a given stage we mean that most of the person's reasoning is at this stage. Progression is made from one stage to the next by listening to and understanding the reasoning of someone at the next higher stage. Let us look first at a brief outline of the three levels and their respective stages and then give closer attention to each of the six stages.

I. Preconventional level

At this level the child is responsive to cultural rules and labels of good and bad, right and wrong, but interprets these labels in terms of either the physical consequences of the action—punishment, reward, exchange of favors—or in terms of the physical powers of those who make the rules and labels. The level is divided into two stages:

Stage 1—*The Morality of Obedience:* "*You do what you're told.*"[1]

The physical consequences of action determine its goodness or badness. Avoidance of punishment and unquestioning deference to power are valued in their own right.

Stage 2—*The Morality of Instrumental Egoism and Simple Exchange:* "*Let's make a deal.*"

Right action consists of that which instrumentally satisfies one's own needs. Human relations are viewed in terms like those of the marketplace. Elements of fairness, reciprocity, and equal sharing are present, but they are always interpreted in a physical, pragmatic way. Reciprocity is a matter of "you scratch my back and I'll scratch yours."

II. Conventional level

At this level, maintaining the expectations of the individual's family, group, or nation is perceived as valuable in its own right regardless of the consequences.

The attitude is not only one of conforming to the social order but of being loyal to it and actively maintaining, supporting, and justifying the order. The following two stages comprise this level:

Stage 3—*The Morality of Personal Concordance:* *"Be considerate, nice and kind, and you'll get along with others."*

Good behavior is equated with whatever pleases or helps others and with what others approve of. Stage 3 people conform to stereotypic ideas of how the majority of people in their group behave. Being a "good boy" or a "nice girl" or a "good neighbor" comes at this stage.

Stage 4—*The Morality of Law and Duty to the Social Order:* *"Everyone in society is obligated to and protected by the law."*

Right behavior consists of doing one's duty, showing respect for authority, and maintaining the given social order for its own sake.

III. Postconventional (principled) level

At this level people reason according to moral principles that have validity apart from the authority of groups to which the individuals belong. This level has the following two stages:

Stage 5—*The Morality of Societal Consensus:* *"You are obligated by whatever arrangements are agreed to by due process procedures."*

Right action tends to be defined in terms of general individual rights and standards that have been examined critically and agreed upon by the entire society. Stage 5 provides a rationale for choosing among alternative social systems and supplies guidelines for the creation of new laws and arrangements.

Stage 6—*The Morality of Universal Ethical Principles:* *"How rational and impartial people would organize cooperation is moral."*

Decisions result from an obligation to self-chosen ethical principles that apply to all mankind regardless of age, sex, race, nationality, socio-economic status, ability, or contribution to society. Stage 6 people emphasize human rights and the respect for the dignity of each human being as an individual person.

A closer look at each of the stages will reveal the progression that occurs in understandings as one advances from lower to higher expressions of moral reasoning.

Small children have no say in what the rules will be, nor do they understand that restrictions imposed by parents reflect the norms of society. Unable to see the purpose or plan behind the rules, they focus attention on the consequences of behavior and judge rightness and wrongness on the basis of the end result. What is rewarded must be good; what is punished must be bad. The *stage 1* child obeys parents out of fear of a spanking or the withdrawal of affection. Focusing on the physical consequences of the act means that the value of punishment becomes greatly exaggerated, and the young child will advocate painful discipline even for minor infractions. If "might makes right," it follows that the value of human life is dependent on the social and physical attributes of the possessor. A person who is strong and has the power to command others has greater worth than a person who is weak or in a subservient position.

Stage 2 children have advanced to an understanding that other people have interests and needs that may or may not be the same as their own. Although the basic motive is to satisfy one's own desires, there are times when this can be done best by entering into an agreement with someone else. Social interaction becomes possible and is a step up from the first stage in which the child is not involved in the decision-making process. Human relations, however, are viewed in terms of the marketplace, and bargaining is expressed in instrumental and physical terms. One is obligated only to those who are in a position to return the favor, and obeying the law or following regulations becomes important if doing so is personally profitable. This attitude, that an act is right only if it enhances one's own pleasure or meets one's own needs, obviously leaves much to be desired. Sometimes called the *selfish-need* stage, there is no genuine concern for the welfare of others apart from a kind of temporary mutual satisfaction. The value of human life is seen as it relates to the needs of the possessor.

In *stage 3* the person is aware that certain commitments and social norms must be maintained in order for group living to be orderly. "Right" is no longer a matter of meeting one's own interest but rather of living up to the expectations of others, of helping and supporting family and friends, and of maintaining the social system for its own sake. The shift from "let's make a deal" at stage 2 to "let's have an understanding" at stage 3 begins for most people during preadolescence and is prominent throughout the adolescent period. Studies show that stage 3, along with stage 4, remains the dominant stage for most people during adulthood. Being able to understand and care for others requires a higher level of cognition than that established previously, for it demands that people step outside themselves, so to speak, and be concerned with what others *think* of them, not just what they might *do* to them. The stage 3 person understands that "no man is an island" and that loyalty to the groups to which one belongs is necessary for positive and stable relationships. Selfishness is wrong because it does not include a mutual commitment to others. The value of human life is based on the affection of family and friends toward the possessor rather than on one's social standing in the community (stage 1) or on the ability of the person to satisfy the needs of another (stage 2).

Part of one's obligation to society is to respect and obey the laws of the land as this assures that all citizens meet the same standards of conduct and receive equal treatment. This *stage 4* attitude is more advanced than that of stage 3, for it takes into consideration not only one's immediate or primary relationships such as family, neighbors, and friends, but also provides a way of living with strangers or those one may not like or wish to associate with. Laws are binding on everyone and are necessary for the maintenance of life and property. A pluralistic society necessitates that rules and regulations take precedence over personal wishes or the enhancement of any particular group. It is only in this way that we can coexist. Those delegated to enforce the laws also deserve our support and loyalty for without them the system could not hold together. The value of human life is seen as it relates to the rights and duties of the individuals in the larger society.

But sometimes laws conflict or are unclear, and sometimes laws that are agreed upon by the larger society place an undue burden on some of its citizens. The question then asked is whether there are principles that will determine what is right in such instances. The answer is found at the next two stages of moral judgment.

Stage 5 reasoning recognizes that there are a variety of ways to arrange the social order and that guidelines must be created for choosing among alternative systems so that everyone within the society will want to cooperate. The stage 5 person is like an impartial spectator judging the social system in terms of community welfare, making sure that the laws reflect the will of the people and that safeguards are built into the operation so that all, minority as well as majority, are guaranteed certain inalienable rights. The United States Constitution is a stage 5 document, for it makes provision for changing legislation that is not fair to everyone and for interpreting the intent of the law so that justice is maintained. The essence of morality is not so much in unquestioning obedience to the law (stage 4) but in changing those laws which do an injustice to a portion of the citizenry. Man was not made for the law, but the law was made for man.

Stage 5 provides a more democratic view of individuals and their respective roles than is possible at stage 4. James Rest (1975) explains the difference.

> One aspect of principled thinking is that people in leadership roles are not seen as a different breed of humankind, nor as infallible, but are seen as individuals having certain prerogatives in order to perform certain functions in society's division of labor. Accordingly, one can criticize or question the job performance of an "authority" . . . without being disloyal to the whole group. Moreover, the prerogatives of authority are limited to the necessities of the role. This less exalted view of authority contrasts with the more exalted concept of authority of conventional thinking, which regards loyalty and support of authority as a sign of loyalty and support for the whole social system. (p. 89)

Stage 5 persons having progressed through the previous stages are aware of the importance of social norms and of why a society needs people in leadership roles. They also understand that those who disobey the law will have to face the consequences. But they know that there is a higher law than that devised by humankind, and if a choice must be made one's allegiance should be to the principle of human justice rather than to what is legislated by the courts. Martin Luther King, Jr., faced this dilemma when he conducted the civil rights marches in the South. In a letter written from a Birmingham jail in April of 1963, he said:

> You express a great deal of anxiety over our willingness to break laws. This is certainly a legitimate concern. . . . One may well ask: "How can you advocate breaking some laws and obeying others?" The answer lies in the fact that

there are two types of laws: just and unjust. . . . One has
not only a legal but a moral responsibility to obey just
laws. Conversely, one has a moral responsibility to disobey
unjust laws. . . . Any law that uplifts human personality is
just. Any law that degrades human personality is unjust.
(King, 1964, pp. 84-85)

Some confuse stage 5 and stage 2 because reasoning at
either of these stages may lead to a rejection of the law.
The difference is considerable, however. Persons at stage 2
take the attitude that the law interferes with their freedom, keeping them from doing as they please. They do
not understand why anyone would experience anxiety over
breaking the law, nor do they ponder the difference between just and unjust laws. They would not say that one
has "a moral responsibility to obey just laws."

Moral reasoning at *stage 6*, the highest stage possible,
considers that human life is sacred and that individuals
are ends in themselves rather than means for some other
good. The moral test is one's willingness to apply the same
principles to oneself as to others. This means people at
stage 6 must have the intellectual ability to imagine themselves in someone else's place, to consider the claims that
person would make, and then be willing to act toward
that individual as they would feel it appropriate were they
in the same situation. This application of the Golden Rule
is not just to family and friends (stage 3) but to all people
everywhere, regardless of their circumstances. It includes
a concern for both the culprit and the victim, for the preg-
nant woman as well as her unborn child, for the rich and
the poor, young and old, male and female, Soviet and
American. Stage 6 provides no easy answers or quick responses to the question of what is just. Justice for one
group must not be at the expense of justice for another.
Nor is legislation that serves to close discussion on these
matters the answer. Ethical principles indicative of stage 6
are different than rules or commandments (stage 4). A

commandment says, "Thou shalt not kill." A principle says, "Thou shalt love thy neighbor as thyself."

Few individuals in any society reach stage 6 reasoning, and those who do find themselves greatly misunderstood. If they make a significant impact on others as did Socrates, Mahatma Gandhi, and Martin Luther King, Jr., they may suffer martyrdom. Society does not like people who are too good or too bad. Jesus was crucified and so were two thieves. One was too good, the others too bad. Although Kohlberg believes only a handful of people have reached stage 6, research studies indicate that from 2 percent to 10 percent of the adult population make statements indicative of this stage.

The postconventional level, as we have seen, allows for judging right and wrong, good and bad, not in terms of one's own interests (level 1) or in terms of what is best for one's group (level 2), but rather by what is best for all mankind (level 3). Justice, equality, and the dignity of human life are higher than one's own needs or any given law. The individual at the highest level has progressed in moral reasoning from one who is directed by the consequences of behavior (stages 1 and 2), to what society says is right (stages 3 and 4), and finally to a self-directed, socially responsive and responsible person who has an integrated set of values that apply to the whole human race (stages 5 and 6).[2]

Techniques Employed

The method used to determine a person's stage of moral judgment is to present a story with a moral dilemma and to listen to the reasoning as it is related to the dilemma. The story may be one used by Piaget a half century ago, one developed by Kohlberg, or one taken from a local newspaper. There are also booklets and filmstrips that present a variety of moral dilemmas.

A typical story is one in which a conflict occurs between the needs of the actor in the story, obedience to the law or to an authority, and the welfare and interests of others also portrayed in the story. One such story is of a man named Heinz who lived in Europe. His wife was near death from a special kind of cancer, but there was one drug, a form of radium that the doctors thought might save her. The druggist in the town was charging ten times what it cost to make and told Heinz he could not have any of it unless he paid two thousand dollars in advance. Heinz said that even if he borrowed all that he could, it would only amount to a thousand dollars. He asked the druggist to either sell it for less or let him pay the rest later, but the druggist said no. So, Heinz, being desperate, broke into the store and stole the drug for his wife.

The question is asked, "Did Heinz do right or did Heinz do wrong?" It is the reasoning behind the answer rather than the answer itself that determines the stage of moral reasoning. A child at the first stage who interprets an action as good or bad according to its physical consequences may say, "He shouldn't have done that because then he'd be a thief if they caught him and put him in jail." The stage 2 child, believing that right action consists of that which instrumentally satisfies one's own needs, may say that Heinz did right to save his wife's life because "if she dies there will be no one to cook his dinner." Kohlberg has done considerable cross-cultural research and finds that a typical stage 2 response in some countries is that Heinz did right because "if she dies it will cost him too much for the funeral." However, if Heinz does not love his wife or if she would not do the same for him under similar circumstances, then the stage 2 child will say he should not have done it. The stage 3 person, who is oriented to social conformity, may say that Heinz did wrong because a person should not steal or that Heinz did right because he should take care of his wife. In either case the judgment is made on the basis of what society expects of its members.

The person at stage 4 being oriented to show respect for the law and to maintain the social order will probably say that Heinz did wrong. As one stage 4 child put it, "It was wrong because he was breaking the law no matter how you look at it, and although I can see why he would have done it, I don't think he was justified in doing it." Those who progress to stage 5, believing that the purpose of the law is to preserve human rights, may say that even though it was wrong for Heinz to steal, it would be more wrong to let his wife die. For those who reason at stage 6 and believe that morality is grounded, not in legality or specific rules, but in abstract principles of justice and respect for the individual, the answer will probably be that "Heinz was wrong legally but right morally."

Although presenting a moral dilemma is the usual technique employed in determining the level of moral judgment, it is not the only way. People face decisions every day and make comments as to desirable solutions on a variety of issues. Given sufficient familiarity with the stages, one may listen to what is said and assess the level of moral reasoning. Is one's desire to enhance self (stages 1 and 2), conform to social expectations (stages 3 and 4), or be concerned with the rights and humanity of others (stages 5 and 6)? Listening to one's own speech may prove an interesting exercise.

The Cognitive Theory Answer

In chapter 1, it was said that regardless of the view taken of the nature of the human condition, psychologists accept the basic premise that the infant is amoral, not knowing right from wrong. The question asked is how the child advances from a state of innocence to a state in which moral maturity is attained. The desire of moral development theorists is to analyze processes operating within the child which produce optimal results, describe external events which contribute to these processes, and assess where any individual may be along the way. Cognitive psychologists, as we have seen, emphasize the reasoning or intellectual functions that occur in moral development and measure the stage or level of morality by what the person says.

Piaget perceived reasoning as proceeding from a morality of constraint, based on unilateral respect of the child for the parent, to a morality of cooperation based on the mutual respect of peers. Egocentrism is replaced with reciprocity as the child learns to take into account, not only his or her own point of view, but the perspective of others as well. Kohlberg, by testing older children and adults, has shown that there are higher stages of moral judgment than those observed by Piaget. As a person enlarges the numbers and groups of individuals to which respect is given, reciprocity with peers is expanded to include a concept of justice that applies to all people everywhere.

The cognitive answer to the question of how moral development takes place is that *the amoral infant becomes capable of morality as he or she advances in thinking processes "from an egocentric, but externally directed being, to a self-directed but socially responsive and responsible person"* (Simon, 1976, p. 173). The egocentric, externally directed child is the one who is able to assume only his own view and judges good and evil on the basis of what will happen to him as a consequence of behavior. This is Piaget's heteronomous child and Kohlberg's stage 1 individual. By contrast, the self-directed but socially responsive and responsible person has a morality that comes from within and judges right and wrong, not so much by how one is affected personally, but on the basis of consequences to society and to the people that make up that society. At early stages this is Piaget's autonomous child and Kohlberg's stage 2 individual interested in concrete forms of reciprocity. At later stages the child exchanges reciprocity for altruism and becomes concerned with the rights and privileges of an ever-increasing segment of humanity, feeling personally responsible for developing a just society for all.

Problems

The work of Jean Piaget and of Lawrence Kohlberg has been evaluated by both advocates and opponents of cognitive psychology. Advocates, having accepted the basic assumptions of cognitivism, opt for methodological changes or call for a more careful analysis of how a person moves from one stage of moral judgment to the next. Opponents, questioning the very foundation of a morality based on reasoning, prefer a behavioral or affective approach to a study of morality, or they object to the non-relative stance of the cognitive theorist that says that higher stages are more moral than lower stages. Occasionally an aspiring scholar will conduct research that does not support the findings of Piaget or Kohlberg and will assume that, as in the story of David of old, a giant Goliath has been felled with one blow. Such, of course, is not the case. But whether any particular criticism points to a genuine problem will depend in large measure on the orientation of the evaluator. The reader is invited to decide which of the following concerns merit serious consideration.

The assumption that the course of moral development is the same as the course of development in other areas of cognition has been challenged. Although people who are more intelligent also tend to be higher in moral judgment, there are many exceptions. An individual may be a brilliant scientist and yet not make moral judgments at the postconventional level. Given the nature of the task of responding verbally to moral dilemmas, no one would refute a relationship between moral judgment and general cognitive ability, but it remains difficult to show just what this relationship is.

Both Piaget and Kohlberg would concur that although there are similarities between the cognitions involved, they are not the same. Piaget speaks of a parallelism between morality and intellectual thought but defines intelligence in terms of his own epistemological theory rather than on the basis of standardized ability tests. Kohlberg (1963) states that "these relations between cognitive development of morality and its internalization are not matters of simple cognitive learning of cultural norms. Such simple cognitive learning fails to take account of the sequential qualitative transformation through which moral thinking procedes" (p. 322). Kohlberg goes on to say that the cognition involved in moral thinking is not "a simple matter of mental age" and that the level of moral development is only moderately correlated with IQ. Thus it would seem that there is little discrepancy between what the critics are saying and what the cognitive theorists report. Needed are definitive studies which would give a clearer understanding of just what cognitions are necessary for moral reasoning.

A second concern often cited in the literature has to do with the relationship between moral judgment and moral behavior. What a person does affects others more directly than what a person thinks or says, so the charge is made that unless higher stages of moral judgment are accompanied by moral acts not seen at lower stages, an understanding of the reasoning processes has little value. A person may make sophisticated judgments without ever acting upon them; and conversely, a person who is lacking in intelligence but is well trained may act in socially respectable ways. Some critics say that for a theory of moral development to be relevant, it should predict distinctive patterns of behavior for each of the stages or levels of moral judgment. The assertion also is made that people act according to acquired behavior patterns that are rela-

tively fixed and that being asked to respond to hypotheti-
cal moral dilemmas has little correspondence to a world
of reality.

Cognitive theorists are aware that to know the good is
not necessarily to do the good and that thinking about
moral issues is not a substitute for moral living. They
agree that moral reasoning is only one part of a much
larger picture and that a connection needs to be established between judgmental processes and moral behavior.
"The sheer capacity to make genuinely moral judgments
is only one portion of moral character. . . . One must also
apply this judgmental capacity to the actual guidance and
criticism of action" (Kohlberg, 1967, p. 179). But cognitive
theorists would not agree that "the claims . . . regarding
the relationship between moral judgment and action are
greatly overstated" (Scharf, 1978, p. 76) or that "there appears to be a wide gap between moral judgment and moral
actions" (Wynn, 1977, p. 67). Numerous studies on this
matter have been conducted, and although specific behaviors do not relate exclusively to specific stages, there are
positive correlations between the two. Golda Rothman
(1980) has summarized the research on the relationship
between moral reasoning and behavior, and her article is
an excellent source for anyone who wishes to pursue this
topic in depth.

A third criticism is that what one says may depend as
much on the particular situation one is in at the time as
it does on an enduring disposition or attitude. If situations
are similar, responses also will be similar; if situations
vary, responses likewise will vary. Piaget saw constancy
as being related to age. A child understands morality first
on a practical level and later on a theoretical or hypotheti-
cal level. When small the child will often imitate the
speech and actions of an adult. But unless there is an accompanying change in convicton, which is not apt to occur in one so young, the desirable speech and performance
may not continue when the adult is absent. As age in-

creases and moral understanding is on a higher level of cognitive organization, greater stability results. Whereas disequilibrium with its accompanying changes is essential for the child to advance to higher stages, stability is increasingly desirable as higher levels of moral reasoning are attained.

Kohlberg has found that most people are about half in one stage of moral judgment and half in the two surrounding stages. This would indicate that the particular situation does make a difference in what the person says. Even so, the person also has a part in the process and brings some consistency based on attitudes or beliefs. Given the range of situational contingencies and the variety of belief systems, it is impossible to reach a definitive conclusion on the relative effects of a changing environment and an enduring disposition. But as research continues, closer approximations to an answer will be forthcoming, although one must keep in mind that both variation and constancy will always be present.

A fourth criticism of the cognitive approach is that the affective components of morality are not given sufficient consideration. Opponents say that emotions are essential to moral development, and one cannot be certain that a moral concept is grasped unless there is an emotional accompaniment. "When someone, for instance, fails to have remorse for voluntarily harming an innocent person, it would be reasonable to say that the individual has not fully grasped the concept of harm. Or if an individual commits premeditated murder and experiences no guilt for his act, then he is likely not to have a well developed concept of murder" (Rich, 1980, p. 82). An inappropriate emotion, such as showing glee over someone's misfortune, also indicates a lack of moral understanding. Emotions play a vital part in the judgmental process, and whether they influence the person in desirable or undesirable ways, they cannot be ignored.

It is true that cognitive psychologists have not stressed

the emotional aspects of moral development, but this does not mean the affective has been ignored. An emphasis on cognition does not exclude other elements of the moral process. Both Piaget and Kohlberg have acknowledged the importance of emotions in moral reasoning. Piaget (1932) writes that "the relations between parents and children are certainly not only those of constraint. There is a spontaneous mutual affection, which from the first prompts the child to acts of generosity and even of self-sacrifice, to very touching demonstrations which are in no way prescribed. And here no doubt is the starting point for that morality of good which we shall see developing alongside of the morality of right or duty" (p. 192-194). Kohlberg, likewise, recognizes the significance of emotions on moral development. Aware that his theory has been criticized for ignoring affect, he has closely linked the cognitive and the affective in his more recent writings. The following statement reflects his views:

> Discussions of cognition and affect usually are based on the assumption that cognitions and affects are different mental states, leading to the question, "Which is quantitatively more influential in moral judgment, states of cognition or states of affect?" In contrast, the cognitive-developmental view holds that "cognition" and "affect" are different aspects of, or perspectives on, the same mental events, that all mental events have both cognitive and affective aspects, and that the development of mental dispositions reflects structural changes recognizable in both cognitive and affective perspectives. It is evident that moral judgments often involve strong emotional components. (Kohlberg, 1980b, pp. 39-40)

Kohlberg continues by saying that an emotion such as fear is more apt to occur at stage 2, whereas the emotion of guilt is more apt to be a stage 4 phenomenon. Anxiety may be included in both fear and guilt. Kohlberg's statement has been supported by a number of researchers, including

Ruma and Mosher (1967) and Ziv (1976) who have found highly significant correlations between guilt and moral reasoning.

These criticisms of a morality based on reasoning are but samples of those found in the literature. Some writers disagree with one or more of the basic assumptions and cite insufficient or conflicting evidence to support the view that stages of moral judgment are invariant, hierarchical, and universal or that morality is a fully scientific claim about human nature or that conflict is necessary for moral development to occur. Others dissent from a position in which character traits such as honesty, courage, and determination compare unfavorably with principles such as justice (Peters 1971), or "justice" is narrowly interpreted to mean "social morality" (Wilson 1980). Some accuse cognitive theorists of creating a moral aristocracy composed of individuals with superior verbal skills and excluding those who may have an intuitive grasp of ethical components but are not able to articulate them. The aristocracy would favor the middle class over the lower class and girls over boys, thus creating unfavorable and unnecessary class and gender comparisons. Fraenkel (1976) questions the fundamental premise that higher stages are always preferable to lower stages and argues that children may take rules too lightly if adults discuss with them the conditions in which rules should be obeyed and in which rules should not be obeyed. He indicates that getting a child to the conventional level may be as much as we can hope for and that discussions at the postconventional level serve to confuse the child and may result in socially unacceptable behavior.

Still others have reported problems with administration and scoring. It takes a relatively long time to give Kohlberg's Moral Judgment Instrument, and analyzing open-ended verbal statements and placing them at appropriate stages requires special training. But the effort is worth it for some like Edmund Sullivan (1975) of the Ontario Institute for Studies in Education who comments, "We have found Kohlberg's instrument for the psychological assessment of moral judgment the most sophisticated and reliable instrument that psychological assessment devices have to offer. The instrument can be reliably scored and its validity is argued within the perspective of cognitive developmental theory" (p. 95). Objectively scored tests are now becoming available, which will be helpful to researchers and educators, and pedagogical and curricular materials are being made easier to utilize.

Practical Applications

A cognitive theory of morality is founded on the premise that some values are to be preferred to others, and Kohlberg as the principal exponent of this theory has provided a philosophical-developmental basis for the hierarchy of moral thought. Parents, teachers, and ministers need not be caught in the bind of a relativity of ethics for according to the moral reasoning approach, what *is* at higher stages is what *ought* to be. Cognitive psychologists also hold that true morality, by definition, must come from within the individual rather than being imposed from without. But the environment may impede or facilitate this development. It is to a consideration of the environment in the home, the school, and the church that we now turn.

Application to the Home

How can parents help the child progress to more mature levels of moral understanding? Let us consider first the implications of the findings of Jean Piaget. In *The Moral Judgment of the Child*, Piaget is critical of the way parents relate to the child. For example, he notes that the average housewife "in the very poor districts where we conducted our work" showed more anger over several cups being broken than over one regardless of the circumstances in which the damage occurred. By fixing attention on the consequences of an act and ignoring whether the act was accidental or intentional, the adult "leads the child to the notion of objective responsibility and consolidates in consequence a tendency that is already natural to the spontaneous mentality of little children." Piaget says that unless a child has more mature models to emulate in other adults or older peers, he may grow to be "as stupid with his own children as his parents were with him" (Piaget, 1932, p. 37, 189, 191). Whether such criticism is deserved, it does point to the fact that parents need to exemplify in behavior and speech mature patterns of moral judgment. Accidents should not be dealt with in the same manner as deliberate acts even though the amount of damage may be the same. Parents who punish or reward on the basis of consequences rather than taking into consideration the circumstances make it difficult for the child to progress in moral reasoning. Piaget refers to this as *intentionality,* and it is one of several ways in which Piaget saw younger and older children differing in moral reasoning. Let us look at the others.

Children differ in ability to engage in *relativism.* Relativism does not mean that one view is as good as another or that truth is relative. Rather, it means that a person is able to put himself or herself in the place of others, to see events from perspectives quite different than one's own, to be empathic with the thoughts and feelings of other people. Parents need to be capable of relativism, to understand how a child feels when scolded or sent to bed without supper or told there will be no television for three days. Whether the punishment is appropriate will depend on the misdeed, the age of the child, and whether a person should be dealt with in this way. Parents who consider the feelings of the child and who recognize that children are people and should be treated as such are parents who provide a just environment in which the child can grow. But being a good model and providing a just environment are not sufficient in themselves. We all have seen good parents who love and care for their children, bestowing upon them kindness and consideration. But they do not insist on the same kind of treatment from their offspring. The results are unfortunate indeed! Even as parents need to be considerate of their children, children need to learn consideration for their parents and for siblings and peers. Asking the child questions such as, "How would you feel if everyone in this family yelled 'shut up' at you like you just did to your brother?" or "Did everyone have a good time at the party?" will probably do more to encourage relativity than asking, "Do you want to get spanked for fighting all the time with your brother?" or "Did you have a good time at the party?" Children enjoy playing house or school and often imitate community helpers such as police officers and fire fighters. Or they may pretend to be one of the cartoon characters seen on Saturday morning television. Such role-playing is important in the development of relativity. Relativity also may be encouraged by reading stories to children and discussing with them the feelings and thoughts of the characters in the story. On occasion, episodes depicted on television also lend themselves to discussions of this nature.

Independence of sanctions implies that an act or attitude is not determined to be good or bad solely on the basis of whether it is sanctioned by someone in authority. There are times when children are told to do something they should not do. They need some way of sorting out when they should obey an adult and when they should not. We caution our children not to accept a ride with a stranger even though the stranger may tell them to do so. A teacher may insist that members of the class reveal who caused the commotion and upset one of the desks. Must the children tell the teacher because they are ordered to do so? Some would say yes. The teacher is in charge and children should obey. But what happens to the mutual trust among peers if they comply with the demand? How can children proceed from heteronomy to autonomy under these circumstances? The very young child is unable to understand any criterion other than obedience, but as children grow older, parents need to help them determine who they should obey and under what circumstances. In homes in which obedience is the *only* measure of right and wrong, where "I told you so" is the only reason given, children will be hindered in the development of moral reasoning.

Parents may enable the child to go from immature to *mature forms of reciprocity*. To the small child, justice is an eye for an eye and a tooth for a tooth. To tell young children that two wrongs don't make a right makes no sense in their world. Hitting someone who has just hit you *does* make it right in their eyes for it evens the score. What could be more fair? Little by little parents need to show the child that sometimes it is best to overlook a wrong or give a soft answer or turn the other cheek. As difficult a principle as this is for any of us to learn, we know that meaningful and lasting relationships with others necessitates taking into consideration past favors and friendships, not just the most recent action on their part. Nor can we reply in kind when to do so would escalate ill will.

Punishment must be in keeping with the misdeed. To punish with the intent to hurt rather than with the intent to change unacceptable behavior or to bring restitution to one who has been wronged serves to lengthen the time the child is at the stage of heteronomy. "The little ones prefer the most severe [punishments] so as to emphasize the necessity of the punishment itself; the other children are more in favour of the measures of reciprocity which simply serve to make the transgressor feel that the bond of solidarity has been broken and that things must be put right again" (Piaget, 1932, p. 225). Some parents favor the attitudes of "the little ones" and advocate a back-to-the-woodshed approach to keep the child in line. It is as though the only way to correct the child is by inflicting pain, by coercion imposed from without. But both observation and research tell us that "in homes where heavy punishment predominates and rules are stringent, the children continue to believe in the effectiveness of punishment, or retributive justice, much longer than children who move toward more advanced stages of distributive justice" (Windmiller, 1980, p. 17). Parents need to exemplify mature rather than immature forms of punishment, to secure "the bond of solidarity" between themselves and their children, to see that things are "put right again."

Children also need the help of parents in understanding that there are *many causes of misfortune.* We know that trouble may come because of negligence or disobedience or because of judgmental errors. Sometimes problems occur through no fault of our own. We are simply in the wrong place at the wrong time. Or disaster may strike naturally as in the case of fire or flood. Children need direction in sorting out the circumstances so they can differentiate between immanent justice and natural causes. If they have had a bad day at school, having been scolded by the teacher, it may be that they were unruly and deserved the punishment, or it may be that the teacher is emotionally unstable and should be replaced. When the child's grandmother dies the child needs to know that her death is in no way related to the fact that he sometimes forgot to pray for her at night before going to bed. Although God may speak to us through misfortune, and the child should be sensitive to this possibility, to believe that all trouble is willed by God because of wrongdoing only serves to keep the child at an immature level of moral reasoning.

Many would not agree with Piaget's view that peers are more influential than parents in the development of moral judgment, but most people would agree that a child's friends do play an essential role. It becomes important for parents to give attention to the kind of companions the child has. It is easier to guide children in their choice of friends during the early years than when they are in adolescence and spend more time away from home. The key is to guide rather than to tell. The direct approach of telling children whom they may spend time with and whom they may not will hamper the kind of development that comes from being involved in the decision-making process. Discussion of possible consequences of friendships with certain types of people sets the stage for cognitive decisions that enable moral development to take place.

A mature sense of justice seldom comes before the adult years. But we can not wait until our children are grown to express mature views. We continue to state principles our children may not understand with the hope that in later years they will remember what we have said and will adopt similar values. By far the most effective way to encourage moral development in the home is by the creation of a just environment—an environment in which intentions are considered, relativism is practiced, mutual trust is stressed, and mature forms of reciprocity are practiced. Punishment should fit the misdeed, and misfortune should not be linked automatically with wrongdoing. Treating children with respect and expecting no less from them in return will facilitate development from heteronomy to autonomy and finally to the mature process of equity.

Kohlberg said less about the influence of the parent than did Piaget. This may be due in part to Kohlberg's having studied older children and in part to evidence that stage of moral reasoning in parents is not highly correlated with stage of moral reasoning in their children. Kohlberg stressed, however, the importance of the parent as a role-model. Children pattern their ideas and behaviors after the people they know—parents being among this group. How much influence the parent has relative to the peer group or other adults will depend on the significance of each person to the child. However, parents provide the child's first encounter with an environment that is either just or unjust and the first example of speech and behavior that is either morally mature or morally immature.

Other writers have expanded on Kohlberg's view of parents as role-models (Lande & Slade, 1979; Woodward, 1976). Parents who are familiar with Kohlberg's stages can determine where the child is in the hierarchy of moral thought and verbalize ideas at the next stage. Does the child do what is right to avoid punishment (stage 1), because it brings pleasure (stage 2), so family or friends will be pleased (stage 3), because it is a rule (stage 4)? The parent should appeal to the next stage. A stage 1 child may be told, "When you finish picking up your toys, I'll read you your favorite story," rather than being told, "If you don't get your toys picked up, you'll wish you had!" A stage 2 child who takes the attitude, "Make it worth my while," when asked to help around the house needs to understand that being a member of a household includes mutual consideration and responsibility. A home is no longer a home if everyone goes his or her own way. Belongingness mandates caring about what others think of us and caring for them in return. Once the child is strongly entrenched at stage 3, the next step is to realize that the maintenance of order goes beyond the seeking of approval. Rules for behavior are established in the home, the school, and the society for the smooth functioning of the group. Laws are to be obeyed not to avoid punishment, but to create a world in which we can live together in harmony.

Although helping our children attain stages 3 and 4 is difficult, especially with others telling them to "look out for number one," "do your own thing," and "you only go around once, so you owe it to yourself," the conventional is not sufficient. We breathe a sigh of relief when our children come to care for family and friends and willingly obey the laws of the land. But so much more is needed. Do we encourage our children to weigh alternatives before deciding on a course of action and to look forward to the time when they can participate directly in democratic decision-making (stage 5)? Do we communicate to them on a regular basis that all people have rights and should be treated with respect regardless of gender, age, race, lifestyle, or contribution to society (stage 6)?

Two publications (Krebs, 1980; Ward, 1979), both written from a Christian perspective and in a style that all parents can understand, apply Kohlberg's three levels of moral reasoning to child-rearing techniques. Ted Ward (1979) in *Values Begin at Home* emphasizes the importance of the family as a "just and moral community" (p. 81) in which children are treated fairly, experiences for social interaction are provided, discussions of moral concerns are open, and opportunities for role-playing are given. Ward advocates rewards and punishments for the child at level 1, models and rules for the child at level 2, and dialogue and interpersonal transactions for the young person at level 3 (p. 79).

How to Bring Up a Good Child by Richard Krebs (1980) is similar in emphasis but more detailed in that the entire book is an application of Kohlberg's theory to child-rearing procedures. By using anecdotes and nontechnical terms, Krebs effectively explains to the reader how to relate to children at each of the three levels. The child at the preconventional level should not be called bad for the young child is premoral, not immoral. "With a premoral child, we are not teaching morality; rather, we are laying the groundwork for later moral development. By consistently rewarding honesty, truthfulness, helping, or whatever moral traits we would like our children to display, we are establishing patterns of behavior that can develop at the next level, the conventional level, into true morality" (p. 45). The premoral child needs care, consistency, fairness, and both reward and punishment.

Children at the conventional level, which encompasses the school years, begin to understand societal standards of right and wrong. Krebs suggested that it is especially important for children at this period to have adequate models of morality. Parents and other legitimate authorities, like teachers and police officers, should supply this need. Interaction with age-mates also matters as the child must learn that interpersonal relationships with equals are affected by violating a trust. At the postconventional level the adolescent or young adult will come to understand the principles behind the rules and regulations imposed on a society. Young adults also come to realize that some actions are immoral even though the actions remain within the law, whereas other actions are immoral if a law is obeyed without regard to the underlying principle. If there is a discrepancy between the law and the principle, the principle should take precedence. Krebs gives the example of breaking down a neighbor's door to warn of fire. It is the spirit of the law, not the letter, that makes for moral action. "While principled children obey specific laws and obey them more consistently than children at either of the earlier moral levels, principled children are also capable of standing against an illegitimate authority of law and bringing about social change and justice" (p. 119).

Lickona (1983) and Duska and Whelan (1975) give a number of practical rules for parents who would encourage the development of moral reasoning in the child. Lickona writes that parents should respect their children and require respect in return. Parents teach by example and can help children take on responsibilities and acquire positive self-concepts. Duska and Whelan include making a distinction between rules for good manners and issues of moral substance, being attentive to the child's reasons for moral judgment, not reacting with more aggravation to the child's carelessness than one would to the same action committed by an adult, and respecting the child's right to an apology when parents have been unjust. Older children should be able to discuss what they consider to be fair or unfair in family relationships, and should feel free to talk with parents about contemporary issues that involve moral decisions without fear of censure. Parents need to remember that although they may encourage moral development by creating a just environment, they cannot imprint their values on their children. Each person must construct a system of beliefs, rethinking the views given by others, and deciding to accept or reject those views in accordance with one's own pattern of moral reasoning.

Application to the School

Curricular programs based on moral reasoning are increasing in popularity. The method used in the classroom is to present a story with a moral dilemma and ask each child to state a position on the dilemma and tell why that position is taken. Teachers also may respond to the dilemma, but they are not to indicate that one response is right and another response is wrong. In this way indoctrination is not used, but children are drawn to the reasoning of someone at the next higher stage. The teacher is aware that just because people do have different moral values does not mean that they ought to have different moral values. Higher stages are preferred to lower stages. Ethical relativity and value neutrality so prominent in some approaches are not accepted in moral judgment. Nevertheless, one does not expect children to reason at stages higher than their cognitive development would allow, nor does one expect moral development to take place by telling children what their values should be.

The story presented should be one the children can understand and to which they will relate. All children at the elementary level are able to respond to the following story adapted from Ziv (1976): "Let's pretend there is a boy (girl) just your age who is walking down the street and suddenly discovers a wallet on the sidewalk with $5.00 in it. He (she) looks around. Do you think the boy (girl) will keep the money?" After the child has answered yes or no, the question that follows is Why? It is the answer to this question that determines the stage of reasoning, not whether the child says the one in the story will keep the money or will not keep it. A stage 1 child may say the girl in the story will keep the money, "because she noticed nobody was around and thinks she can get away with it," or she will not keep the money, "because if her mommy finds out she'll really get it." A child at stage 2 will usually say that the child in the story will keep the money, "so he could spend it—maybe buy a baseball bat or mitt," or "so she can save it and some day buy a new car." One fifth-grade student, also responding at stage 2, said the child would not keep the money, "because if you return it you may get more."[3]

At stage 3 the child is concerned with being a good person in the eyes of others and will probably say that the boy or girl in the story will not keep the money. As one third-grader put it: "Because she's not supposed to. That's what we're told not to do is take someone else's things." Another third-grader, however, replied that the child would keep the money, "because my mom doesn't care if I find something." There are not many responses at stage 4 at the elementary level. A number of children talk about taking the wallet to the police station, but it is not always possible to tell whether the reason for doing so is a concern for the consequences if one does not tell an authority (stages 1 and 2), a way of pleasing others by doing what others would want one to do (stage 3), or a respect for the law and for police officers who are the enforcers of the law (stage 4). An occasional statement may reflect postconventional thinking with its concern for the welfare of another human being. "It may be an old man's money" was one child's response. "It might be someone else's lunch money," said another. The same child may make statements at more than one stage, so it is important to remember that no one should be labeled as being "at" a particular stage unless the majority of responses are reflective of that stage. Several stories are usually given to which the child responds, and in this way an overall assessment may be made. It is also important that one not judge a child at a lower stage of moral reasoning as being less moral than a classmate who is at a higher stage. Emphasis is given to what a person may become rather than to one's present state.

As children discuss a story in the classroom, the stage 1 child will be attracted to the reasoning of the child at stage 2. Keeping or not keeping the money is viewed as related to concerns other than whether someone has seen what has happened. The stage 2 child, in turn, will listen to the judgment of the child at stage 3. He or she begins to understand that "finders keepers, losers weepers" is not quite right. What others think of our actions is also important. We live in a world with parents, neighbors, peers. How do they feel about what we have done? Getting along with them is essential for a good life.

Moral dilemma stories may be taken from booklets especially designed for this purpose, from the local newspaper, or from the experiences of the children themselves. For several years each issue of the *NEA Journal*, published by the National Education Association, featured an unfinished story designed especially for students in grades four through seven. School corporations with adequate resources may elect to purchase films or filmstrips. The moral-reasoning approach has generated so much interest among educators that a number of companies have produced stories on film. News magazines and television broadcasts are excellent sources from which to draw. Dilemmas stemming from problems of labor and management, industry and environment, nationalism and internationalism have moral implications. Students may wish to bring before the class problems they have encountered with the hope that a discussion with peers will produce new ways to cope.

Students at the high school level also engage in discussions of moral problems. Because they are older, more statements will be made at stage 4, and some stage 5 and 6 comments will be heard. A typical heterogeneous group of teenagers should provide a plus-one model for almost everyone in the class. Historical incidents such as Watergate or My Lai are especially interesting to students at this age for they bring up the question of when loyalty to a political party (stage 3) or duty to a commanding officer (stage 4) disregards human rights and violates principles of justice and mercy.

In discussing any social issue it is important to know the facts. Peter Scharf (1978) presents statements made by military personnel involved in the My Lai massacre. High school students need to know what happened at My Lai and to become familiar with the reasons given by those involved. Some students will agree with the preconventional statements of Meadlow, a soldier who admitted killing Vietnamese civilians in order not to be punished for disobedience (stage 1) and as revenge for his friends who were killed (stage 2). As he put it, "During basic training if you disobeyed an order, if you were slow in obeying orders, they'd slap you on the head, drop-kick you in the chest and rinky-dink stuff like that. If an officer tells you to stand on your head in the middle of the highway, you do it," and "I was getting relieved from what I had seen over there . . . my buddies getting killed or wounded" (p. 59).

Other students will take the position of Lieutenant Calley, the officer charged with ordering Meadlow to shoot and whose reasoning appeared to be at the conventional level. To Calley a "good" officer was one who tried to please his superiors (stage 3) and who did what he considered to be his duty (stage 4). "I was a run-of-the mill average guy. I still am. I always said people in Washington are smarter than me. If intelligent people say Communism is bad, it's going to engulf us. I was only a Second Lieutenant." (p. 60), and "I was ordered to go in there and destroy the enemy.

That was my job on that day. That was the mission I was given" (p. 62).

Still other students will argue the position of Bernhardt, a soldier who refused to obey Calley's orders and who made the following postconventional statements: "The law is only the law, and many times it's wrong. . . . It's not necessarily just, just because it's the law" (stage 5); and, "Nothing needs an excuse to live. The same thing goes for bombing a village. If there are people in the village, don't bomb it" (stage 6) (p. 64).

The concern that some adults express who are oriented to the conventional level is that discussions of this nature will lead to anarchy—to the absence of order and control. Although most parents and teachers find it highly desirable for children to attain to stages 3 and 4, they fear a society in which people feel they have the right to make their own judgments. Many conventional adults do not understand the difference between the preconventional and the postconventional, seeing only the danger posed to law and order. Faced with an increasingly lawless society and being the victims of that lawlessness, it is understandable that responsible citizens would oppose any ideology that might contribute to this sorry state of affairs.

Such concern appears to be unwarranted, however, for members of the society who reason at the postconventional level. Granted that these principled individuals may demonstrate against an industry that pollutes the atmosphere or may march on Washington to demand equal treatment for minorities or may refuse to shoot civilians in Vietnam; nevertheless, they understand the importance of getting along with other people and in conforming to societal regulations. Laws are not challenged unless they are seen as working toward the detriment of others. Studies reveal that people who reason at the highest level are less apt to cheat, less apt to hurt others, and more apt to help someone in trouble than either preconventional or conventional individuals. They have a greater resistance to temptation and are less apt to conform to group pressure. Rather than condemning the postconventional members of the society, one would do well to listen to what they have to say, to note the personal sacrifice some have borne in acting on their convictions, to weigh the consequences of their ideas, and then to judge their reasoning as having merit or not having merit. Being a good citizen and a moral person involves a determination of what changes need to be made in this world of ours and then setting about by word and deed to institute those changes.

Another approach at the high school level is the creation of the "just community school." Devised by Kohlberg, there are prepared guides for organizing and administering the program which calls for sixty to ninety students and five to six teachers. According to Graham (1975), the program has two objectives: to make the school a happier place to be and to help students come closer to principled thinking. Membership in a just community is voluntary, leadership is democratic, and the group must have a sense of shared goals. Students, teachers, and administrators together decide on issues of fairness and morality—issues such as stealing, cutting classes, disruptive behavior, grading procedures, and the use of drugs. The opportunity for participatory democracy is in contrast to the structure of traditional programs in which students have little to say as to the policy of the school and in which they are expected to conform or be punished. To insist that young people adhere to established rules regardless of perceived fairness makes for administrative ease but does not encourage moral development. By contrast, the implementation of a just community is time-consuming, necessitates careful planning, and involves the expertise to resolve problems as they occur. But it gives students the opportunity to think through value-related issues.

Kohlberg (1980a) says that a student should emerge from high school at stage 4. "Unless a person leaves high school already at the fourth stage and with corresponding interests and motivations, he or she is unlikely to be in a position to have the capacities and motivation to enter positions of participation and public responsibility later" (p. 466). It would be preferable, of course, for students to be at the postconventional level, but it does not appear that this is a realistic expectation. During the 1970s it was thought that educating students for principled thinking would be possible. Implementation of the just community and the development of social studies programs integrating Kohlberg's techniques into the classroom (Fenton, 1976) were expected to move students in this direction.

But the 1980s have found us no farther along. Perhaps too few schools have used the programs. Perhaps other forces are at work that undermine the development of principled thinking. In any event, there are indications that progress—or what appeared to be progress—has not taken us far, making the mood of some proponents of the moral-reasoning approach more guarded and less optimistic. "My 1976 lecture on education for justice stressed a retrenchment from my 1968 Platonic stage 6 to a stage 5 goal and conception of justice. The present paper reports a further retrenchment to stage 4 goals as the ends of civic education" (Kohlberg, 1980a, p. 459).

Even more serious are signs that our young people may be regressing to the level of the preconventional. Patricia McCormack (1981), United Press International education editor, has written of the changing values in our high schools. An investigation ordered by the federal government's National Center for Education Statistics and carried out by the National Opinion Research Center of Chicago surveyed fifty-eight thousand high school seniors across the nation and compared their values with those of the high school graduating class of 1972. "Working to correct social and economic inequalities" was cited as "very important" by only 13 percent in 1980 compared to 27 percent in 1972. "Having lots of money" was rated "very important" by 31 percent in 1980, up from 19 percent in

1972. Young people appear to be interested primarily in what will serve their own interests. The parents of these teenagers also applaud these goals. They, too, want for their children the acquisition of this world's goods. This is why they say their children should graduate from high school and why they will send their children to college. If they want more for their children than that they make a good living, it is seldom expressed. During the Vietnam era, many young people decided to go into one of the helping professions. Now, by comparison, fewer appear to be interested in areas such as social work and more are interested in areas such as business.

As important as it is to earn a living, the goal of having enough money falls far short of principled morality. "If schooling is only oriented toward preparing students for assuming preestablished occupational slots, then the educational system will have failed one of its most crucial functions in a democracy" (Rest, 1979, Sec. 1, p. 24). Yet schools are a part of the communities they serve and reflect the will of the people. A society at the conventional level will demand schools at the conventional level. Some preconventional attitudes are considered to be in accord with reality and some postconventional beliefs are recognized as important, but moral reasoning that is either lower or higher than that of the populace must be limited or it will be perceived as a threat.

What does the future hold for educational programs based on the cognitive approach of moral reasoning? The answer depends on who is being asked. Those who play down the importance of the judgmental in contrast to the behavioral or the affective, or who say that moral training should be the province of the home or the church and not of the school, or who feel that time spent in a discussion of moral issues leaves too little time for teaching the basics will answer that moral reasoning programs should not be encouraged. They are just a passing fad and probably not worth the effort. Conversely, those who are intrigued by

Piaget's and Kohlberg's insights and who grasp the import of what it would mean to a society for more individuals to be at higher stages of moral judgment will insist that the present trend of including moral discussions in all types of subject matter must continue. If moral reasoning is not a part of the curriculum, there will be less opportunity for children to profit from a plus-one model and development in the hierarchy of moral thought will be less apt to take place. It is necessary that all institutions that affect the child; the home, the church, and the school, be involved in the development of moral reasoning. "The task is to 'give the psychology of moral development and education away' to as many teachers, administrators, parents and interested others as possible. That will begin to make morality a common cause. . . . It is time to 'mainstream' moral education as one means to enhance overall human capability" (Mosher, 1980, p. 221). Unless this is done, those at the preconventional level who seek no good other than their own, and those at the conventional level who do not understand that morality may exceed getting along with neighbors and obeying the law, will never realize their potential. The enterprise is of such magnitude that assistance is needed from as many sources as possible.

Application to the Church

That great body of believers called the church is composed of people at all stages of moral reasoning. Yet, whatever the stage, the Christian message is meaningful. Some come to Christ to escape the fires of hell and obtain the blessings of heaven (stage 1). Others see the Christian life as a good bargain. They will acknowledge Christ now, and Christ will acknowledge them later (stage 2). Still others think of Jesus as their friend, and the fellowship of the saints takes on great importance (stage 3). Those at stage 4 look to Christ as the Lord of their lives and to the Scripture as their guide to faith and practice. Stage 5 Christians emphasize Christ as the Redeemer of the world and endeavor to follow his example of putting people before the law. They are usually more creative and more flexible than those at stage 4. Believers at stage 6 see God as the One who holds together the universe, and they believe that every individual is created in the image of God and has personal worth. They emphasize that true religion is loving others even as Christ loved us.

Some of the problems within the church occur because Christians at one stage or level are unable to understand Christians at a different stage or level. Believers at the preconventional level focus on what God has done for them and on how much better off they are now than before they accepted Christ. Their favorite hymns are songs of personal testimony, "I was lost in sin but Jesus found me," "From sinking sand he lifted me," and "I've reached the land of corn and wine." Those at the conventional level not only see themselves in an advantageous position because of what Christ has done for them, but they also have an appreciation of the family of God and of the fellowship of the saints. Joining hearts and hands with brothers and sisters in the Lord, receiving encouragement, and sharing joys and sorrows gives meaning to their lives. "Blest be the tie that binds" and "Come, we that love the Lord" are enjoyed.

Being at the conventional level also means taking seriously the ceremonies and traditions of the church. Conformity to a particular mode of baptism or a way of taking communion or the manner in which the worship service is conducted is important. For some believers these forms take on such significance that they become part of church doctrine, and church doctrine, in turn, becomes all important. Some stage 4 Christians believe that losing the tradition or the form is tantamount to losing everything. They say that if one domino falls, they all will fall. Such believers are often the pillars of the church and display a loyalty that is most impressive. They are true to what they believe, and they believe fervently. "A charge to keep I have" and "Come, thou almighty King" have special meaning. However, they seldom understand a morality other than their own, and for this reason they do not move to higher stages of moral thought.

Postconventional Christians, having traversed through the previous stages of moral reasoning, appreciate what Christ has done for them personally. They value the fellowship of the saints, and they understand the importance of tradition. But they appreciate, value, and understand far more. If they follow convention—and they usually do—it is done out of conviction, not because they are told they must. They weigh alternatives and judge what is best in a given situation. They will implement innovative methods of witnessing or of teaching a Sunday school class if past methods are shown to be ineffective. If a minister brings new ways of doing things to the church, postconventional Christians will not be perturbed providing the new ways do not become "gospel." When the young people of the church adopt unconventional dress and hair styles, it is overlooked. Worshiping God in spirit and in truth takes precedence over form and custom. Favorite songs are "This is my Father's world" and "Love divine."

Stage 5 Christians are a blessing to some and a cross to others. They are often more caring and accepting and loving than those at stage 4. They are concerned not only for fellow church members but also for a world that needs Christ. They understand that evil comes not only in the form of personal sins like drunkenness, deceitfulness, and infidelity but also in the form of social sins like racism, poverty, and sexism. An enigma to fellow parishioners and a thorn in the side of church leaders at stage 4, the stage 5 Christian may be accused of hindering the Spirit of Christ, of not having a proper respect for authority. From the perspective of the postconventional member, authority *is* respected and church policy *is* understood. But this does not mean that the minister or the church board has a special line to God that others cannot tap. All believers may go directly to God in prayer and to the Scripture to determine God's will and to know what is right and what is wrong in God's sight. Some churches have been known to penalize believers for behaviors based on principled morality when these conflicted with the church's conventions or convenience. When this occurs, postconventional Christians do not feel compelled to stand before a tribunal to be judged for their "liberal" ways. To one's own Master one stands or falls.

Believers at stage 6 will not discriminate against the poor, the less educated, or the less socially aware. All who are true Christians are welcomed into the church. "Sixes" do not take the attitude that families are more important than singles, that the Men's Bible study class has more favor with God than the Women's Bible study class, or that representatives of one's own race are preferable for church membership to those of a different complexion. Nor do stage 6 believers consider that they are better Christians than those who reason at other stages of moral development. All people have equal worth in God's sight, and God uses Christians at all stages. Emphasis is on what one can become rather than on one's present state.

Jack Pressau (1977) in his carefully reasoned *I'm Saved, You're Saved—Maybe* makes a case for the ideal Christian being one who functions, not at the conventional level and not at the postconventional level, but *"at all moral levels at once."*

> Ideal Christians . . . are persons who consciously affirm that there are valid moral reasons at many moral stages. . . . They try to do what they do at the highest Level possible, but they are more concerned about responsible behavior than perfect motivation. . . . I believe the condescension and suspicion between the different moral Levels of salvation understanding is a scandal to the church. By keeping in touch with all those reasons-for-believing pos-

itively we improve our chances of hearing and being heard
by others who need our ministry. (p. 111).

One is not a better Christian for reasoning at a higher
level. Rather, the advantages come in being able to function at more levels at a time, in achieving greater equilibrium when problems occur, and in finding more effective
ways to cope.

Duska and Whelan (1975) write of difficulties faced by
older Catholics who, having spent all their adult lives at
the conventional level, were faced with recent changes in
the church. Loyalty to them meant an unswerving attachment to the practices of worship. "The good thing to do
is that which the Church approves . . . bowed heads after
communion, somberness and seriousness in church, not
eating meat on Friday, fasting during Lent, etc., etc." But
then these people were told that the church did not really
care about these forms of worship. Confused after a lifetime of fidelity, they asked what practices they should
engage in now and were told that they would have to
decide for themselves. At their age, this was impossible.
"Their road map for doing good was taken away and nothing was put in its place" (p. 87).

Younger people find independence attractive but may
suffer from a similar type of problem, a problem that
DiGiacomo (1979), an educator in a Catholic high school
calls "a Stage Four cop-out." Rather than trying to understand the principles behind the moral life, such as *why*
premarital sex, stealing, and lying are wrong, they just say
that their religion is against it. "For this mentality, religion becomes the arbiter of morals, and church membership is a short-cut to enlightenment by way of the
unexamined life. Dogmatism in any form is unacceptable
to the post-conventional mind, and should be" (p. 69).

Such a mentality is not unique to the Catholic church.
It is found in Protestant groups as well. Progression to the
level of the postconventional comes slowly, and many

never attain it. For those in churches where the list of dos and don'ts is exceedingly long and strongly enforced, the letter of the law may take precedence over an understanding of the law. "If God says it, I believe it, and that settles it" is a favorite expression. But those who search the Scriptures do not always agree on what God has said, and so divisions come with each group insisting that it knows the mind of the Lord.

Other problems also may occur. Some churches have been forced to close their doors due to mergers at the national level, leaving members of the local congregations confused and angry, or the minister may be found to have dipped his fingers into the offering plate or to have engaged in sexual immorality. The believer at the conventional level whose loyalty is with the local congregation and who looked to the minister as one sent from God is often at a loss to know how to cope. Postconventional members of a congregation are less disturbed by such events. If the district church folds, they recognize that the cause of Jesus Christ is far greater than the local congregation. If the minister is run out of town, their less exalted view of authority serves to help them pick up the pieces, put them together into a new design, and continue to serve a God who is perfect and who will never leave them or forsake them.

The cognitive view of morality may be applied as well to the teaching of children in the Church school or Sunday school. Bible stories are an excellent source of moral dilemmas. The teacher finds it important not only to present the lesson, but to listen to what each child has to say, recognizing that children are not passive organisms shaped only by the environment but active human beings involved in their own development and understanding. Concepts taught must be at the child's level of cognition, or the result will be unrelated bits and pieces of information. As children respond to the lesson, the teacher should respect what is said as being appropriate to their level of cognition. A child's words should not be reinterpreted so they make sense to the adult mind, for to do so is to misunderstand what the child knows. Nor should a child's ideas be laughed at as being cute or criticized as being wrong. An atmosphere of acceptance and affirmation does not imply value-neutrality, however. Quite the contrary, the teacher will endeavor to help pupils understand the truths of Scripture and relate these truths to a more mature relationship with God. Creating conditions whereby ideas at the next stage of moral reasoning can be presented will foster both cognitive and spiritual development.

The stage 1 child is afraid of God's anger and sees him as the great punisher. An appeal to stage 2 is in order where God's love and care are taught. As a shepherd cares for the sheep, God cares for us. As he clothes the flowers of the field and feeds the birds of the air, so he will clothe and feed us. He loves us and wants us to be happy. Favorite stories are how God rescued Moses from Pharaoh, David from Goliath, and Daniel from the lions. "Jesus loves me" may be sung again and again and not lose its message. Playing the part of one of the characters in a Bible story appeals to the active nature of children and will help them learn that others have thoughts and feelings similar to their own. Role-playing helps the child *decenter*, that is, to see things from the perspective of another. This, in turn, enables the child to move from a morality of constraint at the preconventional level to a morality of cooperation at the conventional level.

Older children, at the junior high level, are ready for conventional thought. It is at this age that belonging to a group with which one can identify and to which one can be loyal takes on special significance. Unless the church has such a group, the young person may give allegiance to friends outside the church community and thus be lost to the influence of the gospel message. Young people also need adequate models after whom they can pattern their lives. The personality and lifestyle of the teacher or class leader becomes as important as what is said. A church library with good Christian fiction or biographies of missionaries also provides role-models for pupils.

The Sunday school class or junior church not only supplies a home base for its members but also defines the rules and duties by which the members of the community must abide. The student learns that God has laws, and these laws must not be broken. If the law is broken then someone must pay. This is what sent Jesus to the cross— to pay for our sins. The Scriptures become the rule book for how one is to live, and the community provides the social pressure to conform. The commandments of God are true and righteous and must be followed. Role-taking may continue through skits and plays but is more apt to occur by dialogue as ideas and beliefs are shared. Moral dilemmas in the Bible take on a larger dimension than was possible at the preconventional level. Moses' escape from Pharaoh and David's encounter with Goliath, of special interest to the preconventional child, are superseded at the conventional level with Moses as the leader of a great nation giving out the commandments of God, and David as a representative of the people of God, of right against might. Daniel's experience with the lions now becomes one of a series of incidents in the lives of a group of young men who encouraged each other to be true to God in the face of incredible odds.

Teachers of senior high students and of adults should endeavor to develop postconventional thinking in their classes. This precludes that the teacher is capable of such thinking and is allowed by church officials to conduct a class in this way. Discussion of why the Scriptures condemn certain behaviors and attitudes will enable members of the class to develop more advanced understanding than was possible at stage 4. Emphasis at the postconventional is also on internal control and self-chosen principles. Moses stood alone even when his own people were against him. David, likewise, knew what he had to do in spite of the ridicule of his brothers. Daniel prayed before God in full view of the enemy, even though disobedience to the king's law could cost him his life. Worship takes on a deeper meaning than is possible at previous levels of cognition for one now serves a God who is interested not only in the worshiper and in the worshiper's friends and family but also in all people everywhere. Jesus told his disciples to go to the ends of the world and witness to every person, bringing to all the good news of salvation.

Theology and the Cognitive Approach

When God created the world, he said, "Let us make man in our image, in our likeness" (Gn. 1:26). Rationality is part of the divine image and has an ethical component. We read that we are not to be like other created beings who have no understanding (Ps. 32:9) or as children who lack knowledge (1 Cor. 14:20). Rather, we are to be as adults in our thinking processes. As Christians we are admonished to set our minds on things above, to be renewed in knowledge in the image of the Creator, and to let the Word of Christ dwell in us richly in all wisdom (Col. 3:16).

The Scriptures present numerous comparisons between cognitive development and spiritual growth. For example, as children become adept in the use of language, they develop the capacity for verbal exchange, words become internalized, and thought processes emerge. Likewise, Christian development thrives in an atmosphere of thinking upon the Scriptures and on that which pertains to Christ. New believers may accept without question the doctrines of the church, even as children in Piaget's stage of heteronomy may accept without question a morality taught them by their parents. But if spiritual growth is to take place, Christians must study God's Word for themselves and decide which beliefs to keep and which to reject, even as children who proceed from heteronomy to autonomy must come to their own conclusions as to what is right and what is wrong. The processes of heteronomy and autonomy "might mingle and overlap more or less" (Piaget, 1932, p. 171) as the believer accepts some external constraints while internal controls are developing. Morality by definition is never imposed, and belief in Jesus Christ is never mandated. God wants us to choose freely—to decide for ourselves. He gave us minds—minds that can accept or reject, believe or disbelieve, love or hate. He knew full well that by giving Adam and Eve the freedom to choose, there would be unleashed infinite possibilities for evil. But that is the risk God was willing to take for he wanted those who follow him to do so freely, not as robots who obey their masters without giving thought to the matter.

There are marked similarities between our Lord's teachings and Piaget's concept of moral maturity (Clouse, 1978). Jesus taught the importance of *intentionality* by saying that one should look at the thoughts and intents of the heart rather than at outward forms and ceremonies (Mt. 23:27). He practiced *relativism* in judgment for he knew everyone's thoughts and was aware of all possible views (12:25). He showed that right and wrong may be *independent of sanctions* by teaching that the weightier matters of justice, mercy, and honesty are more important than the Pharisee's interpretations of the law (23:23). In the Sermon on the Mount he taught a *reciprocity* that called for a turning of the other cheek, going the extra mile, and loving the enemy (5:39-44), thus surpassing Piaget's view of autonomy and even of equity. *Punishment as restitution or reform* is preferable to punishment that would not make for a changed life; so when the teachers of the law brought to Jesus a woman caught in the act of adultery, rather than saying she should be stoned to death, which the law required, he said to her, "I do not condemn you . . . but do not sin again" (Jn. 8:11, TEV). Jesus also taught that a belief in immanent justice (which Piaget held to be immature) is sometimes in error and should be replaced by a concept of *naturalistic causes of misfortune* (the mature view). He gave as examples the time when Pilate killed the Galileans and the time when the Tower of Siloam fell on eighteen people, not because they were more wicked than others (Lk. 13:1-5), but because they happened to be in the wrong place when the misfortune occurred. Jesus knew all things and represented the most advanced thinking possible in the area of moral judgment. Those who hold to the historic Christian position would do well to look to the life of Jesus as the supreme example of moral conduct and to his words as the ultimate in moral discernment.

Kohlberg's stages of moral reasoning have been used by writers to show God's progressive dealings with his people. Jack Pressau (1977)[4] writes that when the Israelites left Egypt, God dealt with them at stage 2, promising blessing if they followed him and judgment if they turned away. After being established in the promised land, the morality of stages 3 and 4 was instituted with laws governing transactions of land and services. In time, the rich found ways to circumvent the law and oppress the poor, making it necessary for God to raise up prophets like Amos and Hosea, who spoke at the postconventional level. During the captivity, the people reverted to a stage 2 morality, the stage which becomes dominant whenever survival is threatened.

A similar approach has been taken by Dan Motet (1978) who pictures Kohlberg's developmental theory as "analogous to what we find in Scripture, where we can follow God's work to raise human moral judgment through the six stages" (p. 18). After seeing Pharaoh's army annihilated, the Israelites "feared the Lord," a stage 1 response. During the wilderness wanderings they were most concerned with their own needs, desiring the food they had had in Egypt (stage 2). Stage 3 is illustrated by Aaron's making a golden calf for the people, seemingly wanting their approval. The law and order of stage 4 comes with the giving of the Ten Commandments. "It is at this fourth stage that later the Pharisees remained fixated, and many of the conflicts between them and Jesus arose because He tried to bring them to the superior level of moral judgment" (p. 19).

As evangelicals become familiar with the cognitive approach to morality, there is increasing interest as to how to interpret research studies that show those adhering to basic Christian truths as more apt to score at the conventional level and less apt to score at the postconventional level than those who are agnostic or liberal in their religious views (Clouse 1982; Ernsberger & Manaster, 1981; Haan, Smith, & Block, 1968; Lawrence, 1978; Moore, 1979; Sanderson, 1973).[5] The natural reaction is to take the offensive. When one is a member of a group considered to have less of some desirable characteristic than another group one does not wish to be a member of, this is tantamount in the minds of some to saying that the research must have been conducted poorly or the theory on which the research is based is in error or the characteristic deemed desirable is not really desirable after all. How could believers be less mature in moral judgment than those who do not know Christ? The research should be carefully analyzed, Kohlberg's theory of moral reasoning may be challenged, and the virtues of conventional reasoning may be emphasized as opposed to the ideals of postconventional thought, but if the cognitive approach to morality does in fact have merit, none of these approaches will enable the Christian to advance in moral judgment. To lock ourselves into less mature stages of moral reasoning in order to feel good about ourselves and experience greater equilibrium will not in the long run profit either us or others.

The line of skirmish between the benefits of the conventional as opposed to the postconventional appears to be drawn between stage 4 and stages 5 and 6. Stage 4

Christians emphasize conformity to the church and to church doctrine. They have the true faith and rightly divide the Word. "With inerrant Bible in hand [they] busily dot the i's and cross the t's of fixed systematic theology which places the legal view of salvation at its center" (Pressau, 1977, p. 55). They believe that a good Christian will accept without question the teachings of the elders of the congregation for they are the ministers of God. The Fours are often suspicious of Christians at stages 5 and 6 because postconventional believers are less dogmatic, less structured, and sometimes deviate from the rules. They accuse the Fives of leaning toward socialism and the Sixes of flirting with humanism, ideologies the Fours feel to be in opposition to the Word of God. They point to Jesus and Paul as being concerned, not about the issues of poverty and slavery, but about bringing into the Kingdom those who would be saved.

Believers at the postconventional level place love above law, choice above conformity, social concerns above institutional profit. Having already traversed through stage 4, they are cognizant of conventional attitudes and may look with nostalgia to a time when they had more answers than questions, and life fit into a neat doctrinal pattern. But given the choice, they would not return to a cognition that demanded submission without examination and an obedience to the letter of the law apart from the spirit of the law. "To bind Christians by rules and regulations is unworthy of our tradition. It was from such legalism Christ came to set us free. . . . Morality is not so much rules as it is a calling from God" (Wynn, 1977, pp. 72-73). Postconventionals criticize the Fours for having too narrow an understanding of the cause of Christ. They say that the Fours will ostracize a true believer who does not meet their specifications or remove from the denomination any church that does not agree on every point of doctrine. By contending for the faith the conventionals become contentious, forgetting that the Bible says love is greater than faith (1 Cor. 13:13) and concern for the individual more important than conformity to the law (Jn. 8:3-11).

Both conventional Christians and postconventional Christians love God and want to further his cause. Both have a grasp of truth and can support their respective positions with Scripture. What may not be realized is that each needs the cognitions of the other. The believer at the conventional level needs to understand principled level thinking so he or she may relate to a larger number of people in love and enjoy the freedom that is in Christ. The believer at the postconventional level needs to be reminded that love alone is not enough. Generous thoughts and liberal attitudes will not bring one into the Kingdom, and an acceptance of universalism (should one go so far) is not in keeping with the words of Jesus, "I am the way and the truth and the life. No one comes to the Father except through me" (Jn. 14:6). When the young lawyer asked what he could do to inherit eternal life, he was told that the law was not enough (stage 4). He must love his neighbor as himself (stage 6) (Lk. 10:25-37). Conversely, the disciples were told that obedience is the confirmation of love. "If you love me, you will obey what I command" (Jn. 14:15). "Love needs law to guide it. It is rather naive to claim that love has no need of any direction outside itself. . . . Love is not infallible. Indeed, it is sometimes blind. So God has given us commandments to chart the pathways of love" (Stott, 1970, p. 151).

Thus, we see that the two moralities of law and love are inextricably combined. In the Old Testament we read, "Thou *shalt* love the Lord thy God" (Dt. 6:5, KJV), and in the New, "The entire law is summed up in a single command: 'Love your neighbor as yourself' " (Gal. 5:14). Jesus explained in the Sermon on the Mount that he did not come to destroy the law but to fulfill it (Mt. 5:17). He then proceeded to add a principled statement to the mandates of the law. "Do not murder" is a law; "do not be angry" is a principle. "Do not commit adultery" is a law; "do not look on a woman to lust after her" is a principle. The law regulates behavior; a principle monitors the cognitions that precede behavior.

The Pharisees had an obsession with keeping the law so they could be seen of men (Mt. 23:5). They took it upon themselves to watch not only their own behavior but everyone else's. They often asked the question, "Is it lawful?" Is it lawful for a man to put away his wife (19:3)? Is it lawful to pick corn on the Sabbath (12:2)? Is it lawful to pay taxes to the Roman emperor (22:17)? But Jesus confronted them face to face. He chided these men for attending to the lesser elements of the law (conventional) and neglecting the more important matters of the law—matters of justice, mercy, and faithfulness (postconventional) (23:23). When asked if it was lawful to heal on the Sabbath, Jesus responded that it was lawful to do well on the Sabbath (12:10-12).

The more important matter of justice is central to Christian theology even as it is the focal point of the cognitive approach to morality. Justice originates in the righteousness of God and is revealed in both the Old and the New Testaments, having been taught by Amos and Hosea and by our Lord himself.

> When one reads both Kohlberg and the prophets, therefore, it is striking that ancient men were in possession of a conception of justice as the Divine character in times when there was no substantial sample of Level III reasoning in the human population from which to infer those attributes. Yet the Piaget-Kohlberg descriptions of "justice" are virtual carbon copies of the Divine character as described. (Joy, 1983, p. 57)

The Christian should have little difficulty in making common cause with cognitive psychology on the subject of justice.

As believers we should be able to function at all levels

at the same time. At the preconventional level we appreciate a personal relationship with a God who will bless and keep—with one who has our best interests in mind (stage 2) (Jer. 29:11). At the conventional level we enjoy the fellowship of the saints (stage 3) and delight "in the law of the Lord" (stage 4) (Ps. 1:2). At the postconventional level we care for a world that needs Christ and are willing to reach people where they are rather than expecting them to fit into a prescribed pattern (stage 5). Finally, we respect each person as one for whom Christ died. Discrimination is condemned, for in God's sight all are equal and should be treated as such (stage 6) (Jas. 2:1). Having competencies at all levels places the Christian in a better position to "understand what is right and just and fair" (Prv. 2:9). Thus, it is apparent that the cognitive approach to morality and the revelation of God to his people have many similarities.

Notes

1. The statements within quotation marks following each stage are taken from *Development in judging moral issues* by James Rest (1979). Minneapolis: University of Minnesota Press.

2. Lawrence Kohlberg (1973) in *The Gerontologist, 13,* 497-502, has written of a possible seventh stage based on a sense of oneness with the cosmos. This union of the mind with nature, the feeling of being an integral part of all creation is more apt to occur during life's later years and is the successful resolution of the despair we all feel at one time or another when we picture ourselves as an insignificant speck in a vast universe. Kohlberg refers to this cosmic perspective, or feeling of oneness with infinity, as a reversal of figure and ground. Rather than seeing ourselves as finite beings, alienated and alone, we come to view ourselves as a part of all that exists, as a portion of the totality of life. Many people have experienced this rush of mystic awareness, perhaps when watching the ocean or listening to beautiful music, but moments like this are fleeting. Although not a true *moral* stage, for it has no definable structure nor is it logically or cognitively more adequate than the previous stage, this seventh stage is nevertheless a

phenomenon of psychological or religious significance that brings a sense of meaning to those who have experienced it. It has been known to enable the elderly to face death confidently and without fear.

3. The statements in quotes are verbatim responses of elementary school children in Vigo County, Indiana.

4. For a more detailed examination of Kohlberg's stages and Christian belief, Jack Pressau, (1977) *I'm saved, you're saved—maybe* is recommended. Atlanta: John Knox.

5. Not all studies report a negative relationship between stage of moral judgment and adherence to Christianity. For a positive correlation between moral reasoning and literal scriptural belief, see Brown, M. B., & Annis, L. (1978), Moral development level and religious behavior, *Psychological Reports, 43,* 1230; and for moral judgment and religious background, see Bull, N. J. (1969), *Moral judgement from childhood to adolescence,* Beverly Hills: Sage Publications. Two unpublished doctoral dissertations show moral reasoning related to religious knowledge (see O'Gorman, R. P. (1979), *An investigation of moral judgment and religious knowledge scores of Catholic high school boys from Catholic and public schools,* Boston College), and to religious education (see Stoop, D. A. (1979) *The relation between religious education and the process of maturity through the developmental stages of moral judgments,* University of Southern California).

References

Clouse, B. (1978). The teachings of Jesus and Piaget's concept of mature moral judgment. *Journal of Psychology and Theology, 6,* 175-82.

_____. (1982). *Moral judgment as related to politics and religion.* Unpublished manuscript, Indiana State University, IN.

Dewey, J. (1895). What psychology can do for the teacher. In R. D. Archambault (Ed.),(1963). *Dewey on education.* New York: Modern Library. (Cited in Kohlberg, L. (1973). Implications of developmental psychology for education: Examples from moral development. *Educational Psychologist, 10,* 2-14).

DiGiacomo, J. J. (1979). Ten years as moral educator in a Catholic high school. In T. C. Hennessy (Ed.), *Value/moral education: Schools and teachers* (pp. 51-71). New York: Paulist Press.

Duska, R., & Whelan, M. (1975). *Moral development: A guide to Piaget and Kohlberg.* New York: Paulist Press.

Ernsberger, D. J., & Manaster, G. J. (1981). Moral development, intrinsic/extrinsic religious orientation and denominational teachings. *Genetic Psychology Monographs, 104,* 23-41.

Fenton, E. (1976). The cognitive-developmental approach to moral education. *Social Education, 40,* 187.

Fraenkel, J. R. (1976). The Kohlberg bandwagon: Some reservations. *Social Education, 40,* 216-22.

Graham, R. (1975). Moral education: A child's right to a just community. *Elementary School Guidance and Counseling, 9,* 299-308.

Haan, N., Smith, M. B., & Block, J. (1968). Moral reasoning in young adults: Political-social behavior, family background, and personality correlates. *Journal of Personality and Social Psychology, 10,* 183-201.

Joy, D. M. (1983). Kohlberg revisited: A supra-naturalist speaks his mind. In D. M. Joy (Ed.), *Moral development foundations* (pp. 37-62). Nashville, TN: Abingdon.

King, M. L., Jr. (1964). *Why we can't wait.* New York: Harper & Row.

Kohlberg, L. (1963). Moral development and identification. In H. W. Stevenson (Ed.), *Child psychology: 62nd yearbook of the National Society for the Study of Education* (pp. 277-332). Chicago: University of Chicago Press.

_____. (1967). Moral and religious education and the public schools: A developmental view. In T. R. Sizer (Ed.), *Religion and public education* (pp. 164-83). Boston: Houghton Mifflin.

_____. (1973). The contribution of developmental psychology to education—examples from moral education. *Educational Psychologist, 10,* 2-14.

_____. (1976a). The quest for justice in 200 years of American history and in contemporary American education. *Contemporary Education, 48,* 5-16.

_____. (1976b). This special section in perspective. *Social Education, 40,* 213-15.

_____. (1980a). Educating for a just society: An updated and revised statement. In B. Munsey (Ed.), *Moral development, moral education, and Kohlberg: Basic issues in philosophy, psychology, religion, and education* (pp. 455-70). Birmingham, AL: Religious Education.

_____. (1980b). Stages of moral development as a basis for moral education. In B. Munsey (Ed.), *Moral development, moral education, and Kohlberg: Basic issues in philosophy, psychology, religion, and education* (pp. 15-98). Birmingham, AL: Religious Education.

_____. (1981). *Essays on moral development: The philosophy of moral development.* (Vol. 1). New York: Harper & Row.

_____. (1984). *Essays on moral development: The psychology of moral development.* (Vol. 2). New York: Harper & Row.

Krebs, R. (1980). *How to bring up a good child.* Minneapolis: Augsburg.

Lande, N., & Slade, A. (1979). *Stages: Understanding how you make moral decisions.* New York: Harper & Row.

Lawrence, J. A. (1978). *The component procedures of moral judgment-making.* Unpublished doctoral dissertation, University of Minnesota.

Lickona, T. (1983). *Raising good children: Helping your child through the stages of moral development.* New York: Bantam Books.

McCormack, P. (1981, April 23). Values change in high schools. *The Terre Haute Tribune,* Sec. B, p. 16. UPI press release.

Moore, M. E. (1979). *The differential effect of a church-related college environment and a state college or university environment on the moral development of self-described students.* Unpublished doctoral dissertation, University of Virginia.

Mosher, R. L. (1980). Moral education: Let's open the lens. In L. Kuhmerker, M. Mentkowski, & V. L. Erickson (Eds.), *Evaluating moral development: And evaluating educational programs that have a value dimension* (pp. 213-21). Schenectady, NY: Character Research.

Motet, D. (1978). Kohlberg's theory of moral development and the Christian faith. *Journal of Psychology and Theology, 6,* 18-21.

Peters, R. S. (1971). Moral development: A plea for pluralism. In T. Mischel (Ed.), *Cognitive development and epistemology* (pp. 237-67). New York: Academic.

Piaget, J. (1932). *The moral judgment of the child* (M. Gabain, Trans.). London: K. Paul, Trench, Trubner, & Co.

Pressau, J. R. (1977). *I'm saved, you're saved—maybe.* Atlanta, GA: John Knox.

Rest, J. R. (1975). Recent research on an objective test of moral judgment: How the important issues of a moral dilemma are defined. In D. J. DePalma & J. M. Foley (Eds.), *Moral development: Current theory and research* (pp. 75-93). Hillsdale, NJ: Lawrence Erlbaum Associates.

_____. (1979). *The impact of higher education on moral judgment development.* Technical Report #5, Minnesota Moral Research Projects. Minneapolis.

Rich, J. M. (1980). Moral education and the emotions. *Journal of Moral Education, 9,* 81-7.

Rothman, G. R. (1980). The relationship between moral judgment and moral behavior. In M. Windmiller, N. Lambert, & E. Turiel (Eds.), *Moral development and socialization* (pp. 107-27). Boston: Allyn and Bacon.

Ruma, E., & Mosher, P. (1967). Relationship between moral judgment and guilt in delinquent boys. *Journal of Abnormal Psychology, 72,* 122-27.

Sanderson, S. K. (1973). *Religion, politics, and morality: An approach to religious and political belief systems and their relation through Kohlberg's cognitive-developmental theory of moral judgment.* Unpublished doctoral dissertation, University of Nebraska at Lincoln.

Scharf, P. (1978). *Moral education.* Davis, CA: Responsible Action.

Simon, F. (1976). Moral development: Some suggested implications for teaching. *Journal of Moral Education, 5,* 173-78.

Stott, J. R. W. (1970). *Christ the controversialist.* London: Tyndale.

Sullivan, E. V. (1975). *Moral learning: Some findings, issues and questions.* New York: Paulist Press.

Ward, T. (1979). *Values begin at home.* Wheaton, IL: Victor Books.

Wilson, J. (1980). Philosophical difficulties and 'moral development'. In B. Munsey (Ed.), *Moral development, moral education, and Kohlberg: Basic issues in philosophy, psychology, religion, and education* (pp. 214-31). Birmingham, AL: Religious Education.

Windmiller, M. (1980). Introduction. In M. Windmiller, N. Lambert, & E. Turiel (Eds.), *Moral development and socialization* (pp. 1-33). Boston: Allyn & Bacon.

Woodward, K. L. (1976, March). Who should teach your children right from wrong? *McCall's,* pp. 97, 154, 168, 170.

Wynn, J. C. (1977). *Christian education for liberation and other upsetting ideas.* Nashville, TN: Abingdon.

Ziv, A. (1976). Measuring aspects of morality. *Journal of Moral Education, 5,* 189-201.

4

The Humanistic Approach
Morality as Moral Potential

He is like a tree planted by streams of water,
  which yields its fruit in season
and whose leaf does not wither.
  Whatever he does prospers. (Ps. 1:3)

Humanism, as the term implies, reflects the idea that the greatest of all attributes are those that make people distinctly human. Awareness of self, sensitivity to others, appreciation of the potential within humankind, and ability to express and analyze feelings are traits stressed by humanists. Being human sets us apart from all other forms of life and provides a sharp contrast to any other creature. People may be similar to animals in some ways, but they are, nonetheless, quite superior in other ways. Animals cannot fall in love, express themselves verbally, or plan for the future. Nor are people like the objects they create. A machine or computer may do some things better and faster than a person, but a machine is not an emotional being having self-awareness, and a computer is not an intelligent creature with a mind of its own. Only people possess those qualities that are of greatest worth.

Although humanism as a philosophy goes back to the time of classical Greece, humanism as a psychology began to emerge in the 1940s as a reaction against the two leading psychologies of the day, namely, behaviorism (learning theory) and psychoanalysis. Accepting neither the behavioristic position that a person is the product of the environment nor the psychoanalytic view that a person is born depraved and in need of cultural alteration, humanists affirm that each of us becomes what we make ourselves by our own perceptions and by our own actions. Inner qualities are stressed, but these are seen as positive rather than negative. This reaction earned humanism the title of *third-force* psychology. Although a cousin to cognitive theory in that both humanism and cognitivism stress the potential of humankind, humanism places greater emphasis on the emotional, motivational, and social aspects of human existence, whereas cognitivism stresses the intellectual or reasoning processes.

Humanism continued to develop in the 1950s, spread rapidly in the 1960s and 1970s, and now claims that time is on its side as more and more people are joining the movement (Morain, 1980, p. 10). Carl Rogers, one of the pioneers of today's humanistic movement, has said that humanistic psychology will never go down in history for what it is *against* but rather for what is *for* (Rogers, 1978, p. 45). Those who joined the movement in the 1960s may have joined because "humanistic psychology tied in nicely with various other protest movements" (Kolesnik, 1975, p. 47), but those who are adopting humanism today come from all walks of life and are attracted not so much by what humanism rejects as by what humanism accepts. An emphasis on becoming, fulfillment, realization, purposefulness, peak experiences, joy, and transcendence is finding universal appeal.

There are several varieties of humanism, each taking a different form and each having a different emphasis. Humanism may be linked with a type of psychotherapy or with educational reform or with the study of humanity's struggle throughout history. Humanism is a vital part of many religions, including Christianity, and yet it is claimed by avowed agnostics and atheists. To place all humanists under the same framework would therefore do a great disservice to an understanding of the differences that exist between them. But there are commonalities as well, and a lack of agreement as to the meaning of the term does not preclude the fact that all humanists are concerned with the development and welfare of that being called "man." Part of man's welfare includes the realm of the ethical or moral, and a number of assumptions of what constitutes morality would be accepted by the majority of humanists even though they come to the position from a variety of backgrounds.

Basic Assumptions

Humanists place emphasis on the positive aspects of the human condition. Infants are born goodly creatures and are equipped with self-generative abilities that enable them to perceive the environment, interact with it, and put it together in meaningful ways. The striving for creativity, identity, meaning, and psychological health is all part of the potential present at birth. This capacity to grow, to develop, to mature encompasses every area of life, including the realm of the ethical. *Human beings are born with the potential for moral development.* They will strive for goodness, truth, wholeness, perfection, and for norms to guide their lives. They have the capacity to be self-critical and self-correcting. "They can recognize their mistakes, aberrations, and transgressions. . . . It is a part of our ethical nature to keep watch over our egotistic, selfish, or criminal impulses" (Kolenda, 1980, p. 4). The inherent dignity of people makes this force-for-moral-growth a part of the intrinsic nature of humankind.

Changes occur when a person perceives the world in a new way. *Moral development comes from within the individual and is dependent on the perceptions available at the time of development.* The real world is each person's phenomenal world—the world as each one sees it. One's awareness of self, one's concept of his or her own values and the values of others, one's conscious beliefs, are part of the perceptions acquired in the progress toward moral maturity. Morality, by definition, must come from within the person rather than being imposed by an outside source. As the child grows, the perceptive field increases to include, not only one's own needs, but the needs of others as well. But the basis of all development is personal, subjective, and introspective. Overt manifestations of morality, although visible, are not the principal concern. "Humanism . . . regards behavior only as symptom, the external manifestation of what is going on inside a human being. The humanist believes that effective understanding of persons requires understanding, not only of behavior, but also the nature of an individual's internal life" (Combs, 1978, p. 301). As important as moral behavior is, emphasis remains on the source of the development—on people themselves as conscious, perceiving organisms.

Although moral development must come from within, *the environment may facilitate or impede one's strivings for morality.* A warm, accepting, positive, nondirective environment provides the occasion for moral growth to take place. By contrast, an oppressive, authoritarian, punitive environment will hinder moral maturity. What a person needs is encouragement not judgment, assistance not opposition, facilitation not threat, friendship not hostility. Fewer restrictions or controls will enable individuals to develop their own potential. Those who provide an accepting milieu are themselves moral for they are giving support to the growth of others. Affirmation frees the perceptual system of distortions and lays the foundation for healthy adaptation.

Human beings are integrated wholes, not a number of compartments. Thus, *morality cannot be separated from other areas of the person's life.* All development is interrelated, each individual having an internal locus of control which integrates every portion of the personality. To develop morally is to develop cognitively, affectively, and behaviorally. Whatever one experiences or perceives has an effect upon the whole organism. What one learns translates to values and a sense of direction. What one feels becomes the basis for future learning and activity. What one does is integrally related to attitudes and beliefs. The realm of morality cannot be considered apart from the totality of all that makes us human.

Morality has many forms of expression. Moral expression may take the form of joyful and creative emotions such as openness, spontaneity, exhilaration, prizing, and love. Or it may come in the form of increased awareness of self and the quality of our existence. As we reflect on our experiences, analyze and integrate our thoughts, find meaning from the past and hope for the future, we become aware of the value of many things previously not recognized. Life becomes more than a day-by-day existence that goes on and on as it has always gone on before. Rather, each day brings wonders and surprises if we but tune in to the possibilities. Morality finds expression as we share with others in a multitude of ways, communicating our attitudes, motives, and expectations to them and listening in turn to their hopes, feelings, and beliefs.

The importance of friendship—of letting others know of our interest in them, of wanting to be a part of their world, of helping them whenever they have a felt need—becomes the basis for the assertion that *morality finds its greatest meaning in relationships between people.* "The fully-functioning, self-actualized person, whom the humanists hold up as an ideal, experiences a deep feeling of identification with others, has strong feelings of sympathy with and affection for them, and a genuine desire to help them. He perceives his interests as being not in conflict but in harmony with those of his fellow man" (Kolesnik, 1975, p. 45). Self-interest must not take precedence over interests in others. Moral maturity means an inclination toward being generous, altruistic, and cooperative. Democracy is highly prized and freedom is cherished. But freedom is not a license for selfish, self-centered behavior. "The watchword of Humanism is service to humanity" (Lamont, 1957, p. 189). The humanist condemns any ideology that would make people less than human, that would strip them of their dignity and worth. Developing morally sometimes will result in a greater adjustment to society, but sometimes it will mean opposing or challenging the existing structure. Any discrimination on the basis of race or religion or national origin is contrary to the tenets of humanism. The ideal society is one "that would free humans to be themselves while retaining love for and attachment to others" (Elkind, 1981, p. 521). Humanists say that these two, self and others, must not nor need not be separated.

Clarifying Values

Moral choices are made when we clarify our values. The word *values* is used often by humanists, and it is recognized that each person's values come from a number of sources—some old and well known and others new and waiting to be tried. The old includes organismic needs each of us possesses as a member of the human race and interpersonal relationships shared with family and acquaintances. The new incorporates a variety of lifestyles portrayed for us through the mass media and the trend to accept all people everywhere regardless of background or culture or religious preference. The old and the new combine to provide a greater number of options for valuing than was known a generation ago. As Carl Rogers (1964) expresses it: "It is no longer possible, as it was in the not too distant historical past, to settle comfortably into the value system of one's forebears or one's community and live out one's life without ever examining the nature and the assumptions of that system" (p. 160).

Values are inferred from the choices we make. We choose how to use our time and how to spend our money. We choose what to wear, whom to be with, and where to go. We choose what book to read, what cassette to listen to, what television program to watch. Our desires, our motives, our needs, our attitudes, our beliefs all affect in some way the kinds of choices that we make. Whenever we choose we are expressing a value. We are saying that a particular object or person or behavior is more acceptable or more desirable or more right for us than another object or person or behavior. Some values may be means to an end and are called instrumental because they help us to accomplish those ends. Other values may be ends in themselves and are called terminal because they are culminating experiences or states. Being ambitious, capable, courageous, and helpful are examples of instrumental values whereas happiness, equality, self-respect, and wisdom are terminal values (Rokeach, 1973).

Values are personal. By definition they must come from within the individual. Although a person may possess many of the same values that others possess, this in no way detracts from the private nature of these internalized guides. Because of the intimate nature of values, they cannot be imposed by an outside source. The direct approach of telling someone what values he or she should have or the indirect approach of modeling those values that are of greatest worth will be effective only if the person decides to adopt those values as his or her own. No one can make another person accept certain values—a fact most parents, ministers, and educators find difficult to keep in mind.

Although humanists would not separate moral values from other values, care must be taken not to make a moral issue of all the choices one makes. Indeed, valuing encompasses so many aspects of a person's life that values that are assuredly moral in nature comprise only a small portion of the total valuing process. Whether a woman buys a Ford or a Chevrolet, studies to become an accountant or a teacher, prefers white curtains or yellow curtains in the kitchen, prides herself on being financially independent or on being a careful manager of her husband's paycheck is not within the realm of the moral. Judgments of right and wrong should not be applied to matters of personal taste. Yet, the moral part of the valuing process is of great importance for it prepares the way for those cognitions, motives, and behaviors that are directly related to issues of good and bad, to matters of right and wrong.

Humanistic psychologists place emphasis on the *process* of valuing, thus following in the progressive tradition of John Dewey. Although not discounting either the content of values or the product of values, the focus of attention is on the procedures whereby one becomes aware of values already held as well as values in the process of emerging. This stress on process rather than product, on becoming rather than being, on potential rather than current state brings optimism and confidence. We are told that life can be more productive, more satisfying, more enjoyable, and more meaningful. But in order for this to take place, we must be aware—aware of our feelings, our thoughts, our beliefs, and aware above all of what we can become.

The ultimate of this potential is called self-actualization, a favorite term among humanistic psychologists. The word "self" designates that the process comes about through changes that occur within the person, or self, rather than by changes imposed from without. "Actualization" has the meaning of having arrived at a desired state, of making realistic the possibilities one has by virtue of being human. By fastening on the goodly aspects of human nature and by holding up as a model those individuals within the society who are psychologically well adjusted, humanists have produced a list of characteristics of people who are self-actualized.

The principal source of this information comes from the writings of Abraham Maslow, who was interested in the needs people have and in the way people go about meeting their needs. Maslow (1970) notes that there appears to be a universal order in which needs are satisfied with earlier and more basic needs having to be met, at least in part, before later or higher order needs will emerge. First in the hierarchy are *physiological needs* such as the need for food or drink or shelter. Life cannot be sustained without the physiological needs being met. Next in order are the *safety needs* of security, protection, and stability. When the safety needs are met, a person is then in a position to move on to a satisfying of the *love needs*, which include a feeling of belonging, of being accepted, and of receiving affection. The *esteem needs* of gaining prestige and recognition, of feeling competent, and of having social status are next in line, followed by the *aesthetic* and *cognitive needs* of appreciating beauty and order and of desiring knowledge and understanding. Meeting the need for *self-actualization* is contingent upon an individual's having met to a certain degree those needs that have preceded.

According to Maslow (1973), self-actualized people tend to accept themselves, others, and the natural world for what they are. They are realistically oriented and yet spontaneous and creative in their thinking and behavior. Although they enjoy close relationships with other people and are democratic in their attitude toward others, they tend to be loners in the sense that they have a need for privacy, for autonomy, and for resisting conformity to the culture around them. They have a continuous appreciation of the world, a sense of awe for much of nature that most people seldom notice, and a feeling of oneness with all humankind. They will devote themselves to a task or mission, centering their attention on their work rather than on themselves. Humor is enjoyed, but never at the expense of another, nor is it expressed in a hostile or vulgar manner. People who are self-actualized have a highly developed sense of ethics that is apparent in both speech and action, are more aware of their values than are other individuals, and have a better understanding of why they think and act and feel as they do. They have clarified what is important to them and have determined what pattern of life will make for a rich, happy, and fulfilling existence.[1]

All of us have values, but not all of us are aware of our values. We are left less knowledgeable and less alert than we should be. We may be confused, apathetic, withdrawn, or overly conforming. Or we may be flighty, aggressive, and overbearing. We may want to relate to others in a serious and meaningful way, but we do not know how to go about establishing such relationships. In today's complex world, we need more than ever to clarify what we really believe, to bring to the surface those values that will give our lives greater significance and direction. We need more consistency and more confidence. We need to discover the discrepancies that make for confusion and dismay, and we need to establish guidelines as to what to do when values are found to be conflicting. In short, we need to clarify our values.

The expression of values has always been pervasive within a society, but only in recent years have there been organized programs to guide in the process of valuing. The approach best known was designed by Louis E. Raths who, with his students Merrill Harmin and Sidney Simon, developed a number of creative ways to implement what is now known as values clarification. Their book *Values and Teaching* (1966) brought attention to how the approach may be used in an educational setting. Since that time numerous books, journal articles, and workshop manuals have been published that give careful directions for conducting values clarification sessions in any context.

Seven criteria must be met for a person to clarify a value. One must

1. Be able to choose freely without restriction;
2. Consider viable alternatives;
3. Choose only after thoughtfully considering the consequence of each alternative;
4. Be happy with one's choice;
5. Affirm the choice publicly;
6. Act on one's choice; and
7. Incorporate the choice into one's life pattern.

The first three criteria involve the act of *choosing* a value; the next two signify a *prizing* or celebrating of the value chosen; and the last two mean *acting* upon the value chosen, making it a regular part of one's life.

The clarification of moral values will go through the same steps as the clarification of all other values. One must choose freely with no hint of coercion, alternatives must be considered, and possible consequences of each alternative must be weighed. Once the choice has been made, the value must be prized and cherished along with a desire to let others know the decision that has been made. The person must then be willing to act on that decision, to change his or her behavior, not just on occasion, but on a regular basis.

Techniques Employed

Values clarification as a seven-step process is only one of many techniques used by humanistic psychologists. Much of the popularity of the humanist movement comes from a variety of programs and therapies designed to help individuals deal with emotional problems. As people learn to strip away the facades that mask their true natures and reveal their innermost thoughts, feelings, and aspirations, they begin to understand who they really are. Hypocrisy, unresolved hostility, crippling guilt, and unexpressed love are exchanged for a nonjudgmental acceptance of themselves and of others. Each of us needs to see ourself as a human being, to understand the importance of being a part of the human race, to approve of those characteristics that make us a representative of that species called "man." We must learn to accept ourselves—even to *like* ourselves. And, as we accept and like ourselves, we learn to accept and like other people. Liking others follows directly from liking oneself.

The purpose of the techniques, then, is to unlock the potential that lies within each person and to make the person aware of what he is and who he is. Encounter groups, transactional analysis, primal scream therapy, Gestalt therapy, and psychodrama, to name a few, enable the individual to become more in touch with the self, to become, in essence, more human.

Since the 1950s, *encounter groups* have sprung up in homes, community centers, churches, and motels. The term "encounter" refers to an interaction or confrontation with others for the purpose of exploring the affective component of life. The appeal of these groups appears to be great. Although it is true that most of us encounter others on a daily basis, joining a special group composed of ten to fifteen people and a trained leader with the intent of finding out more about ourselves is quite different. The encounter group is a way of filling a void created by an emphasis in our society on social adjustment rather than on personal adjustment, on duty rather than pleasure, on the intellect rather than the emotions. We have been taught since childhood to be polite and pleasant, to say we are fine even when we are not, to compliment even when we do not mean what we say. We are told not to wear our feelings on our sleeves and not to reveal too readily our likes and dislikes. We are trained to keep under wraps the kind of persons we really are. The result is a deficit in our lives, a lack of authenticity. We scarcely know who we are.

Encounter groups are designed to meet the needs of normal people. They are not intended for individuals suffering from deep-seated emotional deficits. The group may include a housewife who feels confined to a clean house and an uncommunicative husband, an executive who is contemplating a new business but fears he may lose his life's savings, a couple who are uncertain about patching an unrewarding relationship, a career woman who is tired of one-night stands and has the need to be treated as a person. Almost all are lonely or frustrated in some way, and they come together to share their concerns. It is important to know that someone cares, that someone understands and wants to help. The catharsis of revealing hidden fears, forbidden desires, and secret hopes keeps some individuals going back again and again to these groups. Sessions last for hours, continue all night, or are set up for a three-day weekend. The more elaborate sessions are sometimes held at luxurious resorts complete with beautiful accommodations, elaborate meals, and possibilities for yoga, dancing, and nude swimming.

Another popular technique is that of *transactional analysis*. Often referred to as TA, transactional analysis was developed by Eric Berne in the book *Transactional Analysis in Psychotherapy* (1961) and popularized in his *Games People Play* (1974). Berne holds that the personality is composed of three ego states which he calls Child, Adult, and Parent. The Child within each of us reflects the desires and feelings we developed while young and includes such emotions as joy, sadness, love, anger, fear, and elation. Each of us has a somewhat different Child because each of us had a somewhat different childhood. In the process of growing up children are pressured to mask or suppress the Child. The Adult ego state represents the rational component of the personality and functions as an independent agent making decisions that are in the best interest of the person. In analytic sessions one is helped to recognize and understand the Child within the self and then is trained to put the Adult in charge. The Parent, or third ego stage, resembles a boss that commands others and judges the behavior and attitude of others. The Parent may or may not be effective, depending on the manner in which it operates (James, 1976). Each person has all three ego states and will be Child, Adult, or Parent, depending on the circumstances. Any interaction with another person can be diagrammed as an interaction of ego states: Child to Child, Adult to Adult, Parent to Parent, Child to Adult, Child to Parent, and on and on. The purpose of TA is to help people recognize both their own state and the state of another during any particular interaction. In TA, participants are educated to train the Adult and diminish Child and Parent.

In *I'm OK, You're OK*, Thomas Harris (1969) further popularized transactional analysis by constructing four attitudes toward any interaction. These are: (1) "I'm not OK, you're OK," a position often taken by young children in relationship to their parents and by adults who have poor self-concepts and feel they are at the mercy of others; (2) "I'm OK, you're not OK," the view held by bullies and tyrants who get status by negating the rights of others; (3) "I'm not OK, you're not OK," in which the person is depressed and does not enjoy self or others; and (4) "I'm OK, you're OK," the ideal position in which a person is confident and accepting of both self and others. By analyzing what people say and do, a person can begin to feel OK and can learn to help others feel OK, too. All three ego states: Child, Adult, and Parent may be OK or not OK, depending on the mode of functioning, although the combination of Adult to Adult and I'm OK, you're OK produces the most optimal results.

Transactional analysis is widely used in schools and as a trouble-shooter in the world of business. Thousands more use it as a parlor game, analyzing themselves and others at home or at work or at a party. The fascination shown in transactional analysis by people from a large variety of backgrounds may be as interesting a phenomenon as the technique itself.

Another humanistic procedure is *primal scream therapy*. Developed by Arthur Janov (1970), this therapy is a way to relive the primal pain that occurs in infancy when physical or psychological needs are not met. As a baby, one may not have been held enough or rocked enough or fed when hungry. As a toddler one may not have been comforted when frightened or talked to when lonely. As the child grows older, and pressures to conform increase, the pain becomes intolerable. Finding no relief, the pain is masked and neurotic defenses develop. What the therapist must do is to take the person back to the troubled time, help the person relive the unfortunate events (even birth trauma may be experienced), enabling him or her to feel in full force the primal pain. Relief is gained by an outpouring of moans, screams, utterances, and cries. Therapy may take weeks, months, or years.

Gestalt therapy, pioneered by Fritz Perls (1969), places emphasis on helping the client live fully in the here-and-now and encourages an avoidance of excessively dwelling on the past or anxiously waiting for the future. Self-awareness is the key to therapy. As clients grow in self-awareness, they find they can take the support given during therapy and translate it into self-support. They realize that they alone are responsible for the life they live and that they must accept the challenge to experience it fully. Personal wholeness is aided by throwing off (acting out) internal restrictions such as anger, pain, and guilt and by being aware of social restrictions that have robbed them of an adequate self-concept. Perls saw therapy as a way of plugging up the holes of the personality put there by a repressive environment. Psychoanalysis, Gestalt psychology, and existentialism are all part of Gestalt therapy. In method it is decidedly humanistic, and, as in other humanistic therapies, people are seen as basically good and society is viewed as essentially oppressive.

Psychodrama is yet another technique used. Designed by Jacob Moreno (1944), psychodrama is a means for acting out the private world in which we live. The logic of psychodrama is that by actually simulating an experience we will be able to cope more adequately with that experience. By bringing an event into the open, we can get a closer look at it and find release from the anxiety or guilt or dread that accompanied it. If psychodrama is done by a group with a trained leader, strangers may help one another find relief from painful and traumatic events and provide encouragement to try new endeavors. By taking the part of someone in an event and acting out the sequence of events, new perceptions are possible and new solutions can be acquired. By putting ourselves in the place of another and endeavoring to work through the thoughts and emotions of another, we learn to understand others in a way we did not before. We become for the moment someone else. The parent "becomes" a child, thus seeing himself or herself through the eyes of the child. A couple during a quarrel engages in role-reversal, the husband "becoming" the wife and the wife "becoming" her husband. Each is acting the part of the other, thus learning to see things from the perspective of the other. The parent who can "be" a child will be a better parent, and the couple who can "be" each other will not quarrel long.

As with all psychological theories, a person need not accept the philosophy of humanism to apply the techniques. Encounter groups, transactional analysis, and psychodrama, for example, have been used in a variety of settings by those not necessarily in sympathy with humanistic thought. A strong disagreement, however, with the basic assumptions of any psychological theory may place an individual in a position whereby some methods cannot be used, some areas of life cannot be enacted, and some conclusions must be reinterpreted. The code of ethics of the leader or therapist is important in deciding how a session will be conducted and in determining what inferences will be drawn.

Humanistic psychologists do not see morality as separate from other concerns. Whatever is a part of being human is basically good. Whatever detracts from living life fully must be exorcised. Humanistic therapies are designed to repair the damage of a restrictive environment and bring about an awareness of the true potential within humankind.

The Humanistic Theory Answer

In chapter 1 the question was raised as to how the amoral infant becomes capable of morality. It is an inquiry into the process whereby the young child learns what is right and what is wrong. How can a child become the kind of person who acts morally rather than immorally? Humanistic psychologists would agree that young children are amoral in the sense that they do not understand moral concepts, nor do they always know what is expected of them. Humanists would not agree, though, that children are amoral in the sense that they come into life neutral; nor would they say that children have a bent toward doing the wrong thing. Rather, they feel that human nature is inclined naturally to go in the right direction. People come into this world as beautiful creatures with the potential to understand and appreciate the best in themselves and in others.

Humanistic theory has its roots in the philosophy of Jean-Jacques Rousseau who saw the child as a noble savage. Children are noble in that they are goodly or godlike. They are savage in that they do not adhere to social custom but seek to go their own ways and make their own decisions. Society is not willing to accept either the nobility of the child or the child's savagery. Instead, from infancy on, the child is pressured to conform to stereotypic ways of behaving and to adopt societal standards of acceptable conduct.

Mothers are especially culpable because they are the first to begin the civilizing process. Later, other adults continue to thwart the child's normal propensity toward self-actualization. The consequence is a stifling of the creative potential and an increase in confusion, frustration, and neurotic behaviors. This unfortunate state may be somewhat ameliorated by the use of humanistic therapies, although a better way would be for parents, educators, and other adults to show a proper respect for the developing child and to affirm the child's natural tendency to do what is best.

Humanistic psychologists would say, then, that *the amoral infant becomes capable of morality as he or she is allowed to choose, affirm, and act upon those values that make a person a fully functioning individual. Each child is born with the potential for good citizenship, responsibility, creativity, and intelligent behavior, and these characteristics will develop naturally if adults provide an atmosphere of encouragement and opportunity.*

Problems

Perhaps no psychological theory has come under greater attack than has humanism. There have always been those who would not accept the view that people are basically good and are able to decide for themselves what is right and what is wrong. But the number of opponents appears to be increasing, or at least they are becoming more visible. Some critics see humanism as so dangerous they feel compelled to write and speak in constant condemnation of the movement. Tim LaHaye's *The Battle for the Mind* is a case in point.

Most of the evils in the world today can be traced to humanism, which has taken over our government, the UN, education, TV, and most of the other influential things in life. (Introduction)

Today's wave of crime and violence in our streets, promiscuity, divorce, shattered dreams, and broken hearts can be laid right at the door of secular humanism. (LaHaye 1980, p. 26)

In response to an outpouring of anathemas, humanists have doubled their efforts to explain their position, defend their views, alert others to the errors of their opposition, and make their own appeal for converts. Paul Kurtz (1976), former editor of *The Humanist,* in a special issue on "The Evangelical Right: The Attack on Secular Humanism" has this to say:

This form of religious intolerance and bigotry threatens the very basis of our pluralistic democratic society: it could be the beginning of a new tyranny over the mind of man and of a new inquisition. . . . The fact is that humanism— in the broad sense—is the deepest current in Western civilization. . . . It . . . was influential during the founding of the American republic (where humanistic giants emerged, such as Jefferson and Paine). . . . Humanists have sought to cultivate a large number of . . . key moral values: a compassionate concern for others, freedom, equality, justice, creativity, dignity, and tolerance. These values are fundamental to our national democratic tradition and are widely shared. . . . Humanism is the movement to achieve democracy in all phases of our social life. (pp. 4-5)

Antihumanists and humanists both say that their ideas are best—best for the individual and best for society. Both feel they have the truth and speak of mystic religious experiences. Both are asking people to join with them, to spread the word, and to resist the opposing view. Among the most vocal is a subgroup of nonhumanists who call themselves the Moral Majority and a subgroup of humanists who call themselves secular humanists. Both the Moral Majority and the secular humanists are minorities within the opposing ideologies, but they have, nevertheless, commanded considerable attention. Although the arguments of these groups are interesting, we will turn our attention first to nonreligious objections.

The first problem is that definitions of humanism are vague and numerous. Based on nebulous propositions, humanism means many things to many people. After studying the literature, Wertheimer (1978) found at least three distinguishable meanings of the term. First, humanism is a curricula within the liberal arts that focuses on an understanding of the human race and includes such subjects as anthropology, sociology, history, economics, and biology. Second, the term *humanism* is used to refer to the human potential movement with its psychotherapies and with the theories of humanistic psychologists such as Arthur Combs, Abraham Maslow, and Carl Rogers. Third, the term *humanism* focuses on the person as an integrated whole. People are greater than the sum of their parts and are actively involved in an integration of the parts. This antimechanical view of human beings is adopted by many who do not espouse humanistic psychology (even as many professors within the liberal arts do not accept humanism as a philosophy). If one is critical of humanism, the question may be asked what the person has in mind when the term is used. Is the person opposed to a liberal arts curriculum, to the human potential movement, to the holistic and antimechanical nature of human beings? All three meanings of humanism have been challenged, although the bulk of criticism has been leveled at the second of these, namely, a psychology that emphasizes people as being sufficient within themselves to achieve self-actualization.

Even as the term *humanism* has a variety of meanings, words used by humanists also are vague and may be used in a number of ways. An example of this is the word *values*. Values are never precisely defined, nor are we told their origin. Are they from without? From within? Humanists emphasize the internal nature of values, but one may ask how this is possible. Can any of us generate values independent of our circumstances? To what are our values tied? To our own best interests? To the best interests of friends? To society as a whole? And, what are the ground rules for accepting some values and rejecting others? Do we not need a value system rooted in a source other than ourselves? "If two people were to disagree as to what we ought to do, there is no transcendent ground of value to which we may appeal in order to arbitrate between them. We are thrown into the relativity of conflicting values at a time when absolute decisions about the one future of humankind need to be made" (Peters, 1978, p. 146). Kohlberg states that "values covers everything under the sun" (Kohlberg and Simon, 1972, p. 19), and in *Morality and Mental Health*, Mowrer (1967) says:

> "Values" is . . . an essentially useless term, which has recently come into vogue because it serves as a sort of lowest common denominator for all who recognize, however vaguely, the reality of some sort of axiological dimension in human existence but who don't want to be pinned down to anything too specific. Everyone, I suppose, values something, regardless of how perverse or self-defeating it may be. So the term, unless extensively qualified, verges on meaninglessness, and certainly lacks power and precision. (p. viii)

A second problem is that humanism lacks a well-defined theory to support its assumptions. How do we know that being human is better than being something else? On what basis can it be said that people have worth and that personal growth and development are of utmost importance? Why does it matter what a person thinks or

how a person feels or what a person does? "Psychologists
. . . have not offered a theory of man that explains the
dignity of his being or justifies the concern society pro-
fesses to have for his development and protection" (Silber,
1975, p. 197). Humanists have not faced squarely the issues. This becomes apparent in their unwillingness to differentiate between what is moral and what is not, and in
their lack of interest in "ought" as well as in "is."

Without a well-defined theory, humanists are hindered
in an understanding of other relationships as well. What
is the place of reason in relation to the emotions? By
stressing affective states it would appear that humanists
relegate cognitive processes to a lesser position. Goals and
objectives also lack specificity. On what basis can it be
said that one goal is better than another or one purpose
should be pursued rather than another or one state of being
is optimal rather than another? How can objectives be
stated in behavioral terms if feelings have priority over
what one does? Without a carefully reasoned theory we
are left without satisfactory answers to these questions.

A third problem, closely tied to the second, is that humanistic claims are based on testimonials rather than on
empirical data and hard evidence. The nature of a testi-
monial is such that it can be neither verified nor falsified.
Publicly agreed upon norms cannot be applied to individual preferences and feelings, nor can the scientific method
be used to show the position of the testifier to others also
expressing preferences and feelings. Furthermore, it is
against the spirit of humanism to conduct a study in such
a way that people are placed in one experimental group or
another and then manipulated in some arbitrary fashion.
Independence, autonomy, and self-determination are not
to be violated. This ethical stance on the use of human
subjects translates to fewer external controls and a greater
reliance on introspective reports.

Given this orientation it might be expected that humanists would not emphasize the role of science or give

credence to the scientific method. Such is not the case. Paul Kurtz (1976) expressed the humanist position in this way: "Humanism has supported and encouraged the development of the scientific method as a way of understanding nature and applying the findings of the sciences to the betterment of humankind, and the scientific world view has had immeasurable success in the contemporary world" (p. 4). One might ask at this point how humanists can allow for validating some facts through personal testimony yet praise the use of science, which for more than half a century has spoken out against introspection as a valid technique. Is this not a contradiction? Opponents of humanism would say that it is. Supporters of humanism would say it is not. Let us look at these opposing views.

Paul Vitz (1979), an opponent, states that "humanistic selfism is not a science but a popular secular substitute religion, which has nourished and spread today's widespread cult of self-worship." Vitz continues:

> In spite of the non-scientific character of humanistic selfism, it has frequently claimed to be or allowed itself to be taken as a science and, as a result of this misrepresentation, it has gained greatly in money, power, and prestige. ... The selfist response to ... attacks is to attempt to redefine science so as to include their position. This ends up making the concept of science vague beyond any usefulness. (pp. 103-4)

That science has been redefined would not be contested by supporters of humanism. That it is "vague beyond any usefulness" would, of course, be rejected. Humanists claim that their way of understanding science is far superior to that of the behaviorist (learning theorist). According to the humanists, true scientists are "men of courage who are willing to study the difficult, not men who are terribly proficient in techniques but have no vision and who study less and less important things with more and more skill"

(Welch & Rodwick, 1978, p. 341). Carl Rogers (1969) is critical of graduate schools that "attach enormous importance to turning out 'hardheaded' scientists, and strongly punish any of the sensitive, speculative, sportive openness which is the essense of the real scientist" (p. 181). Humanists argue that the greatest scientists of all time—men like Aristotle, Einstein, and Leonardo da Vinci—were men of vision and courage who refused to be restricted to the logic and techniques of their day but rather used their genius and individuality to work toward new insights and new methods.

The arguments of both the antihumanists and the humanists can be quite convincing. Is there a place for both views of science? The reader is invited to decide.

A fourth problem, according to some critics, is that an adoption of humanistic views will make a person egocentric and selfish. The argument is: If I'm OK what right has anyone to be critical of what I say or what I do? And, on what basis need I be critical of myself or seek to change my ways? If you're OK, the same thing holds. You should receive praise and adulation and not be questioned as to motive or performance. Humanistic ideas are attractive because they appeal to our vanity. We all like to be flattered and told that we are intrinsically wise and good and master of our own lives. But what kind of people will we be if we accept this as truth? Humanism implies that we must do what is best for ourselves before we can do what is best for others, that we cannot love and appreciate and respect others until we love and appreciate and respect ourselves, that we cannot bring happiness to those around us until we know true happiness ourselves. But is this really so? Are these the only options—myself and others or neither myself nor others? What about the man who feels he would be happier with another woman but leaving his wife would create loneliness and financial difficulty for her? What about the woman who may not wish to remain in an unrewarding job but quitting would mean her children would not have nourishing food? The results of some decisions do not appear to profit both the decision-maker and others. To choose the best for oneself may mean that someone else is left with less than the best. The high divorce rate and a lack of proper care of dependents are examples of the consequences of selfism. Opponents say that humanism has contributed to the "me generation" of the 70s and has encouraged an age of narcissism. In *The Culture of Narcissism*, Christopher Lasch (1979) has portrayed the dire effects of an egocentric mind-set that has pervaded every aspect of American life.

Humanists feel that to be charged with contributing to selfish behavior is unfair. They say that one is not to harm others for the benefit of the self, that "the emphasis on the self . . . carries with it no implications of selfishness as that term is ordinarily used, or of any unhealthy, unsocial kind of self-centeredness" (Kolesnik, 1975, p. 45). But one may well ask how far past egoism and self-gratification humanism and humanistic techniques really take us. If one perceives that self-denial and self-sacrifice result in a blocking of self-actualization, what direction should that person take? In the practical everyday world in which we live, it would seem than an emphasis on the rightness and beauty of the self would encourage an attitude popularized by such expressions as "looking out for number one," "doing your own thing," and "creative selfishness."

The concern with "me-ism" applies to the rearing of children as well. What kind of children will we have if they are brought up in accordance with humanistic views? If children are basically good, as humanists say, and if they know intuitively the right direction to go, and if what they need is affirmation and encouragement rather than judgment and control, the logical inference is that adults should be careful not to place many restrictions on them. Parents are to take good physical care of the child, be friends and companions, and serve as models of good behavior, but they are not to make demands upon the child or insist on orderly behavior. Parents who follow these ideas are said to be permissive because they permit the child to do almost anything the child wishes. They are seldom punitive and may even succeed in hiding their annoyance and impatience with the child. If children were like flowers in the garden, growing and blooming when fed and watered, it would be worth the effort for parents to use permissive techniques. Studies in child psychology (Ausubel & Sullivan, 1970; Baumrind, 1977), however, show that rather than being lovely creatures for all to see, children reared in permissive homes are often uncooperative with adults, overbearing with peers, and lacking in purpose and motivation. It appears that nonjudgmental behavior on the part of parents does not provide a basis for children to develop their own self-critical abilities. Consequently they consider whatever they do is all right. If not corrected at home, they feel unjustly treated when corrected elsewhere. Although some children reared permissively are a joy to their parents and an asset to society, this does not appear to be the norm.[2]

A fifth criticism or problem is that humanists claim too much. They promise more than they can deliver. This criticism is mentioned in the literature especially as it relates to humanistic techniques and therapies. Is the group leader or therapist qualified? Are sessions conducted discretely? Are participants really helped by attending the sessions?

Some leaders and therapists are experienced mental health professionals, well trained, and eminently qualified. They know what questions to ask, when to probe, and when to withdraw. They are able to recognize the one in the group who is too disturbed to profit from the encounter and should be removed. They are able to use the personalities of group members to work for the good of all. Other leaders, however, are self-appointed, have little or no training, and may know nothing about the technique other than what they have witnessed as a member of a group. They are unable to function effectively as leaders and would not know how to handle an emergency should one occur. Some of these amateurs are well-meaning individuals who wish to help others. Others are charlatans and hucksters out to make a fast buck. They con the public into believing that a session will leave them glowing and happy. Judging from the numbers who flock to these sessions, deceiving the public appears to be relatively easy. Everyone warms to a promise of love and brotherhood and caring. We all like to be told that we are truly beautiful and that we owe it to ourselves to discover our true selves. We all want to hear that we are capable and can do anything we wish to do.

The session may or may not proceed in accordance with humanistic principles. Humanists hold that every individual must be treated with respect. But some therapists who give lip service to humanism act in inhumane ways in conducting their sessions. If it is good for people to talk about how they feel, the argument is made that people should be *made* to talk about how they feel. Pressure is put upon group members to participate, to talk about their feelings, to "let it all hang out." But such pressure, whether flagrant or subtle, is in violation of the tenets of humanism for it does not respect the person as an autonomous individual who should choose freely and without coercion. No leader or therapist should insist that group members reveal their innermost thoughts, show emotion, or become intimate with others by physical contact. It is an intrusion into one's privacy to expect the person to tell what he or she ordinarily would not tell or to engage in a "feely-feely" if the propriety of doing so is questioned.

What occurs during an encounter or therapy session should not be confused with what happens in real life. A short-term intense emotional experience cannot become a long-term affective state. To maintain such a "high" indefinitely would consume the individual. The body and

the psyche are not made for continuous elation and endless passion. A bride with stars in her eyes and a young
man who receives a promotion soon learn that the excitement of the moment all too quickly gives way to a world
of reality with its unceasing demands. In the same way,
a client who expects the closeness of the encounter to last
will find that after the session is over or the weekend is
past, one must return to the world from which one came.
The low that follows the high may put the person in a
worse state than before.

Therapists would say that if a session enables a person
to have a better self-concept and to live more fully, that
is fine. If it does not, it cannot be helped. A temporary
high to those who live boring and unfulfilled lives is better
than no high at all, and a little happiness and caring, though
shortlived, is better than no happiness and no caring. Besides, does not all of life have risks? Why should participation in therapy sessions be different? But some
participants may not understand this. They have been given
a taste of what they thought was possible on a regular
basis, and by raising their expectations they have found a
new level of discontent.

Do humanists really claim too much? Both humanists
and nonhumanists agree that some people are helped by
humanistic techniques, others remain as they were, and
still others may be harmed. The disagreement comes with
the numbers given to each of these categories, humanists
being more generous than nonhumanists in the number
of people they say are helped.[3] More studies need to be
conducted before it can be determined to what extent
therapists and group leaders are qualified, whether sessions are conducted properly, and what percentage of participants are benefited.

Criticisms of humanism are not confined to those that
have been mentioned. Nevertheless, the problems dis-
cussed serve to show valid reasons for the concerns many
have about this increasingly popular movement. To decide

which or how many of these problems apply to any particular humanistic theory would be an interesting exercise and much preferred to a blanket condemnation of all humanistic psychology.

Practical Applications

A humanistic theory of morality is founded on the premise that morality is not a separate component of the personality but rather an integral part of every aspect of life, interwoven with the physical, the cognitive, and the social, as well as being related to the affective, the creative, and the spiritual. Humanism emphasizes those characteristics that make us distinctly human, thereby giving us a better understanding of ourselves and of others. The humanist emphasis on each person's taking responsibility for his or her own life and the assumption that morality comes from within the individual rather than being imposed by an outside source are views adopted by many individuals whether or not they consider themselves in the humanist camp. Parents, teachers, and ministers who are effective in their respective positions often adopt humanistic concerns and employ a number of techniques commonly linked with third-force psychology.

Application to the Home

It is a well established fact that showing delight in the growing child and affirming the child's strivings for competence enhance development and becomes what is often referred to as a self-fulfilling prophecy. The more the child is encouraged, the better the child does. The better the child does, the more confident the child becomes. The result is increased motivation and a healthy self-concept. Children also tend to be like their parents. If parents are warm and cordial, excited about life, and respectful of others, children are more apt to be pleasant, interested in learning, and considerate in their relationships with others. Humanists want their children to live purposeful, satisfying lives; to be open to new experiences; and to have close, rewarding friendships with others. Surely there can be no quarrel with these goals for children everywhere.

Thoughtful people also adopt the humanistic view that to be fair with others and to understand them, one should try to see things from their perspective. Parents will endeavor to put themselves in the place of the child, to see the world as the child sees it. They will wonder what perceptions and emotions the child is experiencing. They know that providing for the child's physical well-being is not enough. The child is a unified whole, a complex organism with many needs. Parents also will be aware that each child is different and should be respected for his or her own individuality. To decide what kind of child one wants and then to pressure the child each moment to conform is not to reckon with the child's uniqueness as a person or to show respect for the child's dignity as a member of the human race. Individual temperaments, abilities, and interests must be taken into account if parents are to deal with their children in humane ways.

The Board of Directors of the American Humanist Association (AHA) has taken the following position relative to the family (AHA's Statement on the Family, 1980).

> Families . . . are the well-spring of human interaction, compassion, love, productivity, and creativity that the individual bequeaths to the larger society. The family provides the security and germinates and fosters the altruism that makes civilization possible. . . . A safe, healthful environment, balanced nutrition, adequate housing, medical care, and quality education are minimum family requirements. . . . The family is a creative, vital force that can meet the challenges of the future as it has met the demands of the past. (p. 40)

Few parents would disagree with this position.

Other portions of the statement are less palatable—especially to those of a more conservative persuasion, although those holding liberal views would agree with many of them.

> Any two people or group of people wishing to make a commitment to one another over time and to share resources, responsibilities, goals, and values should be considered a family. . . . Child-care programs, encouraged by government, for the children of working parents have been too long postponed. . . . And no law or regulation should require women to bear unwanted children. Children have a right to be wanted and a right to be born into the bosom of the family, not into an unnatural, unloving atmosphere. . . . Equality for women and human rights for children should be the law of the land. (p. 40)

Today's families are described as "pluralistic, intergenerational, multi-racial, and multi-cultural" (p. 40), a condition endorsed by the American Humanist Association.

Control and guidance of the child are major parental tasks. Humanists take the view that the only discipline that is truly effective is self-discipline, not a discipline imposed by others. As one might expect, humanists differ in the degree of permissiveness considered optimal but generally agree that adults should try to solve the problems of parenting in less authority-centered, power-based ways. Friendship with one's children is encouraged. Children should be self-confident, curious, and independent— traits developed best in an atmosphere of openness and mutual concern.

Humanists readily admit that there are risks involved in rearing children permissively, as some children will adopt values in contradistinction to the values of the parents. But these are risks parents must be willing to take. Unless children are allowed to develop their own moral sensitivities and choose their own ways, they will never be free, self-directed persons, cognizant of the reasons for believing as they do and capable of developing responsibility for their behaviors. Robert Hall (1976), writing for *The Humanist*, links the opposing position of stricter controls with deficits in moral understanding. "It is because morality has been promulgated as rules rather than as reasons that so many people today seem to have so little sense of right and wrong. . . . Parents who want their children to be taught 'the only one right way' in contrast to liberty and toleration want, in effect, to live in a closed society; this is not, however, what America is, nor, it is hoped, what it shall become" (p. 45).

Parents who agree with Hall will have little difficulty using humanistic methods. Parents, however, who believe there truly is only one right way and therefore reject a relativity of truth and ethics will be obligated to sort through humanistic suggestions and strategies and adopt only those that enhance rather than conflict with their own beliefs. Furthermore, humanistic values have been held for centuries by those who do not espouse humanism as a philosophy. Humanists do not have a monopoly on humanistic qualities. Many parents and other adults show love and respect for the children entrusted to their care. They provide an atmosphere of encouragement and sensitivity to others and are aware of qualities both within themselves and in others that make people distinctly human.

Sidney Simon and Sally Olds (1976) in *Helping Your Child Learn Right from Wrong: A Guide to Values Clarification* have presented in interesting and understandable fashion exercises parents may use in the home. Written from a humanist perspective, the authors believe that all of us need guidance in learning how to analyze ideas and situations and that we learn best in an atmosphere of openness and freedom. Although moralizing (invoking guilt, religion, and patriotism), manipulating (limiting the child's options by rewards and punishers), and modeling (expecting the child to act as we do) are all appropriate at times, these methods are the "Three Misleading M's" (p. 18) because they do not help children work out their own values and develop their own understanding of what is right and what is wrong. Values cannot be taught directly but the process for arriving at values can be.

The parent may start by saying at the dinner table something like, "Let's talk about everyone's high point of the day," or while riding in the car, "Let's play a game. Each one will tell which season of the year is his or her favorite and why." (this could just as well be a favorite food or color or flower, and the like). Each member of the family then responds appropriately. The idea is that by answering such questions, children learn to understand themselves and others. There are ground rules to be followed, and these may be explained to family members either before the game begins or applied as the need arises. The rules are: (1) No one jumps on anyone else (the ideas of another are to be respected); (2) there are no right or wrong answers, attitudes, or responses; (3) only one person talks at a time and nobody interrupts; (4) everyone has the option of passing at any time (this safeguards one's privacy); (5) no "killer-statements" that put down other people; (6) no self put-downs (self-denigrating statements are not allowed); and (7) changing one's mind is a sign of growth (pp. 43-45). It is through this sharing of feelings and opinions that children learn to examine life rationally, consider possible options, make choices based on those options, and consider the consequences of their decisions.

The exercises suggested in *Helping Your Child Learn Right from Wrong* are delightful, may be enjoyed by all members of the family, and serve to bring the family closer together. The rub may come if the discussion turns to ethics and religious belief, for these are areas that many feel are not subject to relative judgment and subjective preference. Some may not care to discuss with their children the question, "Are there times when it is right to cheat?" (p. 196) or, "If you were going to convert to another religion, which one would you choose and why?" (p. 198). But eliminating some questions need not preclude the use of clarification strategies for those values not related to morality or to religious commitment. Nor does one need to rule out all questions suggested by Simon and Olds directed to one's faith, such as, "When have you been close to a miracle?" (p. 198) or, "What more could you do to live a holier life?" (p. 199).

Applying the valuing process to the Christian faith is what Roland and Doris Larson (1976) do in *Values & Faith: Activities for Family and Church Groups.* The authors give credit to Simon and others who helped to shape their understanding and use of methodologies in the area of values education and seek to show how the methodologies apply to an examination of "opinions, attitudes, beliefs, and values in a Christian context" (p. 3). In introducing the book, the Larsons express their faith in God as "the absolute, the beginning point of ourselves and of our world" and declare that his revelation comes to us "through the Bible, the Church, the life of Christ, and the activity of the Holy Spirit among us" (p. 5). In this context, values clarification becomes more than the blind leading the blind. It becomes a method for internalizing and clarifying one's faith. We learn to value and prize our relationship with God as we consider what that relationship means to each of us personally. Values clarification was used by Jesus when he told a parable and then asked his disciples to interpret what he had said. Parents also may use it to help their children develop a greater appreciation of the Christian heritage and of a faith that gives meaning to life. Respect for each member of the family is enhanced by the sharing of ideas, and the resulting cohesiveness allows parents more influence in the lives of their children.

The Larsons caution parents not to yield to the temptation of imposing their views on their children. Children know full well how their parents stand for parents also contribute to the valuing sessions. But telling children they must believe as you do is not as effective in the long run as sharing with them the reasons for your faith. They know that after a consideration of other belief systems, you have chosen Christianity as having the greatest value. Prizing the choice made and showing delight in the faith, along with living a life consistent with that choice, will have its influence on the child. But in the end, each person must decide individually. We cannot choose for our children, nor are we responsible for the choices they make. We only hurt ourselves by feeling accountable for their decisions.

Some parents cannot use values clarification procedures. The approach is inimical to their personalities and too far removed from their idea of how children should be reared. Nor are values clarification techniques adaptable to all situations or all topics. But parents who use the technique find it rewarding. These parents liberate as well as control, listen as well as expound, let their children go as well as hold them close. They are willing to risk letting children make their own judgments as to those values having the greatest meaning, and by doing this they encourage their children to take responsibility for their own moral development.

Another contribution of humanistic thought is the holistic health movement. The focus of third-force psychology is on prevention rather than treatment, wellness rather than sickness, doing for oneself rather than relying on a physician. Although it is recognized that at times medical assistance is needed, it is also recognized that doctors cannot always do what we can do for ourselves. Adequate nutrition, weight control, proper exercise, and sufficient rest is each one's responsibility. Wellness is also enhanced by meaningful and productive work and by rewarding relationships with others. Good health is an ongoing process, seldom attained by a pill or a powder or by the surgeon's knife. As parents we guard the health of our children, but as they grow older they must take responsibility for themselves. Encouraging them to say more about how they feel when they are happy and things are going well and less about their aches and pains or psychological hurts will help them focus on the positive aspects of life and bring about a kind of self-fulfilling prophecy. To the humanist a healthy mind and a healthy body are expressions of morality.

Other humanistic ideas that apply to the home include the use of family therapy (Charny, 1974) and the application of transactional analysis to adults who have had unfortunate home backgrounds (Yablonsky, 1976). In family therapy the whole family is included in the sessions even though only one member appears to be having difficulty. In this way family members come to see themselves and each other in ways not previously understood. With transactional analysis, the counselor or therapist may set up role-playing sessions in which other adults play the part of family members, and events in the person's life are reenacted so that childhood trauma can be dealt with openly and in a rational manner. The participant recognizes the Child, the Adult, and the Parent in the self and in others and comes to understand why he feels as he does about the self. By the use of TA the unwholesome attitude of I'm not OK may be changed to the optimal I'm OK position, and the client learns to relate to others in an Adult to Adult fashion. Through encounter sessions participants can learn not to make the same mistakes in rearing children that their parents made with them. The therapist and group members provide the incentive, while the discussions and role-playing activities equip participants with the information needed to become good parents.

Application to the School

The scene is a first-grade class, and at the front of the room are ten chairs arranged in a circle and occupied by the children and their teacher. This is not just any circle. It is a Magic Circle. It is called magic because as the boys and girls share their ideas, express their feelings, and listen to one another, something magic seems to happen. Each child discovers that he or she is not somehow different or inferior to the other children. Rather, the child learns that all people have times when they are happy and times when they are sad. Everyone experiences love and hate, pride and shame, warmth and loneliness. Even big people have times when they feel the way little people do. The teacher may tell of a time when she felt "left out" or frightened or embarrassed or "empty inside."

Each Magic Circle session (formerly known as the Human Development Program founded by Bessell and Palomares, 1973) begins with a topic that centers on one of three themes: (1) an awareness of one's own thoughts, feelings, and actions; (2) a demonstration of mastery of some skill; or (3) the development of competence in social interaction. The subject for the day may be "something that gives me a good feeling" or "something that gives me a bad feeling" or "I had a nice thought when . . ." Or the topic may be, "I did something nice for someone else," or "Somebody got me into trouble." The leader of the group (teacher or student) begins by reviewing the rules. "Raise your hand when you wish to participate. Everyone gets a turn. Listen to the one who is speaking." The atmosphere must be positive with no laughing or smirking allowed. At the end of the twenty-minute session when all who wish have responded, the leader reviews what each child has said, calling the child by name. The teacher then will ask, "What do you think we learned here today?"

What is learned, according to the humanist educator, is an increased respect for self and others, greater responsibility for one's own behavior, better interpersonal relationships, and improved speaking and listening skills. The child's self-concept is greatly enhanced by the use of Magic Circle. Every child upon entering school wants to be successful. It is as though the child asks three questions: "Am I safe?" "Can I cope?" "Will I be successful?" Magic Circle helps the child answer in the affirmative. The child comes to see himself or herself as secure, capable, and lovable—an important member of the class and the community.

Magic Circle is only one of several such programs available for children at the primary level. Others include the Most Important Person (MIP) Series, Developing an Understanding of Self and Others (DUSO), and values clarification (VC), already described. Both MIP and DUSO are multimedia approaches and have special appeal to younger children. Values clarification may or may not use props but is applicable to students at all grade levels. Like Magic Circle, these programs deal with the humanistic themes of accepting self and others, understanding one's own feelings and the feelings of others, achieving mastery and competence, setting purposeful goals, and dealing with choice and the consequences of choice.

To the humanist educator, the child is a whole person, a totality composed of many parts—the physical, the social, the cognitive, the affective, and the moral. All parts are interrelated and an understanding of this relationship must be considered when planning curricula. To fasten attention on only one kind of learning while ignoring others is to do the child a grave injustice. The three Rs are important, but they must not be taught to the exclusion of the fourth R of human relations. Only as children develop an understanding and a caring for others will they endeavor to discipline themselves. They learn that misbehavior makes other people unhappy, and even as they do not want others to make them unhappy, they do not wish to make others unhappy. They learn to behave in ways that are socially acceptable. In essence, they learn to be moral. And importantly, the desire comes from within rather than being imposed by a teacher or an administrator.

In response to those who say there is not enough time in the classroom for such frills as Magic Circle or values clarification, supporters respond that there is no better way to spend twenty minutes a day. A close relationship of the child with the teacher, as well as with peers, will motivate the child to learn in every way, including mastering the three Rs. The teacher sees the child, not as an empty vessel into which information is to be poured or as an inadequate and sinful creature whose will must be bent into conformity, but as a member of the human race having tremendous potential. Furthermore, the teacher understands the task of the educator to be that of facilitator of the child's potential. Learning in all its ramifications is best accomplished in an atmosphere of cooperation and mutual regard.

Values clarification remains the approach most frequently used. The clarification of a value is really the culmination of a three-step process that begins with a knowledge of the facts, details, events, and actualities of the matter and then proceeds to an understanding of the concepts or principles underlying the facts. It is only after the students have gained familiarity with the facts and have integrated the facts into relevant concepts that they are in a position to choose their values based on their feelings, opinions, and interests.

Suppose, for example, a fourth-grade class is studying the Pilgrims (Harmin, Kirschenbaum, & Simon, 1973). The students must learn why the Pilgrims came to America, how they got here, what experiences they had the first year in a new land, and why they decided to celebrate the first Thanksgiving. After learning the facts, the teacher and students discuss the concepts or principles behind the facts. The concepts may include those of prejudice, cultural assimilation, emigration, helping, and ceremony. Unless the unit also includes the values level, it will make little difference in the lives of the students. It is only at this third level that they become personally involved in choosing a value, in prizing the value chosen, and in acting consistently on the value chosen. Each child, for instance, needs to come to terms with the meaning of prejudice, for others and for the self. The child must determine his or her own attitudes and feelings and decide how to respond to those who are culturally different.

Many schools teach only the facts. Some teach concepts as well. By comparison, only a few endeavor to help students cope with a changing world by teaching the process of valuing. The method appears to be gaining in popularity, however, and is mandated for teacher training in some public schools. Nationwide, "the values-clarification movement . . . boasts a network of about one hundred trainers, who have conducted workshops in the method for more than two hundred thousand teachers, counselors, and other helping professionals" (Hall, 1978, p. 7).

In addition to values clarification, other humanistic approaches have been implemented at higher grade levels. "Man: A Course of Study" (MACOS) is designed for teaching social studies to upper elementary and junior high pupils. Developed by Jerome Bruner, the course integrates both cognitive and affective learning and has the central theme of understanding the nature of that being called "man." Students think through what is human about humans, how humans got the way they are, and how humans can become more human. There is an emphasis on the discovery method, and students are encouraged to engage in informed guessing, to use problem-solving techniques, and to contrast humans with other forms of life.

Like other humanistic programs, MACOS has been criticized by those who say that children are not in a position to decide what is good and true or to form independently a sound value system. Rather than discovering what it means to be human, children must be *taught* who they are and how they relate to the rest of God's creation. Some parents feel that a classroom discussion of how humans and baboons are alike in personality traits and in social behaviors undermines the teaching in the home of the person being made in the image of God. Several members of Congress, seeking ways to cut costs, have objected to using federal funds to support the MACOS program. Other groups have criticized MACOS on the grounds that the personal rights of children are violated, claiming that in some cases psychological trauma has occurred.

A way that some educators have met these criticisms is to use a method referred to as *values education.* Values education takes on many forms but often differs from values clarification in that the young person is taught some values and given the opportunity to choose others. Differentiation is made between those values generally agreed upon by the larger society and those values that are highly individualistic. D. L. Barr (1974) uses the terms "consensus values" and "contended values" to distinguish between the two. Consensus values, such as not stealing or not murdering, are inculcated into the lives of students. If young people refuse to adopt consensus values, at least they have been told what these values are and that deviation is accompanied by judicial punishment. Contended values—and most values fall into this category—are chosen by the individual in terms of one's own needs and one's own preferences. "The school's responsibility in regard to these values is not to inculcate, but to clarify . . . to devise techniques and strategies that will help the student in his choice" (p. 19).

There are those who oppose values education programs on the same grounds that they oppose values clarification. They fear that school values may conflict with values taught in the home, or they say that the church is the only place where values should be formally presented. Some critics make the charge that values education, like values clarification, deals only marginally with moral values and so should not be referred to as moral education. Some have cited research showing that school children do not profit from valuing programs (Lockwood, 1978; Perlmutter, 1980).

Humanist educators refuse to accept any blame for failures within the public schools. To their way of thinking very few schools have actually implemented humanistic techniques or established a curriculum based on humanistic principles. Arthur Combs (1981) writes that "the majority of today's teachers and administrators were schooled in some form of behavioristic psychology as the theoretical base for their professional thinking. Such views concentrate attention primarily upon behavior and the external conditions that produce it" (p. 447). In response to those who report that valuing programs do not help students, humanists are quick to cite studies that show that the programs have indeed produced optimal results (e.g., Goldbecker, 1976; Simon & deSherbinin, 1975). Kirschenbaum (1976) states that "there is a growing body of data, over thirty-five studies, which indicate that value clarification can lessen apathy, enhance self-esteem, reduce drug abuse, and contribute to other laudable goals, while simultaneously maintaining just as much or greater learnings in cognitive skills and subject matter as curricula that omit the valuing process" (p. 4).

Humanists emphasize the changes that are taking place in our society and say we must be ready to meet the challenges brought by these changes. They feel that the best educators can do is to prepare the next generation for the world in which they will live, to prize them as persons, to care for them without possessing them, and to assist them in learning methods of valuing that will enable them to live genuine, meaningful, and productive lives.

Application to the Church

The ease with which values clarification may be used with any age group and in any setting has caught the interest of Sunday school teachers as well as teachers in the public schools. "Values clarification already has a solid place in Sunday and church schools, where thousands of teachers are using it. These teachers are face to face with the question of whether moralizing is a suitable way to deal with religious education" (Simon & deSherbinin, 1975). Leaders within the church are aware that true spirituality, like true morality, must come from within the person rather than being imposed by a minister or teacher, and although spiritual values may be taught by those in authority or acquired by association with Christian parents and teachers, unless these values are incorporated by choice within the life of the individual, attitudes and behaviors may not remain secure. Those advocating values clarification feel that more choice and less unquestioning acceptance of what is taught will make for greater cognitive and affective stability when one is in a situation varying from that in which the instruction was received.

The suggestion has been made (Simon, 1973) that the Sunday school teacher or church group leader should use all three levels of teaching when presenting a lesson: the facts level, the concepts level, and the values level. Bible stories are excellent sources with which to begin. When telling of God's dealings with the children of Israel, for example, the teacher will start with the facts. The teacher will explain how God brought the Israelites out of Egypt, supplying them with food and water and protecting them from the enemy. Next will come a discussion of relevant concepts. What does this story tell us about God? What are the attributes of someone who loves and cares for others? Does God love everyone the same? In what ways does God love us? What does deliverance mean? Has God delivered us? If so, from what? The third level of values is then considered, based on a knowledge of the facts and an understanding of the concepts. Values relate personally to each member of the class. What choices will each one make as a consequence of knowing God's love? How will it change each life? Is God's love prized? Will it make a difference in behavior? If so, how?

We read in the Old Testament that Joshua used this approach. He recounted for the people the facts of their escape from Pharaoh, their survival in the wilderness, and their entrance into the promised land of Canaan. (Jos. 24). Joshua then reminded them of the concepts of who God is, of his holy and jealous nature, and of the allegiance he requires if blessings are to continue. Finally, Joshua asked the people to make a value judgment—a choice of whom they would serve. They could value and serve the Lord who had done great things for them, or they could value the gods of their heathen neighbors, turning their backs on Jehovah. Which would it be? "Choose for yourselves this day whom you will serve," Joshua told the people, and then added, "As for me and my household we will serve the Lord" (v. 15). As the people listened, they considered the consequences of choosing the Lord as opposed to the consequences of serving idols and decided to join Joshua in serving the Lord.

In the New Testament, we read that Jesus encouraged people to make choices. He did not force his value system on others but let them know what would happen if they decided one way as opposed to the consequences of deciding another way. The rich young ruler came to Jesus to ask what he could do to inherit eternal life and was told that he could either give up his possessions and achieve eternal life, or he could keep his wealth and not see the Kingdom (Lk. 18). The young man knew the alternatives and that the choice was his, and even though he made the wrong choice, Jesus did not call him back or try to get him to change his mind. Jesus invites but does not pressure; he knocks but does not pound; he offers but does not force. Each of us must do our own choosing and our own valuing.

In *Values & Faith,* Roland and Doris Larson (1976) provide a number of ways values clarification may be used in the church. They feel it important for believers to "take actions to make their behaviors more consistent with their beliefs and values" (p. 3). Using Hebrews 11 as the basis for discussion, a class can look first at the *facts* about faith—how faith is defined, which people showed faith, what they did to show their faith, what their goal was, and why they did not receive all that was promised to them. Next, the class will explore *concepts* related to faith. What kind of relationship did those recorded in the Hebrews passage have with God? What characteristics did they possess that enabled them to act upon their faith? What were the results of their faith? After a discussion of the facts and the concepts, the matter of *values* comes into play. Values are personal, and although one may share what faith means personally or consider how one's faith is like or unlike the faith of another or think of ways that faith may be strengthened, values remain an individual matter. Faith must come from the heart.

Few churches go beyond the facts level. If the lesson for the day is the triumphal entry of Jesus into Jerusalem, most Sunday school pupils will learn only the facts surrounding the event, such as the directions Jesus gave to his disciples or the reaction of the large crowd singing Hosanna or what the Pharisees said about the demonstration (Simon, 1973). But there is more to be learned than just a recounting of what happened. The lesson will take on greater interest if the class considers the concepts of what it meant for Jesus to ride into the city on an ass, what the people who threw palm branches before him expected to have happen, and the ways in which the Pharisees and the disciples differed. Even more exciting and meaningful is the valuing process in which each child thinks through what this event means to him or her. Does the child wish to praise the Lord? If so, in what ways can the child do this? Should a person engage in a demonstration as did the people in Jesus' time? Does it matter if a demonstration makes those in authority angry as it did the Pharisees? Why or why not? Should one demonstrate even if the law says one should not? The possibilities of valuing are great, and each member of the class must decide individually. The questions asked will depend in large measure on the position of the teacher or church leader with regard to religious, social, and political issues. Most churches would welcome a discussion of how each of us can praise the Lord. Fewer would approve of asking children to decide when it is appropriate to demonstrate if those in authority condemn the action.

Children may enjoy role-playing the characters in a Bible story and discussing the values of those whose lives they reenact. They may consider what would have happened if the person in the story had made a different choice or what choice they would have made had they been the one in the story. Reading biographies of Christian missionaries and other men and women of God will set before them values they may decide to adopt as their own; and having a teacher who is open, personable, confident, and fully functioning will produce satisfying results. Songs that are sung should reflect the potential that believers have in Christ, bringing encouragement and hope to young people as they face the life that lies ahead. Such a song is William and Gloria Gaither's "I Am a Promise." A portion follows:

> You are a promise,
> You are a possibility;
> You are a promise with a capital "P,"
> You are a great big bundle of potentiality.
> And if you listen you'll hear God's voice,
> And if you're tryin', He'll help you make the right choices;
> You're a promise to be anything He wants you to be.
>
> You know something?
> It doesn't matter what your name is, where you live, who
>   your daddy is, or how big you are, or what you look like.
> Hey, what do you look like?
> Short? Tall? Are you fat, skinny, got holes in your tennis
>   shoes and freckles on your nose?
> It doesn't matter one bit!
> You can be exactly what God wants you to be . . .
> You're a great big promise, you see!*

*©1975 by William J. Gaither. Used by permission.

At one end of the religious continuum are churches that take the position that it does not matter what values one has or what beliefs one cherishes as long as the person has some values and as long as the person lives by those beliefs. At the other end of the continuum are churches that consider any idea even remotely associated with humanistic thought corrupt by virtue of that association. Both positions are extreme, and neither can be supported from Holy Scripture. Some values *are* basic to the Christian faith and cannot be compromised. In matters of the divinity of Jesus Christ and the inspiration of Scripture no concession can be made. One is not a Christian in the historic sense of the term unless one is a follower of Jesus Christ, and one who follows incorporates within the self the values and beliefs of the one being followed. But did Jesus not turn toward humanistic concerns? Did he not help those in need regardless of their position in life? Did he not see the potential in the disciples long before that potential was realized through their association with him? Did he not say even to the Pharisees, "The kingdom of God is within you" (Lk. 17:21)? And did he not come to redeem a people confused by sin though originally created in his own image? Jesus, by his own words and deeds, showed himself to be a great humanist.[4]

Applying transactional analysis (TA) to the church is the theme of Muriel James's *Born to Love* (1973). Each person may be analyzed in terms of Parent, Adult, and Child ego states, and relationships between individuals or groups may be diagnosed as an interaction between ego states. Why one Sunday school class or church group is successful and another is not is more readily understood if verbal interactions of group members are diagrammed to indicate whether a person is speaking as one in authority (Parent) or as one who views events objectively (Adult) or as one coming from a dependent position (Child). Crossed-transactions occur when a message sent from the ego state of one person elicits an unexpected response from the ego state of another. Crossed-transactions lead to misunderstandings and confusion. Suppose, for instance, that a member of an adult class speaks from the Adult ego state and suggests that lesson material for the next quarter include information on humanism and the technique of transactional analysis. If the teacher responds from the Parent ego state with a diatribe on the evils of humanism, saying that as the teacher of the class he is responsible for keeping heresy out of the church, the result will probably be anger or dismay. The class member making the suggestion may react by thinking, "The teacher knows best and is only trying to help me be a better Christian" (Child), or, "The teacher is speaking from a perspective different than my own because his background and training are different (Adult), or "The teacher is stupid and I'll show him and the rest of the class that I know more than he does" (Parent). If a church group is to thrive and meet the needs of its members, verbal behavior must change so that tensions and divisions are less apt to occur. Understanding TA is one method for bringing about this change.

The four psychological positions of I'm OK, you're OK; I'm OK, you're not OK; I'm not OK, you're OK; and I'm not OK, you're not OK" may be expressed in the plural in order to examine the attitude of one church or denomination to another. According to Muriel James, churches that are accepting of both themselves and other groups, the We're OK, you're OK position, are healthy and vibrant. They appreciate and respect both their own views and the views of others. The second position of We're OK, you're not OK is adopted by many churches that consider their congregation or denomination to be the one true church, and by comparison other churches and denominations propagate falsehood. This position is one of arrogance, and even though these groups say they love all people, hating only their sin, one cannot tell by their actions that this is so. The third position of We're not OK, you're OK is taken by churches that aspire to greatness by copying the methods of other religious groups. Lacking in confidence, they seem willing to try almost any technique in order to grow and be recognized. "We're not OK, you're not OK" churches soon disintegrate, being of little value to themselves or to others (James, 1973, pp. 92-93).

An analysis of ego states (Parent, Adult, Child) and a working knowledge of the four psychological positions relative to one's worth (e.g., I'm OK, you're OK") is met with enthusiasm by some ministers and group leaders and strongly opposed by others. Those fascinated by "the games people play" enjoy analyzing their own and other people's speech and find that using a paradigm such as transactional analysis makes for an engaging interpretation of interpersonal relationships. Pastors and seminary students sometimes take courses in guidance and counseling and many of these classes are based on humanistic assumptions, thus introducing humanist ideology and humanistic methods into the church. By contrast, church leaders who oppose humanistic psychology consider transactional analysis to be silly or outright dangerous. They do not wish to have their motives and statements diagnosed, especially if this is done by someone they consider less knowledgeable and less spiritual than themselves. They believe that parishioners should understand the God-ordained hierarchy within the church and should come to the house of worship expecting to be instructed in the things of the Lord. In TA terminology, this means that the preacher sees the minister's role as Parent and the parishioner's role as Child. There is little room for the Adult, for the one who exhibits a free spirit and independence of thought. Creative ideas and rational analysis are not welcome in many churches if they are perceived as interfering with church polity in any way.

Some congregations assume that to take a position other than "We're OK, you're not OK" will undermine the reason for the existence of their particular group or denomination. Their church is the one true church, stemming directly from apostolic times, and blessed in a special way by God. That so many churches make the same claim does not bother those who "know" they have the truth. It does, however, result in considerable confusion for the seeker after truth, for the one who has not yet found the way.

What does the church have to offer to the child in the Sunday school, to the young person in the youth group, to the adult in the Bible study class? How will it meet the needs of the seeker after truth? Is it a loving, caring community of believers interested in each person as a total individual? Is it a joyful community rejoicing in the Lord, prizing the life they have in Christ, and celebrating the excitement of a commitment to Jesus Christ? Is it a church that sees in each person all the potential that person has as a member or future member of the family of God? Although it may be said that the "I'm OK, you're OK" attitude has invaded some churches to such an extent that there is no longer any basis for judging right and wrong, and this is not in keeping with the Word of God; it also can be said that the church cannot become the healing community it is supposed to be until all individuals are afforded the respect and dignity befitting one made in the image of God. So, the church family will pray together and worship together and celebrate in song, waiting for the day when our potential will be fully realized, for "we shall be like him, for we shall see him as he is" (1 Jn. 3:2).

Theology and the Humanistic Approach

In the minds of many Christians, humanism is a world view that glorifies "man" but leaves out God. If people are basically good, as the humanist claims, and if they have within themselves the potential for self-actualization, there can be no reason for the message of the gospel. We are masters of our fate and captains of our soul. The darker side of our condition—our greed and selfishness—appears not to be recognized apart from an unfortunate environment, thus negating any need for a Redeemer who lifts us from a fallen state and makes us new creations in Christ Jesus.

All humanists do not agree that as members of the human race we have no need for God. Nor would all humanists say that a belief in a personal deity debilitates rather than enhances moral development. But historically there have been humanists who have taken this position, and their number appears to be increasing. Most visible among them is a group who call themselves, quite appropriately, secular humanists and who disseminate their views through publications, workshops, and debates. The notoriety of the secular humanist movement has come in part because those holding this position are now more organized and are seeking ways to add to their constituency, and in part because secular humanism has become the target of a scathing attack by a number of politically conservative preachers who feel called upon to alert "pro-moral, pro-American, and Christian citizens" to an organization that is "leading our country down the road to a socialist Sodom and Gomorrah" (LaHaye, 1980, pp. 100, 143-44).

The most succinct statement of the secular humanist position is found in *Humanist Manifesto II*, published in 1973 and designed as an update to the first *Humanist Manifesto*, written forty years earlier. In keeping with the humanist emphasis on change, those wishing to offer suggestions for the revision of *Humanist Manifesto II* or to have input into a possible third manifesto are invited to do so. "These affirmations are not a final credo or dogma but an expression of a living and growing faith" (Humanist Manifesto II, 1980, p. 10).

Some of the ideas in *Humanist Manifesto II* may be shared by Christians. Especially in those areas dealing with social concern, the follower of Christ will have little difficulty. The Christian sees the need to "fuse reason with compassion in order to build constructive social and moral values," and wishes to "provide humankind with unparalleled opportunity for achieving an abundant and meaningful life" (Humanist Manifesto II, 1980, p. 4). The Christian, as well as the humanist, believes in "the preciousness and dignity of the individual person" and desires to "cultivate the development of a responsible attitude toward sexuality, in which humans are not exploited as sexual objects, and in which intimacy, sensitivity, respect, and honesty in interpersonal relations are encouraged" (p. 7). Christians share in a recognition of the "common humanity of all people" (p. 10) and work toward a "world community in which all sectors of the human family can participate" (p. 9). Christians agree with the wise use of technology, so that "we can control our environment, conquer poverty, markedly reduce disease, extend our lifespan" (p. 5).

Other statements in the manifesto, however, are in direct opposition to the Christian faith, and it is over these statements that the believer in Christ must part company with the secular humanist. The sections that are most offensive are those dealing with religion and ethics, for it is here that secular humanism rejects the foundation of Christianity and makes light of a morality based on an understanding of who God is. The following excerpt will serve as an example:

> We find insufficient evidence for belief in the existence of a supernatural; it is either meaningless or irrelevant to the questions of the survival and fulfillment of the human race. As nontheists, we begin with humans not God, nature not deity. . . . We can discover no divine purpose or providence for the human species. . . . No deity will save us; we must save ourselves. . . . Promises of immortal salvation or fear of eternal damnation are both illusory and harmful. . . . The human species is an emergence from nat-

ural evolutionary forces. . . . There is no credible evidence
that life survives the death of the body. (Humanist Manifesto II, 1980, p. 6)

This denial of basic Christian truths means the secular
humanist will look at morality in a different light than
the believer in Christ. To the humanist there is no sin,
and guilt is something laid on one by others. We create
our own values, are saved by our own efforts, and the final
court of appeal is our own conscience. "Moral values de-
rive their source from human experience. Ethics is *autonomous* and *situational*, needing no theological or
ideological sanction. . . . We strive for the good life, here
and now" (Humanist Manifesto II, 1980, p. 7). Faith is in
ourselves not in God, and guiding principles are drawn
from human experience rather than from the revealed Word
of God. Needless to say, such statements are antithetical
to Christian belief.

To the secular humanist there are many alternative
paths; to the Christian there is only one (Jn. 14). To the
humanist this life is all and enough; to the Christian "if
in this life only we have hope . . . we are of all men most
miserable" (1 Cor. 15:19, KJV). To the humanist "the chief
end of thought and action is to further this-earthly human
interests on behalf of the greater happiness and glory of
man" (Lamont, 1957, p. 189); to the Christian "man's purpose is to know and to love God in this life, and to be
forever happy with Him in the next" (Hammes, 1971,
p. 184). The secular humanist wants no denial of self, but
rather an enhancement and affirmation of one's identity;
the Christian knows that only by denial, by losing one's
life for Christ's sake will one find true identity (Mt. 10:39).
The goal of the humanist is to be self-actualized; the goal
of the Christian is to be restored to God's likeness. The
humanist says, "I can do all things"; the Christian says,
"I can do all things through Christ" (Phil. 4:13, KJV). Herein
lies the difference. Feeling no need for God, the humanist

declares the self to be god and gives to the self those attributes befitting deity. The Christian knows he or she is nothing without God. One's existence is dependent on the creative will of God, and any virtue one possesses cannot be separated from the redemptive power of Christ.

Morality to the secular humanist is on a horizontal plane—the relationship of one person to another. Morality to the Christian is on a vertical plane as well—the relationship of man to God. It is only as we touch God that we can fully understand the enormous worth of every living soul. For the Christian, guilt feelings are relieved not by a denial of guilt, but by a recognition of the sin producing that guilt and by confessing the sin to the One who has promised to cast our sins "into the depths of the sea" (Mic. 7:19). "I'm OK, you're OK" comes not by self-acclamation but by a pronouncement from God.

Secular humanism is but one of many humanistic groups. Some humanists accept deity, some do not. Some believe in the Bible, some do not. There now appears to be a trend for Christians once again to claim the term "humanism" as their own. J. I. Packer (1978) states: "I am a humanist. In truth, I believe it is only a thoroughgoing Christian who can ever have a right to that name. . . . It is part of the glory of the gospel to be the one genuine humanism that the world has seen" (p. 11). Donald MacKay (1979) echoes this sentiment by saying: "Christian humanism affirms that the only true fulfillment is to be found in working out our destiny in line with the will of our Creator through whom alone we can hope to learn what true compassion and healthy self-reliance mean" (pp. 109-10). Dale Brown (1970) puts it this way, "Christianity at its best does not oppose humanism: rather, Christianity is humanism-plus" (p. 54).

These writers are saying that the word "humanism" rightfully belongs to the Christian, that humanism has its greatest meaning in the context of the Christian faith. They have a good case. To relinquish a word simply because it is used by those who do not know our Lord or because it is narrowly defined by some Christians as meaning only a philosophy that places the human race at the center and leaves God out of the picture is not the best approach. We do not cease to use the word "God" because it has been used to refer to deities other than the true God. Nor do we stop using terms like "morality" or "ethics" because these words also are used by those "who call evil good and good evil" (Is. 5:20). Love, joy, peace, kindness, and goodness—fruits of the Spirit (Gal. 5:22)—are words used by those who do not know the Spirit and therefore have only a shallow understanding of their meaning, yet we continue to speak of them when describing the working of the Spirit in the life of the believer. In the same way, "humanism" which is basic to the Christian position of our being made in the image of God should be a part of the Christian's vocabulary. There is no humanism more beautiful, more inspiring, more in keeping with the true nature of the human race than the humanism of the Bible.

A number of Christian leaders including Donald Bloesch, George Brushaber, Richard Bube, Arthur Holmes, Bruce Lockerbie, J. I. Packer, Bernard Ramm, and James Sire have worked with the editors of *Eternity* magazine to prepare a statement entitled "A Christian Humanist Manifesto" (1982). The purpose of the manifesto is to declare "the place of the human species in the universe" and to "seek to recover the term 'humanism' to its traditional lofty meaning and to articulate the Christian world- and life-view against the secular one" (Secular vs. Christian humanism, *Eternity*, 1982, p. 15). An invitation is given for those who wish, to amend or revise the statement "to make it a more perfect expression of the Christian world-view" (p. 15). Even as all secular humanists do not accept every statement in *Humanist Manifesto II*, all Christians will not accept every statement in "A Christian Humanist Manifesto," but the effort to reclaim a term that finds its highest expression within the Christian tradition is to be commended.

The purpose of God as revealed in Scripture is that people will become like him. Made in the image of God, the first human beings were given that potential. But sin entered when they tried to be like God through their own initiative and in their own way. Then God in his infinite love devised a plan—a plan so that the potential within the human species would not be lost. God sent his Son to become one of us, to dignify the human race by becoming a person, making it possible once again for us to be like our Creator. "God made him who had no sin to be sin for us, so that in him we might become the righteousness of God" (2 Cor. 5:21). This is the message of salvation. It is a message of hope and joy. It is a message that says we have value because God has given us value. It is a message that says we are moral, not by our own efforts, but by his Gift of righteousness. It is a message we can *choose* for ourselves, *prizing* it as we tell others of our choice and *acting* upon it repeatedly in our daily lives.

Notes

1. For a more detailed description of the self-actualized person, see J. A. Oakland (1974), Self-actualization and sanctification, *Journal of Psychology and Theology, 2,* 202-9.

2. Ausubel and Sullivan (1970) in *Theory and problems of child development,* New York: Grune & Stratton, used the term "overvalued non-satellizer" to describe the child who has been reared permissively. "The child is installed in the home as an absolute monarch and is surrounded by adulation and obeisance. . . . These eventualities first threaten when the protection offered by his unreal home environment is removed and his hypertrophied ego aspirations are confronted by peers and adults unbiased in his favor" (p. 268). The authors described the overvalued non-satellizer as unable to curb "hedonistic impulses" or acquire "executive independence" and thus not apt to become "invested with moral obligation" (p. 269).

Baumrind (1977), whose research on authority patterns in parents

and instrumental competence in children has gained widespread recognition, wrote that an "assumption that advocates of permissiveness
have made is that unconditional love is beneficial to the child, and
that love which is conditional upon the behavior of the child is harmful to the child. I think that the notion of unconditional love has
deterred many parents from fulfilling certain important parental functions. They fail to train their children for future life and make them
afraid to move towards independence. . . . The parent who expresses
love unconditionally is encouraging the child to be selfish and demanding while she herself is not. Thus she reinforces exactly the
behavior which she does not approve of—greedy, demanding, incon-
siderate behavior" (pp. 254-5). (Some thoughts about child rearing, in
S. Cohen & T. J. Comiskey (Eds.), *Child development: Contemporary
perspectives*, Itasca, IL: Peacock.

3. Richard James in *The Wall Street Journal*, April 16, 1979, 59,
pp. 1, 18, reported that nearly 60 percent of encounter-group members
and 90 percent of encounter-group leaders say the sessions are beneficial. This is in contrast to a study conducted by Lieberman and
Yalom (reported by James) in which two hundred encounter group
participants were given a number of psychological tests, and only
about one-third appeared to receive any longlasting benefits. As the
figure of one-third is close to the number that improves even without
therapy, it would seem that "many, if not most, of the methods may
hardly be better than doing nothing at all" (James, 1979, p. 1). Max
Wertheimer (1978) in *American Psychologist, 33,* 739-45, comes to
the same conclusion for he states that therapy has only "a slight
positive effect" (p. 744) and that the difference between clients and
control groups may be due to a self-fulfilling prophecy; that is, clients
expect to be helped and so report they feel better after a session much
as one would report less tension or less pain after taking a placebo.
In another study (M. L. Smith & G. V. Glass (1977), *American Psychologist, 32,* 752-60), the results of almost four hundred evaluations
of psychotherapy and counseling cited in the literature were surveyed.
Smith and Glass found that humanistic techniques had approximately the same success rate as psychodynamic and behavioristic
approaches. Regardless of type of therapy, clients were better off than
about 75 percent of untreated individuals.

4. Other sources providing suggestions and exercises for using the
valuing process in the church are as follows: *Instructor's resource book
for redesigning man: Science and human values* (1974). San Francisco:
Harper & Row. McEniry, R. (1982). Values clarification: An aid to
adolescent religious education. *Counseling and Values, 27,* 40-51. Sa-
vary, L. M. (1974). *Integrating values: Theory and exercises for clari-*

fying and integrating religious values. Dayton, OH: Pflaum. Simon, S. B., Daitch, P., & Hartwell, M. (1973). Value clarification: New mission for religious education. In S. B. Simon & H. Kirschenbaum (Eds.), *Readings in values clarification* (pp. 241-46). Minneapolis: Winston.

References

A Christian humanist manifesto. (1982). *Eternity, 33*(1), 16-8.

AHA's statement on the family. (1980). *The Humanist, 40*(5), 40.

Ausubel, D. P., & Sullivan, E. V. (1970). *Theory and problems of child development* (2nd ed.). New York: Grune & Stratton.

Barr, D. L. (1974). Is 'moral education' possible? *Eternity, 25*(8), *17*, 19-20, 26.

Baumrind, D. (1977). Some thoughts about child rearing. In S. Cohen & T. J. Comiskey (Eds.), *Child development: Contemporary issues* (pp. 248-58). Itasca, IL: Peacock.

Berne, E. (1961). *Transactional analysis in psychotherapy: A systematic individual and social psychiatry.* New York: Grove Press.

———. (1974). *Games people play. The psychology of human relationships.* New York: Grove Press.

Bessell, H., & Palomares, U. (1973). *Methods in human development theory manual.* San Diego: Human Development Training Institute.

Brown, D. W. (1970). *Brethren and pacifism.* Elgin, IL: Brethren.

Charny, I. W. (1974). The new psychotherapies and encounters of the seventies: Progress or fads? *The Humanist, 34*(3), 4-9.

Combs, A. W. (1978). Humanism, education, and the future. *Educational Leadership, 35,* 300-3.

———. (1981). Humanistic education: Too tender for a tough world? *Phi Delta Kappan, 62,* 446-9.

Elkind, D. (1981). Erich Fromm (1900-1980). *American Psychologist, 36,* 521-2.

Goldbecker, S. S. (1976). *Values teaching.* Washington, DC: National Education Association.

Hall, R. T. (1976). Moral education: A bicentennial defense. *The Humanist, 36*(2), 44-5.

———. (1978). Moral education and secular humanism. *The Humanist, 38*(6), 7.

Hammes, J. A. (1971). *Humanistic psychology: A Christian interpretation.* New York: Grune & Stratton.

Harmin, M., Kirshenbaum, H., & Simon, S. B. (1973). *Clarifying values through subject matter: Applications for the classroom.* Minneapolis: Winston.

Harris, T. (1969). *I'm OK, You're OK: A practical guide to transactional analysis.* New York: Harper & Row.

Humanist manifesto II. (1980). *The Humanist, 40*(5), 5-10.

James, M. M. (1973). *Born to love: Transactional analysis in the church.* Reading, MA: Addison-Wesley.

————. (1976). The OK boss in all of us. *Psychology Today, 9*(9), 31-6, 80.

Janov, A. (1970). *The primal scream.* New York: G. P. Putnam's Sons.

Kirschenbaum, H. (1976). Dialog: Howard Kirschenbaum talks with Lisa Kuhmerker. *Moral Education Forum, 1*(5), 1, 4-6.

Kohlberg & Simon: An exchange of opinion. (1972). *Learning, 1*(2), 19.

Kolenda, K. (1980). Humanism and Christianity. *The Humanist, 40*(4), 4-8.

Kolesnik, W. B. (1975). *Humanism and/or behaviorism in education.* Boston: Allyn & Bacon.

Kurtz, P. (1976). The attack on secular humanism. *The Humanist, 36*(5), 4-5.

LaHaye, T. (1980). *The battle for the mind.* Old Tappan, NJ: Fleming H. Revell.

Lamont, C. (1957). *The philosophy of humanism.* New York: Philosophical Library.

Larson, R. S., & Larson, D. E. (1976). *Values and faith: Activities for family and church groups.* Minneapolis: Winston.

Lasch, C. (1979). *The culture of narcissism: American life in an age of diminishing expectations.* New York: W. W. Norton.

Lockwood, A. L. (1978). The effects of values clarification and moral development curricula on school-age subjects: A critical review of recent research. *Review of Educational Research, 48,* 325-64.

MacKay, D. M. (1979). *Human science & human dignity.* Downers Grove, IL: Inter-Varsity.

Maslow, A. H. (1970). *Motivation and personality* (2nd ed.). New York: Harper & Row.

————. (1973). Self-actualizing people: A study of psychological health. In R. J. Lowry (Ed.), *Dominance, self-esteem, self-actualization: Germinal papers of A. H. Maslow* (pp. 177-201). Monterey, CA: Brooks/Cole.

Morain, L. L. (1980). Humanist manifesto II: A time for reconsideration? *The Humanist, 40*(5), 4-10.

Moreno, J. L. (1944). *Sociodrama: A method for the analysis of social conflicts.* New York: Beacon House.

Mowrer, O. H. (1967). Preface. In O. H. Mowrer (Ed.), *Morality and mental health* (pp. vii-x). Chicago: Rand McNally.

Packer, J. I. (1978). *Knowing man.* Westchester, IL: Cornerstone Books.

Perlmutter, R. (1980). The effects of the values clarification process on the moral and ego development of high school students. Unpublished doctoral dissertation, Boston University.

Perls, F. S. (1969). *Gestalt therapy verbatim.* Lafayette, CA: Real People.

Peters, T. (1978). *Futures—human and divine.* Atlanta: John Knox.

Raths, L. E., Harmin, M., & Simon, S. B. (1966). *Values and teaching: Working with values in the classroom.* Columbus, OH: Charles E. Merrill.

Rogers, C. R. (1964). Toward a modern approach to value: The valuing process in the mature person. *Journal of Abnormal and Social Psychology, 68,* 160-67.

————. (1969). *Freedom to learn.* Columbus, OH: Charles E. Merrill.

————. (1978). Some questions and challenges facing a humanistic psychology. In I. D. Welch, G. A. Tate, & F. Richards (Eds.), *Humanistic psychology: A source book* (pp. 41-5). Buffalo, NY: Prometheus Books.

Rokeach, M. (1973). *The nature of human values.* New York: The Free Press.

Secular vs. Christian humanism. (1982). *Eternity, 33*(1), 15.

Silber, J.R. (1975). Encountering what? In D. A. Read, & S. B. Simon (Eds.), *Humanistic education sourcebook* (pp. 196-200). Englewood Cliffs, NJ: Prentice-Hall.

Simon, S. B. (1973). Three ways to teach church school. In S. B. Simon & H. Kirschenbaum (Eds.), *Readings in values clarification* (pp. 237-40). Minneapolis: Winston.

Simon, S.B., & deSherbinin, P. (1975). Values clarification: It can start gently and grow deep. *Phi Delta Kappan, 56,* 679-83.

Simon, S. B., & Olds, S. W. (1976). *Helping your child learn right from wrong: A guide to values clarification.* New York: Simon & Schuster.

Vitz, P. C. (1979). *Psychology as religion: The cult of self worship.* Icknield Way, Tring, Herts, Great Britain: Lion.

Welch, I. D., & Rodwick, J. R. (1978). Communicating the sciences: A humanistic viewpoint. In I. D. Welch, G. A. Tate, & F. Richards (Eds.), *Humanistic psychology: A source book* (pp. 335-42). Buffalo, NY: Prometheus Books.

Wertheimer, M. (1978). Humanistic psychology and the humane but tough-minded psychologist. *American Psychologist, 33,* 739-45.

Yablonsky, L. (1976). *Psychodrama: Resolving emotional conflicts through role-playing.* New York: Basic Books.

5

The Psychoanalytic Approach
Morality as Moral Conflict

Not so the wicked!
They are like chaff
that the wind blows away.
Therefore the wicked will not stand in the judgment,
nor sinners in the assembly of the righteous. (Ps. 1:4-5)

Psychoanalysis is both a theory and a form of therapy. As a theory, emphasis is placed on unconscious processes that come in conflict with the demands of a real world. Instinctive, irrational, pleasure-seeking impulses present at birth and seething with sexual and aggressive energy are thwarted by societal restrictions and taboos. The result is a constriction of sensuality and a demand for behaviors deemed appropriate by a civilized world. The consequences to the developing organism are frustration and defense. Feelings of guilt for noncompliance, a fear of parental rejection for hating as well as loving, and underlying anxiety for lack of impulse control all take their toll on the child. Growing up is difficult and fraught with danger, for growing up means conflict—a conflict between instinctive forces within and social restrictions

225

without, between a desire for pleasure and a desire to live in a world that limits pleasure, between what one wants and what one can have. Growing up may result in the development of moral character, or it may result in the acquisition of neurotic traits, or perhaps both character and neuroses will be the outcome. But whatever the final state, the process of development from the depraved condition of the newborn to the mature disposition of the adult is fraught with tension and compromise.

As a form of therapy, psychoanalysis brings into consciousness fantasies, ideas, feelings, and events that have been repressed and kept at the unconscious level. The method used is called "free-association" because the patient, after being made comfortable by lying on a couch, freely says whatever comes to mind while the therapist takes the memories, hopes, and dream world of the patient and analyzes their hidden meanings. By bringing into awareness unconscious processes, analyst and patient together can deal with the problems. "By extending the unconscious into consciousness the repressions are raised, the conditions of symptom-formation are abolished, and the pathogenic conflict exchanged for a normal one" (Freud, 1920/1949, p. 377). Psychoanalysis should not be thought of as a catchall for any kind of psychotherapy, for it represents only one type of therapy, one based on the teachings of Sigmund Freud and used by him or a recognized follower. Psychiatrists who are psychoanalysts have gone through psychoanalysis as part of their own training.

The name of Sigmund Freud has become a household word. Founder and father of psychoanalysis, Freud was born on the Continent in 1856 and was well recognized for his accomplishments by the time of his death in London in 1939. A precocious young man, he graduated *summa cum laude* from medical school where he specialized in neurology. He became increasingly interested in the effect of the mind on disorders of the central nervous system, and by using the method of hypnosis with patients in a hospital setting found that depression, anxiety, and hysteria stem from psychological disturbance rather than from physical disease. This discovery opened a whole new area of investigation into the makeup of the personality. Later, using the method of free-association, he developed the theory of "psychic determinism", a view that all behavior, including dreams, fantasies, and even slips of the tongue, are determined by psychic forces rather than by unlawful or random dispositions.

In Freudian psychoanalysis, moral development is an integral part of the total process of personality development. The same forces that bring a child to social maturity bring a child to moral maturity. The developing organism incorporates within the self the dictates and demands of an external world, making societal standards a part of one's own personality and passing them on to one's children when one becomes an adult. In this way the culture is perpetuated from generation to generation. A look at the basic assumptions of psychoanalytic thought with regard to morality will enable us to understand better the process by which this development takes place.

Basic Assumptions

Unlike the learning position that children are born neither good nor evil (note chap. 2), or the cognitive view that children have within themselves the desire for moral understanding (note chap. 3), or the humanistic belief that children are goodly creatures with great potential for moral self-actualization (note chap. 4), the psychoanalytic approach fastens on the darker side of the human condition. *The original nature of humankind is one of depravity.* Born with irrational passions and instincts and desiring only the satisfaction of one's own needs, the person is animalistic, seeking gratification of sensual and aggressive impulses and void of moral direction or desire. In the original state humans are not fit to live with others for they are crude, insensitive, and arrogant. Intervention must take place if a person is to become a moral individual.

Moral development occurs when the child internalizes the expectations and normative demands of the society as interpreted by the parents. The helplessness of human infants puts them in a vulnerable position. Left to themselves they would die. The dependency on the parents for life itself brings about an imitation of parental actions as a way of keeping the parents close. Later, children will identify with parental attitudes and beliefs as well. Children try to be like their parents because this makes them feel more grown up, and growing up is something every child wants very much to do. As representatives of the society, parents constantly explain the "shoulds" and the "should nots" of the social order to their children and use a variety of methods to assure that conformity will take place. It is in this way that children learn to accept the demands of the culture and to make these demands an integral part of their own personalities.

The optimal time for moral development to occur is between two and six years of age. One of Freud's greatest contributions was to emphasize the importance of the early years. This is no better illustrated than in the area of morality. Even before the child's first birthday the child is aware of a world outside his or her own skin that brings pleasure or pain. Pleasure is associated with doing what is good, and pain is associated with doing what is bad. By the age of two, children have begun to imitate the actions of those around them, and by four or five years of age they are well on their way to adopting parental standards. Good and bad, right and wrong, moral and immoral are interpreted for them by the same people who satisfy their personal needs. For the normal preschooler, the world of reality and the world of right and wrong have become an integral part of daily life, and the baser passions inherent at birth are now subjugated to meet these new demands.

Never again will the influence of parents be so strong. Never again will the child be so close to someone who meets both physical and psychological needs while at the same time demanding behaviors considered appropriate by the society.

Moral development may continue after the early years but takes on a different form. As the child becomes less dependent on parents and enters the larger world of other adults and peers, ideas of what is right and what is wrong begin to change. Baby-sitters and teachers will take on some of the authority of the parents, and peers may demonstrate the importance of mutual interdependence, but the child does not rely on teachers or age-mates for survival, nor does the child live with them during the early formative years. Consequently, the variety of influence is less related to an internalization of standards that are normative for every occasion and more related to the consequences of behavior that differ from one circumstance to another. Furthermore, stages of moral development correspond with certain chronological ages and are related to the "task achievement" (Tice, 1980) of that stage. In early childhood the task is to identify with parents, whereas in later childhood tasks include "being able to take a moral point of view more effectively over a wide range of experience" and "further attainment of moral values, rules, principles and ideals" (Tice, 1980, p. 191). As each stage of moral development includes remnants of earlier stages, children who have not developed a strong sense of right and wrong during the early years will be hampered in moral stability at a later time. Middle childhood, adolescence, and adulthood are all important in the development of morality, but each age has its roots in previous ages and as such is contingent on the success or failure of the earlier periods.

Moral development takes place in a context of conflict and defense. The emotional conflict generated by the battle between the natural desire to please self and the external pressure to conform to the society makes for inner turmoil and feelings of guilt. The focus of psychoanalysis is on passion rather than intellect, desire rather than reason. Yet, without this conflict there would be no moral progress. Psychopaths are so named because they do not have a conscience, nor do they experience feelings of guilt. Their pathology stems from a lack of anxiety over their behavior and an unwillingness to adopt cultural standards. Not having experienced the inhibitions that arise when societal restrictions are internalized, they continue their infantile ways of caring only for themselves with no concern for the well-being of others. At the other extreme are neurotic individuals who find the conflict overwhelming, and because they cannot cope, they suffer acute anxiety and distress. Normal individuals also experience conflict, but unlike neurotics they are able to deal with the tensions. Being psychologically healthy, they turn the distress into opportunities for creative and culture-building activities. Nevertheless, the line between neurotic and healthy is not always clear, and for both groups the process of moral growth is painful and fraught with danger and compromise.

Because of the emotional turmoil and distress that accompanies conflict, Freud believed that *becoming a moral person benefits the society more than it does the individual.* "We can demonstrate with ease that what the world calls its code of morals demands more sacrifices than it is worth" (Freud, 1920/1949, p. 377). Yet, Freud recognized that the code is essential for without it would be unleashed "a savage beast to whom consideration towards his own kind is something alien" (Freud, 1930/1961, p. 59). The aggressive nature of human beings emerges wherever it finds an outlet—in lust and killing as well as in revolution and war. Society as we know it could not exist without repressive forces keeping its members in line. But in the long run society does not win either. "This conflict is not resolved by helping one side to win over the other"

(Freud, 1920/1949, p. 375). For both the person and the social order there are only compromises, adjustments, and concessions. Nor will it ever be different. The human race will continue to experience the consequences of its own depravity, and the society will continue to make its rules, written and unwritten, only to find them broken time and again. The person becomes the victim-spectator of greed and lust, tragedy and oppression; and the social order becomes the tyrannical overseer torn by insurrection and strife. This shadow-side of the human race is oppressive and pessimistic, but it is, nevertheless, an aspect of humanity we cannot dismiss. Readily visible all around us are the manifestations of evil. The plight of humanity is described in Holy Writ and found in the musings of great philosophers and poets. Without an acknowledgment of sin and its consquences, we deceive ourselves, choosing to look only at the brighter side of life rather than to gain a total picture of the human condition.

Freud's Analytic View of the Personality

Freud saw the personality as composed of three parts: The *id* consisting of irrational passions and instincts and oriented to pleasurable states of the organism, the *ego* encompassing rational and cognitive components of the personality and oriented to the world of reality, and the *superego* embodying societal values and attitudes and oriented to matters of right and wrong. The id is present at birth; the ego and the superego develop later. Freud believed that all three components should be well formed by the age of six.

The child is born as an "it," or an *id,* a seething mass of energy demanding immediate and direct expression of its needs. As the inherited portion of the personality it is composed of animal-like drives and instincts that are largely sensual and agressive in nature. The id has no mind, no consciousness, and no awareness of anything other than its own desires. Within the id are two classes of instincts, the *eros*, or life instinct, having to do with self-preservation, and the *thanatos*, or death instinct, having to do with self-destruction and aggressive tendencies toward others. The *libido* is the energy of the life instinct and is usually associated with sexual pleasure, which may be expressed either directly in sexual intercourse or indirectly in warm and pleasant relationships with others. The death instinct is destructive, finding release by turning against the self as in self-mutilation and suicide or by turning against others as in sadism and murder. Life and death, love and hate, preservation and destruction are part of the id and constitute one's heritage as a member of the human race. These conflicting forces are destined to remain throughout life, seeking release and working at cross-purposes with each other.

Sometime during the first year of life the infant becomes aware of an external physical and social environment, a world of reality that will not permit the total gratification of id impulses. If the child is to survive he or she must take into consideration not only the world of pleasurable states but also the real world of the external. In order to cope with this situation, part of the id is changed into a rational structure oriented to reality and becomes the "I" or ego portion of the personality. The ego functions as a decision-maker, guiding perceptions and behaviors, and protecting the person against both the dangers of an external world and the harm that would come if id desires remained unchecked. The ego is primarily conscious, having awareness of self and its decisions. Being intelligent and prudent, it weighs the consequences of action in accordance with the situation, provides control of emotion, and generally serves the best interests of the person. By diverting the energy of the id to its own use, the ego is empowered to reconcile the biological demands of the id with the external pressures of a real world. The ego continues to develop through middle and late childhood and even into the adult years, but as reality changes and new problems arise, increased cognitive capacities must be brought to bear and the person must alter perceptions to meet life's challenges and to reckon with the consequences of behavior.

The superego, which contains both conscious and unconscious elements, begins to develop as early as two or three years of age as part of the ego changes to a new structure that incorporates adult attitudes and values. The process is called introjection because the child is introjecting or putting within the self the expectations and normative demands of the society. There are two subsystems operating within the superego, one called the *ego ideal*, which is the self-image of what the person feels he or she should be, and the other called the *conscience*, which is a self-criticizing agent that produces feelings of guilt when parental demands are not met. The ego ideal is positive, creating feelings of esteem and pride when the standard is met; the conscience is negative, bringing punishment for infractions from within the individual. Both the ego ideal and the conscience are important for moral growth, the ego ideal developing when the child is praised and the conscience developing when the child is punished. Unlike the ego, which gains in power and importance after the child starts school, the superego is less apt to develop after the early years, making the first few years of life the critical period for the cultivation of internal controls. Without the stability and trustworthy behavior that accompanies inner restraints, society as we know it could not survive.

Some social learning psychologists have borrowed heavily from psychoanalytic theory and have emphasized the place of the ego as well as the superego in moral development.[1] Both a world of reality and a world of right and wrong must be considered and a healthy balance between them attained if one's conduct is to be moral. The consequences of behavior as well as the press of conviction should be contemplated before a course of action is taken. Adopting the best of both components of the personality, namely, the flexibility of the ego to vary as the situation demands and the stability of the superego to stand firm on matters of principle is essential for moral action to take place. If the ego is present without the constraints of the superego, one's conduct will be opportunistic and unpredictable and may lead to delinquency. If the superego with an overdeveloped conscience is dominant without regard for the consequences of behavior in a real world, the personality will be constricted and life will have little to offer by way of pleasure and creative expression. An ego without a superego is mundane and superficial; a superego without an ego is oppressive and damaging to self and others.[2] Like the id, the ego is interested in what is best for one's self without concern for ethical standards. Also like the id, the superego is blind, unintelligent, and demanding. And so, the ego needs the superego to give it consistency and depth, and the superego needs the ego to give it sight and understanding. Consequently, social learning psychologists emphasize that a balance between ego and superego, reality and ideal, intelligence and conscience is more moral than a preference for one apart from the other.

But a balance between consequences of behavior in a real world and standing firm on matters of principle is not easy to achieve, and the conscientious person who tries to weigh both will find that conflict is inevitable. Yet, without this conflict there would be no growth, and the individual would be relegated either to the superficial life of the here and now or to the tyrannical world of impossible ideals and feelings of guilt. So, the struggle continues—a struggle between the life instinct and the death instinct within the id, between the id and the real world of the ego, between the ego and the dictates of the superego. The id says "I want," and the superego says "Thou shalt," or, "Thou shalt not," and the ego which serves as mediator says, "I will," or, "I won't," or, "I will but only in this socially acceptable way." The methods used by the ego to make concessions to both the id and the superego while keeping them both in line are known as defense mechanisms. It is to a consideration of these mechanisms that we now turn as a way of seeing how moral development may be enhanced or deterred.

Mechanisms of Defense

Some of the desires of the id are so out of keeping with what society will allow that they are not permitted into consciousness. The person is not even aware of having these desires. This is known as *repression*. Repression occurs because the ego, or "I" portion of the personality, is so threatened by what would happen in the real world if instinctual urges were given free expression that these urges are relegated to the realm of the unconscious rather than being recognized and dealt with in a rational way. Freud had much to say about the effects of repression on the personality. He believed that socially unacceptable passions and instincts do not go away simply because the person does not know about them. Instead, they remain within the individual, generating fear and anxiety and feelings of guilt, and seeking outlets of expression in some disguised form such as dreams or neurotic behavior. "The psychology of the neuroses has taught us that, if wishful impulses are repressed, their libido is transformed into anxiety. And this reminds us that there is something unknown and unconscious in connection with the sense of guilt. . . . The character of anxiety that is inherent in the sense of guilt corresponds to this unknown factor" (Freud, 1913/1952, p. 79).

A case in point is the child of four or five years of age who has an incestuous desire for his mother (Freud believed that boys this age feel that way about their mothers). But the child is thwarted in his desire because of the presence of his father. Dad is bigger and stronger than he and already has mother. Furthermore, the child develops castration anxiety for he fears his dad will castrate him if he knows of his intentions. So, like the mythical Greek figure, Oedipus, he grows to hate his father and would like to kill him. But society takes a dim view of boys killing their fathers and having sexual relations with their mothers, so these instinctual desires are not allowed into consciousness but remain rather at the unconscious level, creating feelings of anxiety and distress. Not understanding the turmoil within him, the child knows only that he wants to be near his mother and that he does not wish to share her with anyone. Freud believed that the successful resolution of the Oedipus complex takes place when the child learns to identify with the parent of the same sex. The boy must identify with the father who is feared and hated. In this way, even though he cannot have mother directly, by being like the one who does have mother, he, too, vicariously has mother. Being masculine, like dad, makes him less anxious and helps to satisfy sexual and aggressive urges. The counterpart of the Oedipus complex in boys is the Electra complex in girls. Suffering from "penis envy," the girl of four or five years of age desires her father and is jealous of her mother. Freud believed that the girl wishes to compensate for the loss of the penis by having a child by her father. By six or seven years of age she will have resolved the unconscious turmoil by identifying with her mother.

A second mechanism of defense is *sublimation.* Sublimation takes place when the psychic energy of the id is transferred to the ego so that the person's behavior can be monitored and gradually changed to activities that are considered by the society to be creative and culturally beneficial. Helping others in times of trouble, expressing oneself in writing or in the arts, and engaging in religious exercises are ways in which sublimation may take form.

Unlike repression in which sexual impulses are not admitted into consciousness, sublimation allows for an awareness of primitive drives but mandates that these drives be desexualized. Pearson (1954) gives the example of a small child who wishes to play with his feces but sublimates this desire and plays in the mud instead. In time, the child learns to play in sand and then to collect rocks, arranging the rocks in attractive patterns. Little by little his behavior is being changed to socially more acceptable forms. The original sexual impulse of playing with his own excrement has been turned in the direction of a nonsexual art expression that is pleasing both to himself and to others. He may become a great artist and receive recognition for his accomplishments. The sublimated desire, rather than being kept at the unconscious level, has been given opportunity for demonstration, thus enabling the person to remain psychologically healthy. The energy of the libido is released to the ego so that the individual is free to create and to engage in culture-building activities.

Sometimes a person will revert to an earlier pattern of behavior or mental functioning, usually during a period of stress. This is known as *regression*. The four-year-old begins wetting his pants when a baby brother is born; a nine-year-old sucks her thumb whenever she is scolded; an adult sleeps in a fetal position when he hears he may lose his job. Regression may be so severe that the person must be cared for as an infant, or it may be so mild as to go unnoticed. Mild forms of regression are visible all around us if we are but tuned as to what to see. Adults, as well as children, need security blankets to ease the pressure of everyday living. We find that inner tensions are released when we cuddle up to something soft and warm—a favorite quilt or a person we love. But regression is more apt to refer to extreme behaviors that indicate a return to primitive and infantile ways of adjusting to conflict. Used in this sense, regression is an unhealthy mechanism for dealing with stress for it renders the person ineffectual both to the self and to others.

Projection is another protective device employed by the ego to deal with emotional conflict. Sometimes when people have thoughts or feelings that are unacceptable, they may unwittingly attribute these characteristics to someone else but remain unaware that they possess them themselves and that their behavior is affected by them. When this occurs, projection is used. If we say that someone does not like us, it often means that we do not like that person although we are reluctant to admit our own feelings in the matter. A wife who would like to engage in extramarital sex may accuse her husband of infidelity while thinking of herself as pure and noble. The young woman who is claustrophobic believes that others are fearful while riding in elevators but that she is able to cope quite well. Another example is the small boy, already mentioned, who is at the oedipal phase of psychosexual development and suffers from castration anxiety. His own unconscious hostility for the father is attributed to the father so that he believes it is the father, not himself, who wishes to inflict pain. Freud wrote that projection is a "defensive procedure, which is a common one both in normal and in pathological mental life" (Freud, 1913/1952, p. 61). It helps us to like ourselves better if we attribute our undesirable traits to others rather than recognizing them in ourselves. Although positive attitudes and feelings also may be projected, the term generally is not used in this way.

Introjection is the counterpart of projection. Whereas in projection people believe that their own characteristics are more descriptive of others than of themselves, in introjection they introject, or put within themselves, the qualities and characteristics of others. Introjection begins as soon as the child learns the difference between self and nonself, between what is a part of one's own body and what is external. The infant incorporates milk from the mother and the milk becomes a part of the self, but the mother remains distinct from the self. Yet, because she brings great pleasure and the child would like to be assured that she will always be nearby, she becomes both the object and the subject of the child's affections. As object, she is to be possessed; as subject, she is to be imitated. The child knows her first as object, as the instrument by which needs are satisfied; the child knows her later as subject, as the one whose attitudes and expectations for conduct become a part of one's own personality. By introjecting her attributes and demands, she becomes in the best sense of the word a part of the self.[3]

Freud (1937/1957) writes that introjection also accounts for the depression a person feels after losing a loved one. "Another such instance of introjection of the object has been provided by the analysis of melancholia. . . . A leading characteristic of these cases is a cruel self-depreciation of the ego combined with relentless self-criticism and bitter self-reproaches. . . . The shadow of the object has fallen upon the ego." To lose someone we love is to lose a part of ourselves. "Melancholias . . . show the ego divided, fallen into two pieces, one of which rages against the second. This second piece is the one which has been altered by introjection and which contains the lost object" (p. 187). To love deeply is to experience great pleasure, the pleasure of possession and the pleasure of identification, but to lose that love is to experience great pain for only the shadow remains to haunt and darken our lives.

Other mechanisms used by the ego to satisfy conflicting demands include *rationalization* in which socially acceptable explanations are given for actual, less honorable motives; *compensation* in which success in one area is substituted for weakness in another; *escape* which may be either physical or mental; *denial* or a turning away from reality by ignoring or disavowing its existence; and *reaction formation* in which the behavior exhibited is the exact opposite of the behavior the individual would like to pursue.[4] In every case, the mechanism used enables the person to deal in some way with threat so that inner tensions are released while outbreaks of anxiety are prevented. The defensive maneuver protects the self from instinctual demands within and environmental restrictions without, from a developing superego that brings a sense of guilt and the censorship of acquaintances that would stifle individualism and creative expression. The ego must remain strong for the person to be psychologically healthy. The ego's job is to mediate between opposing forces and defend itself against the conflicts that would destroy it.

There are both healthy and unhealthy ways of dealing with stress, the end result depending on which defense mechanism is used, how often it is used, the way in which it is used, and the age of the person using the defensive procedure. Freud (1937/1957) considered repression to be unhealthy, for it "ramifies like a fungus . . . in the dark and takes on extreme forms of expression" (p. 90). Repressed desires are not allowed into consciousness where they can be dealt with in a rational manner but are kept out of mind, thus rendering the individual unable to recognize and face the problems of life and placing the individual in a vulnerable position should repressed urges find an avenue for direct expression. By contrast, sublimation is healthy for it is at the conscious level, at least in part, making possible a compromise between the individual's own interests and society's insistence that the finished product be of value. In sublimation the energy of the id is used by the ego to pursue a variety of options, thus allowing for creative expression and altruistic contribution. Other mechanisms of defense also may be deleterious or beneficial depending on the mechanism used. Denial is unhealthy for it does not allow the acknowledgment of reality. Compensation is healthy for it encourages the cultivation of socially desirable traits and behaviors. Projection is unhealthy for, as fears and hates are attributed to others, the person becomes paranoid, suspicious, and resentful. Introjection, the counterpart of projection, is healthy for by its use one puts within the self the expectations and normative demands of the society so that one can live harmoniously with others.

Sometimes, however, the unhealthy mechanisms play a role in moral development, and the healthy mechanisms if used in excess are harmful to the formation of character. For instance, repression keeps sexual and aggressive impulses in check so the person can live with others; denial ("I don't believe this is happening to me") alleviates the trauma of disaster which would render the individual incapacitated; and projection paves the way for an empathic understanding of others and their concerns. On the other hand, sublimation "can become a compulsion, a counting compulsion, for example" (Pearson, 1954, p. 186); compensation may cover up the less attractive characteristic rather than acknowledge one's shortcoming; and introjection can lead to "obsessional neuroses, a gratification of sadistic tendencies and of hate" (Freud, 1937/1957, p. 132). Obviously, the way the mechanism is used as well as which mechanism is used determines whether it contributes to or detracts from the development of a wholesome personality.

Defense mechanisms are used by people who are normal and by people who are abnormal, but the way in which they are used and the extent to which they are used will differ. It is normal to escape reality by daydreaming; it is abnormal to escape reality by a psychotic detachment from the world. It is normal to be dependent on others; it is abnormal to regress to the point where we expect others to take complete care of us. It is normal to put our best foot forward; it is abnormal to rationalize by making constant excuses for our behavior. It is normal to say we are fine when we feel poorly; it is abnormal to engage in reaction-formation by washing our hands for hours because we have an unconscious urge to be dirty. Normal uses of defense mechanisms enrich and strengthen the ego for they alleviate stress, allow compromise, and maximize one's interests and potential. Abnormal uses of defense mechanisms impoverish and weaken the ego for they contribute to paranoia, obsessional neuroses, and psychotic withdrawal, thereby limiting the person's ability to enjoy life and to cope with its challenges.

The age of the person also makes a difference. Freud believed that defense mechanisms are necessary for young children but should be resorted to less and less as the person matures. Healthy development calls for replacing unconscious mechanisms which produce anxiety and fear with methods of control that are under the direction of the conscious ego. "Freud's assumption that during the period of the ego's formation the defense mechanisms function as protective devices and may therefore have favourable influences upon its adequate development does not, of course, contradict his other assumption that when they persist in adults they should be regarded as pathogenic" (Sjöbäck, 1973, p. 279). By adulthood people should have mature egos that are able to understand the nature of instinctual demands, the press of conviction, and the coercion of outside constraints, and they should be able to achieve a balance between these forces so that they can go about their daily lives as productive and satisfied persons. Needless to say, many adults are not able to do this and so continue to use defense processes in an effort to protect their weak egos.

In summary, it is apparent from the writings of Sigmund Freud that defense mechanisms contribute to the development of morality when used by children who are younger than five or six years of age. After the age of six, the mechanisms are less effective in producing moral character, and when employed by adults may result in neuroses rather than in socially desirable personality characteristics.[5] The mechanism of introjection is especially important for young children, for it is when children introject societal standards as interpreted to them by their parents that they begin to act in socially acceptable ways. Their conduct stabilizes into trustworthy and acceptable patterns even though adults are not present to monitor their actions. Identification with the parent of the same sex (the resolution of the Oedipus complex) plays a significant role for it allows for a repression of aggressive and sexual impulses which if left unchecked would destroy both the person and the society. Sublimation also is effective in contributing to moral growth for it allows children to express themselves in socially acceptable ways without constricting the personality and creative endeavors. By sublimating id impulses, young people learn to paint pictures, play musical instruments, or engage in religious activities, which bring pleasure both to themselves and to others.

Without the conflict that comes when defense mechanisms are employed, the child would not become a moral adult. Adults in our society who have no conscience and who are therefore sociopathic,[6] have little conflict for they have not introjected the demands of the social order, nor have they repressed sexual and aggressive urges nor sublimated the desires of the id. Consequently, they have weak egos and underdeveloped superegos. Neurotics, on the other hand, have a disproportionate amount of conflict. Unduly concerned about what others think of them and fearful that at any time they may have more anxiety than they can cope with, they introject what they perceive the attitudes of others to be, repress thoughts and feelings that would make them free and creative beings, and sublimate their individualities to oppressive consciences. Neurotics have weak egos and dictatorial superegos.

Healthy adults have come to terms with all three components of the personality: a demanding id, a watchful ego, and an overbearing superego. As children they made use of defense mechanisms to internalize societal demands, but as they matured the repressive forces gave way to more conscious methods of control. Ego and superego have developed together, each fulfilling its purpose and each continuing in a balanced relationship with the other, the ego serving to protect the individual in a world of reality and the superego guarding the mores and standards of the social order. The conscious, rational ego and the unconscious, restrictive superego both have a place in the formation of a healthy personality and a wholesome character.

Techniques Employed

Only those psychiatrists specifically trained in psychoanalysis are in a position to employ psychoanalytic techniques. The method is not usually available to other trained professionals such as counselors, neurologists, ministers, or educators. Even other psychotherapists and physicians schooled in ways of helping people are not in a position to "psychoanalyze" their patients, an expression used far too loosely by lay persons to include any method whereby one tries to understand the hidden meaning of another's speech or behavior. Psychoanalysis calls for bringing into awareness unconscious conflicts that render the person fearful and anxious and for dealing with those conflicts in a rational and reflective way. Extensive training is needed for the therapist to learn how to interpret the underlying significance of what patients say when they recall their dreams or relate whatever comes to mind during a period of free-association.[7]

It has been said, perhaps facetiously, that psychoanalysis is only for the rich and idle. In a sense that is true. The services of a medical doctor carefully trained in an area of speciality command a price, and sessions may take place daily over a period of several years. Furthermore, the arrangement involves only two people, analyst and analysand (the name given to the patient in psychoanalytic literature) working together. Group therapy, so popular today, in which expenses are shared and peers as well as therapist have a role in the healing process, is not the method used in psychoanalysis. The format for reporting in journals and books what takes place during the therapy session is the case study—an in-depth look at one patient and the changes that take place in that patient as therapy proceeds. In this way psychoanalysts share their insights and sustain the dialectic between theory and practice.

The telling of dreams and the sharing of thoughts and emotions demand that the patient be capable of verbal expression. Some people are better able than others to communicate this way. For those who have difficulty, a nonverbal form of symbolization can be used. Children, especially, may need another medium of expression, and neurotic adults with rigid defense mechanisms may become more relaxed if a somatic mode of representation is employed. Avstreih and Brown (1979) write that movement and art therapy provide "the vital tools with which we can extend the work of psychoanalysis into the nonverbal sphere. Body and visual imagery may well be the only viable way in which we can reach that imagistic, preverbal netherworld where words fail; it may then form a link or bridge facilitating the emergence of these images in the verbal sphere, allowing further conceptualization" (p. 67). The use of movement and other art forms does not preclude verbal communication but serves to provide the analyst with cues as to where the problems may lie.

It is not unusual for the patient to transfer the love-hate feelings he or she has for the parent to the analyst or to displace the urge for self-destruction into hostile attitudes during the analytic session. The physician trained in psychoanalysis knows to accept these feelings and interprets them as a sign that repressed sexual and aggressive instincts are coming to the surface where they can be dealt with in an intelligible way. Any difficulty arising from the patient's love or hate for the analyst will be resolved in later sessions. In the meantime the patient experiences a cathartic release as insight is gained and learning takes place as to how to cope with one's problems. Therapy is painful and filled with conflict, but without it there would be no deliverance from the prison of one's own psyche or relief from the pressures of an inhibiting society.

The purpose of therapy is to strengthen the ego's defense system so that it emerges victor over both the animal-like urges of the id and the idealistic but impossible demands of the superego. Freud saw the analyst as coming to the aid of the patient, for it is only with the analyst's help that the patient is able to take charge of his or her own life.

> Our plan of cure is based upon these views. The ego has been weakened by the internal conflict; we must come to its aid. The position is like a civil war which can only be decided by the help of an ally from without. The analytical physician and the weakened ego of the patient, basing themselves upon the real external world, are to combine against the enemies, the instinctual demands of the id, and the moral demands of the superego. We form a pact with each other. The patient's sick ego promises us the most complete candor, promises, that is, to put at our disposal all of the material which his self-perception provides; we, on the other hand, assure him of the strictest discretion and put at his service our experience in interpreting material that has been influenced by the unconscious. Our knowledge shall compensate for his ignorance and shall give his ego once more mastery over the lost provinces of his mental life. This pact constitutes the analytic situation. (Freud, 1949/1970a, p. 430)

A strong ego, then, is the mark of good mental health, for only the ego has the consciousness and ability needed to understand the complexities of life and to appreciate its ambiguity. "The analytic therapist aims not only to help clients feel better and function better but also to extend their perspective—the view of reality—and to recognize and accept that even with improvement, life is inevitably a mixture of comic, ironic, romantic, and tragic elements" (Messer & Winokur, 1980, p. 824). Patients must be set free, not to do whatever they please, but to understand themselves and to appreciate the vicissitudes of the human condition. By strengthening the ego, old conflicts are worked through and new conflicts are challenged. The end result is not so much a feeling of equanimity as one of competency to deal with both the self and with the society in which one lives.[8]

The question may be asked whether good mental health and good moral health are the same. Does the strengthening of the ego during therapy mean that the person is developing in moral character? Does the challenge to the superego with its feelings of guilt contribute to one's sense of right and wrong? Or, is just the opposite the case? Would not a lessening of guilt feelings make a person less inhibited and more apt to do those things of which society would disapprove? The answers are not easy to come by. Freud seemed to see it both ways. In many of his writings he linked morality with organized religious teachings, which he believed constricted the basic nature of human beings and contributed to their neuroticism. Given this view, moral health and mental health are antithetical. In other essays, Freud saw moral development as essential to the continuance of the society and to a person's place within that society. Obviously, one cannot be mentally healthy and at odds with the world in which one lives.

Psychoanalysts who speak to the issue of morality tend to follow Freud's view that morality linked with an oppressive superego detracts from mental health, whereas morality associated with an insightful ego contributes to mental health. A morality of the ego has been given increased attention since the time of Freud as being essential for both moral behavior and optimal psychological functioning (see e.g., Lee, 1948; Lorand, 1972; Pattison, 1968). This is not to say that the superego is not recognized as important, for by it the rules that keep a society together are passed from one generation to the next, and as the superego is internalized, behaviors become stabilized and trustworthy in the young child. But it is to say that moral development must include the ego as well, for without the ego the superego has no voice or consciousness or expression. Without the ego, the person has no way of resolving the oppression that makes one so miserable.

If morality were a function of the superego alone, neurotics would be more moral than those who are not disturbed. Obviously, this is not the case. The strengthening of the ego in psychoanalytic therapy should contribute both to psychological health and to moral health. Karl Menninger (1973), founder of the famed Menninger clinic in Topeka, Kansas, states it well:

> I am a doctor, speaking the medical tongue with a psychiatric accent. For doctors, health is the ultimate good, the ideal state of being. And mental health—some of us believe—includes all the healths: physical, social, cultural, and moral (spiritual). To live, to love, to care, to enjoy, to build on the foundations of our predecessors, to revere the constant miracles of creation and endurance, of "the starry skies above and the moral law within"—these are acts and attitudes which express our mental health. (p. 230)

Mental health and moral health are inextricably linked. Both are made possible by a strong ego and a sensitive superego. In therapy, both ego and superego must be made viable, each relating to the other in optimal ways.

The Psychoanalytic Answer

The question in the introductory chapter was, "How does the amoral infant become capable of morality?" The question recognizes that the young child does not know the difference between right and wrong, but as the child grows older he or she becomes a good person or a bad person. If we knew the process whereby the child becomes a moral or an immoral adult we would be in a better position to help those entrusted to our care become the kind of people who would live dependable lives and be of benefit to the society in which they live.

Psychologists approach the study of human development from different philosophical positions and come to the topic of morality (as to all topics) with different orientations. Yet, they all agree that the newborn is amoral not knowing the right hand from the left or having an understanding of virtue and vice, integrity and depravity. Psychologists who are interested in moral development also agree that it is important to know what factors are present in producing responsible citizens. The answers of psychologists to the question of how the amoral infant becomes capable of morality will differ, however, depending on their respective theoretical viewpoint. As we have seen, learning psychologists (behaviorists) hold to the belief that the child learns to be moral by being conditioned to act in moral ways and by imitating the behavior of appropriate models. Cognitive psychologists emphasize the intellectual or reasoning aspects of morality and see the child becoming moral as he or she advances in thinking processes from an egocentric being to a socially responsive person. Humanists say that the child is basically good and has a natural propensity for doing the right thing, and what is needed from others is encouragement and affirmation to be all that one can be.

Psychoanalysts give yet another answer. Those who follow Freud's teachings believe that the infant is helpless and depraved. Every child is born as an id, or an it, with irrational instincts and passions. In order for the child to become a better person an ego that relates to reality and a superego that relates to matters of right and wrong must be formed. The ego and the superego become part of the personality, working to help the child become a moral person. The role of the ego is to produce mechanisms of defense against the id so as to keep in check sexual and aggressive impulses that would destroy the person and the society in which one lives, and to keep the superego from bullying the person to the point of neuroticism. Later, the ego will use more conscious methods of control to keep the id and the superego in their proper places. The role of the superego is to hold before the person an ideal to strive for and a conscience that condemns when the ideal is not reached. By internalizing the superego, the child incorporates the standards of the society and as an adult passes them on to the next generation. Psychoanalysts would say, then, that *the amoral infant becomes capable of morality as he or she develops an ego that relates to the world of reality and a superego that relates to a world of good and evil. An optimal balance between ego and superego is essential for moral development, and achieving this balance is a constant struggle throughout one's life.* The ego provides flexibility and vision; the superego provides stability and purpose. Both are needed for moral maturity to be realized.

Although Freud believed that the final state of the person is preferable to the depraved condition of the newborn, he did not have good words for adults, either, as seen in a letter written in 1918 to a minister of religion. "I have found little that is 'good' about human beings on the whole. In my experience most of them are trash, no matter whether they publicly subscribe to this or that ethical doctrine or none at all. . . . If we are to talk of ethics, I subscribe to a high ideal from which most of the human beings I have come across depart most lamentably" (Freud, 1963, pp. 61-62). Even after a lifetime of conflict, the person still is not moral, according to Freud. The tension, inhibitions, and restraints have made the person more palatable to others, but he continues to be victim both of his own passions and of the restrictions placed upon him by the society.

The pessimism of Freudian psychoanalysis is great and is not shared by all psychoanalysts, yet the shadow side of the human race is a fact of life and should not be taken lightly by those who would understand the nature of the human condition. In psychoanalytic theory, people are born sinful and will remain sinful all their lives. Improvement is in the offing with the formation of the ego and the superego, but even so, humankind cannot be said ever to become moral in the full sense of the term.

So, the struggle continues—a struggle to be a better person and to live in a better world. It is a struggle that knows no end; yet, without that struggle, life would be empty and void of meaning. Humanity has no choice but to go on, doing the best that it can in the face of incredible odds.

Problems

One of the major criticisms of psychoanalysis is that it does not lend itself to scientific inquiry. Freud presented many of his ideas in such a way that they can neither be verified nor falsified, leaving the student who is committed to an experimental approach at a loss to know what to accept and what to reject. How can it be determined, for example, that the small boy has an incestuous desire for his mother if he has no awareness of this desire? How can any repressed desire be investigated, for that matter? Is it sufficient to take the word of the therapist, trained in psychoanalysis, that the Oedipus complex is indeed present and represents one of Freud's greatest insights? Unless a person already is oriented to psychoanalysis, the answer probably will be negative.

Another concept difficult to measure is that of reaction-formation. If a person's behavior sometimes is the same and sometimes is the opposite of what the person would like for it to be, how can it be known what the underlying motive really is? And, again, if different motives produce the same behavior, how can one know what motive is present? Is the person clean because the person wants to be clean, or is the person clean because of an unconscious wish to be dirty? Psychoanalysis is a closed system for it has a built-in method of explaining away any evidence that is contrary to it. As such, it is empirically unsound and methodologically weak. Data gained from therapy sessions add little, for therapy is clinical rather than systematic in nature, each case being unique, making the information obtained of questionable value when applied to people in general.

Take another example, this one closer to our search for an understanding of how morality develops. Suppose that the small child has acquired a strong superego by identifying with the parents and imitating their behaviors. But as the child grows older parents influence the child less and peers influence the child more, the ego-ideal and the conscience that make up the superego become less important while the ego that looks to the consequences of behavior in a real, external world takes on greater significance. Does this mean that the child is becoming more moral or less moral? How can we tell? Are there measuring instruments to aid us in our search for the answer? What criterion should we use in deciding what it is we want to measure? Shall we look at overt behavior to see if it lines up with agreed upon social norms? Shall we test for emotional stability and mental health? Shall we gauge the strength of the superego by listening to confessions and feelings of guilt? Do we need a longitudinal approach whereby the person is tested at different age periods to see what changes take place at different times in his life? Psychoanalytic theory does not provide us with the answers, nor is it stated in such a way that the answers are forthcoming.

This is not to imply that Freud's ideas have not generated considerable research, for indeed they have. The large number of doctoral dissertations and journal articles on Freudian concepts attest to this fact. Several volumes (Eysenck & Wilson, 1973; Fisher & Greenberg, 1977; Hook, 1959; Pumpian-Mindlin, 1952; Sarnoff, 1971; Sears, 1943) also have been published and represent the conclusions of both supporters and critics of Freudian thought as related to experimental investigation. The supporters say that psychoanalytic concepts can be tested scientifically and argue for "the fruitfulness of a marriage between psychoanalytic concepts and experimental research" (Sarnoff, 1971, p. ix). The critics say just the opposite. "There is not one study which one could point to with confidence and say: 'Here is definitive support of this or that Freudian notion' " (Eysenck & Wilson, 1973, p. 392). Most authors and editors make an effort to show that some of Freud's ideas can be supported by the research whereas other ideas cannot be supported. The topic of how psychoanalysis relates to science is sufficiently detailed and so filled with controversy that interested students will find more than enough material to keep them busy for some time.

Rather than arguing for "a marriage between psychoanalytic concepts and experimental research," some supporters defend psychoanalysis as being above the trappings of the so-called scientific method with its gathering of facts and use of numbers. They argue that the great insights given to a few great minds as to the nature of humankind and the world in which we live cannot be put into empirical molds and judged in accordance with how well they fit those molds. It is a travesty even to suggest that psychoanalytic theory can be cut into pieces and the pieces subjected to operational definitions designed by experimenters who understand numbers better than they understand genius. Erich Fromm (1980), a psychoanalyst, put it like this: "If one tries to study one aspect of the personality apart from the whole, one has to dissect the person—that is to say, destroy his wholeness. Then one can examine this or that isolated aspect but all the results one arrives at are necessarily false because they are gained from dead material, the dissected man" (pp. 13-14).

Be that as it may, most psychologists think of themselves as scientists and tend to take a jaundiced view of any theory that does not lend itself to objective scrutiny. Consequently, psychoanalysis does not have the level of support from academicians that many psychologies enjoy. This does not detract, however, from its acceptance by the person on the street, by clinicians trained in its methodology, or by other intelligent people in disciplines not oriented to scientific verification. Some people are surprised to know that psychoanalysis is not well received in many psychological circles because to their way of thinking Freud's theory must explain areas of human nature that otherwise could not be understood or the theory would not have received such notoriety.

A second criticism of psychoanalysis is that the affective nature of human beings is emphasized at the expense of other important characteristics of the personality. In Freudian psychoanalysis, emotion takes precedence over reason, passion over intellect, and the volitional nature of the person is given no significant role. Like the learning theory view that people have little to say about what they do or what they become (see chap. 2), Freud saw the person as the victim of oppressive forces, the product of a destiny beyond one's control. But unlike the learning view that sees the restrictive forces as only from without, the psychoanalyst views the pressures as coming from within the individual as well as from the social order. Irrational passions and instincts present at birth war against each other, making the person fearful and anxious. Later, the society bombards the person with its demands, thereby providing a double assault upon the organism. As the victim of two warring factions, one from within and the other from without, the person's only available response is one of strong emotion. Reason and free will have little to contribute in such a context. Conflict is basic to our very existence and constitutes our heritage as members of the human race.

Even so, the emphasis on emotion takes away from the dignity of people as thinking, autonomous beings. If reasoning is but a facade, self-determination an illusion, and morality a product of a dictatorial superego adopted early in life, there is little to commend the human race. Freud saw people as basically hedonistic, naturally aggressive, and seeking pleasure wherever it may be found. Nor do people show an interest in a life based on ethical principles. Whether infant or adult, there is little good to be said about the human condition. Health comes when the ego is in control for the ego contains an element of rationality, but for many people that desirable state never will be attained, and they are destined to live out their lives in frustration and defense.

In the area of moral development, especially, an emphasis on the affective without regard for the cognitive renders the person incapacitated. As guilt feelings emerge with the advent of the superego, provision must be made for intellectually dealing with those feelings, or one is left helpless and confused. Nor can people be held accountable for wrongdoing if they are subjected to forces beyond their rational control. For this reason, social learning psychologists and neo-Freudians have put more emphasis in recent years on the ego components of morality and less emphasis on the superego variables in an effort to resolve this problem.

Not only did Freud stress emotion at the expense of other components of the personality, but males were given precedence over females, children over adults, and sexual interests over other desires. Whether these emphases constitute a problem depends on one's perspective, but a number of writers, including some psychoanalysts, are critical of Freudianism with regard to these issues. Granted that males historically have been dominant, that childhood is the critical period for emotional development, and that people are sexual beings, this is not to say that females suffer from penis envy, that the personality cannot change after the age of six years, and that every wish and every object have sexual connotations. Yet Freud's writings would imply that this is so, so that an acceptance of Freud's ideas would relegate women to an inferior position, negate the efforts of educators and others who work with children after the age of six, and direct one's attention to the sexual aspect of all events and all relationships when other factors may have greater meaning. Erich Fromm (1980), a noted psychoanalyst, speaks to this last point as it relates to the Oedipus complex.

> Freud in his discovery of the Oedipal tie to the mother discovered one of the most significant phenomena, namely man's attachment to mother and his fear of losing her; he distorted this by explaining it as a sexual phenomenon and thus obscurred the importance of his discovery that the longing for mother is one of the deepest emotional desires rooted in the very existence of man. (p. 30)

Fromm explains that even the most intense sexual relationship will not last if it is without affection and that "to assume that men should be bound to their mothers because of the intensity of a sexual bond that had its origin twenty or thirty or fifty years earlier is nothing short of absurd considering that many are not bound to their wives after even three years of a sexually satisfactory marriage" (p. 29).

A third problem with Freudian psychoanalysis is that Freud attributed characteristics found in neurotic patients in a clinical setting to all people everywhere. There is reason to question the validity of a theory in which the abnormalities of a few are made normative to the population as a whole. Applying insights derived from disturbed people to the behavior of the rest of the population is dubious at best; at worst it is deceptive, presenting a picture that highlights the less desirable features of the human condition rather than giving a more accurate portrayal that includes both favorable and and unfavorable traits. Furthermore, Freud seldom studied children directly. Instead, he took many of his ideas of what children are like and the difficulties that they face by listening to adult neurotics tell of their childhood memories. One wonders how accurately these early experiences were recalled and the extent to which they can be applied to normal children. During therapy sessions Freud noted that patients often spoke of their relationships with family members and other acquaintances in such a way that the sexual component appeared to be dominant. From this Freud surmised that children go through a series of stages that are psychosexual in nature and that healthy personality development is dependent on the timing and sequence of each stage. Whether one accepts Freud's ideas of what children are like as insightful or rejects them as misconceived, the methodology by which Freud reached his conclusions leaves much to be desired.

The last problem to be mentioned is that any interpretation of Freudian thought, either by supporters or by critics, is subject to error for a variety of reasons. First, Freud's thinking changed on a number of issues over the course of his lifetime. What he wrote early in his career and what he wrote in his later years varies, so that the scholar must determine what should be taken at face value and what should be relegated to a lesser position by virtue of when it was written. Second, supporters accuse the critics of only a superficial understanding of what Freud meant by what he said, and they proceed at length to elaborate on what Freud *really* meant by this or that idea, leaving the inquirer to think that whereas the critic may err on the side of superficiality, the supporter errs on the side of reading too much into Freud's statements. Derek Wright (1971) may be right when he says that "any account that goes beyond a series of quotations from Freud's work is bound to be in some degree an individual interpretation" (p. 31). Third, Freud emphasized some ideas in an effort to counterbalance what he felt to be lacking in the understanding of people at the time. Had he lived in another era his writings might have fastened on other concerns. The importance of early childhood, the sexual nature of man's being, and the psychological basis of neurotic behavior were needed concepts to offset misunderstandings prevalent during the early twentieth century. For instance, in response to criticisms that he overemphasized the shadow side of human nature, Freud (1920/1949) wrote: "We dwell upon the evil in human beings with the greater emphasis only because others deny it, thereby making the mental life of mankind not indeed better, but incomprehensible" (p. 131). Freud thus saw his ideas as providing a balance to the misconceptions of the day.

If it appears that Freud wavered with regard to the consequences of moral development, at times stressing the ills of fear and repression and at other times condoning the social system as a necessity, it was because he saw it both ways. The need to live life freely and the need to submit to civilizing forces are both viable, even though having to accept both only adds to one's conflict. Yet conflict is necessary for moral development. Freud believed that without anxiety and fear and disequilibrium one cannot become a better person.

Whether the criticisms in this section indicate that Freud's contribution to an understanding of human nature and moral development is not as great as generally thought or whether it means that Freud's teachings need more careful study in order to be fully appreciated and understood is left to the judgment of the reader. The lack of scientific rigor, the emphasis on emotion apart from reason and volition, the stress on early childhood and on the sexual nature of man's being, the generalizing from the abnormal few to the normal many and from adults to children, and the difficulty of intepreting Freud's writings are more disturbing to some people than they are to others. But regardless of one's leanings, all would agree that Freudianism has had a noticeable impact on child-rearing procedures and on an understanding of the importance of the affective component of a person's life. It is to an application of psychoanalysis in the home, the school, and the church that we now turn.

Practical Applications

Prior to the time of Freud it was generally thought that young children were mindless creatures, more like animals than like humans, and that whatever happened to them before the age of six or seven years was of little consequence compared with what happened to them after this age. Children also were thought of as innocent beings having neither an interest in sex nor a propensity to engage in sex-related activities. The role of parents, therefore, was to take responsibility for the physical care of children to assure survival and to keep children in line so that they could learn to conform to an adult world. There was little reason to believe that what parents said and did related to the intellectual development of one so young or affected the emotional well-being of the child years later when maturity was reached (Aries, 1962).

Teachers received the child when it was assumed that the child was ready to learn. The teacher's role was defined as one in which the skills would be taught that the child needed to know in order to take his or her place in society. Learning was considered a cognitive endeavor, the affective component taking a back seat in an understanding of how knowledge is acquired. Consequently, the method used to teach, whether severe or gentle, was of little importance. Teachers were hired to teach, not to understand individual differences or to be concerned with the feelings of students.

It was in this milieu that the works of Sigmund Freud fell like a bomb. Freud's ideas were so explosive to educated and lay public alike that his writings were received both with fascination and rejection. Freud wrote that many of the problems seen in adults stemmed from experiences that occurred during the first few years of life. Time and again, Freud noted that his patients would recall events that took place in early childhood—events so traumatic they were affected by them all their lives. It became increasingly clear that children are not mindless, emotionless, sexless beings but are aware of what goes on around them and sense keenly the quality of interpersonal relationships. Freud (1913/1968) reiterated the saying, "The child is father to the man" (p. 183), meaning that the adult personality is determined by the experiences one has as a child.

This emphasis on the early years, as well as Freud's teachings on infant sexuality, the death instinct, the importance of the unconscious, and the role of psychic determinism, made for profound changes in the attitudes of people toward others. Parents began to see that they were responsible, not only for the physical care of the child, but also for the emotional health of their young. Teachers, as well, were told that learning would be enhanced if they became familiar with the defense mechanisms used by children. Repression, regression, and projection are utilized by students to compensate for conflicts within their personalities, and a recognition of this fact and an understanding of behaviors that accompany these mechanisms would aid the teacher in being more sympathetic with students and thus would increase learning in the classroom. As Freud's ideas became more widely accepted, the roles of parents, teachers, and others who work with youth came to have greater significance.

Application to the Home

Freud believed that each person goes through a series of stages that are psychosexual in nature, each stage corresponding to a particular chronological age and forming the basis for the stage that follows. The infant is at the *oral* stage, so named because the mouth serves as the erogenous zone with its functions of breathing, crying, and incorporating milk from the mother. The toddler is at the *anal* stage, an appropriate term considering that children universally are toilet trained at this age. The *phallic* stage is entered when children are approximately four years of age and constitutes the time when the Oedipus and Electra complexes occur, forcing the child to identify with the parent of the same sex in order to resolve the conflict brought on by an erotic desire for the parent of the opposite sex. The child enters *latency* about the time he or she starts school and remains at this stage during the elementary years. The term *latency* implies that sexual interests are latent or dormant, and the child is ready to settle down to learn more about a real world and to form close friendships with peers of the same age. Puberty ushers in the *genital* stage, a time when the genital area becomes the erogenous zone, and the young person enters another period of emotional turmoil in preparation for taking on an adult role.

The quality of care given to the child at each stage of development has a profound impact on social and moral development and will leave an indelible imprint on the adult personality. During the oral stage parents should recognize the dependency needs of the infant, willingly provide for these needs, and encourage the child's sense of trust. During the anal stage, parents need to be aware of the child's strivings for independence, appreciate these strivings as an indication of growing up, and provide an optimal balance between autonomy and control. During the phallic stage, parents can help the child come to terms with his or her own sexual identity as they exhibit sex-appropriate behaviors and model socially desirable male-female relationships in the home. Latency brings a respite from inner turmoil and is a time when social values and practices are conveyed by peers and teachers as well as by parents. During the genital stage the problems of the first three stages again appear, and parents may face the most difficult period of all in the rearing of the child as they work with the teenager to resolve anew the issues of dependence, independence, and identity.

The ego begins to form during the oral stage as soon as the infant is able to differentiate between self and nonself. The superego appears in rudimentary form during the anal stage when the child begins to understand that some behaviors are "good" and other behaviors are "bad." One actually can observe the process of introjection taking place when, for example, the toddler turns away from an object he or she has been told not to touch or when the two-year-old says, "I a good boy" because he sits quietly in church or picks up his toys or whatever else he knows to be acceptable behavior. The internalization of social and parental standards results in children being able to monitor their own behavior and to experience feelings of guilt when that behavior is not in conformity with expected demands. The ego and the superego both continue to develop throughout childhood and even into adulthood, but Freud believed that the most sensitive or critical period for their formation occurs before the age of five or six years.

It is to the social learning psychologist who has studied how the conscience develops that we owe much of our understanding of how psychoanalytic theory can be applied to the rearing of children. The investigations of Robert Sears (1960) and others within the social learning framework have shown that the superego or conscience is more apt to occur if parents are accepting of the normal dependency needs of the child, if they take the time to reason with the child regarding the consequences of behavior, and if they use love-oriented techniques of discipline. Let us look at each of these.

The dependency needs of the child take on many forms. Wanting to be near the parents, touching them, engaging them in conversation, insisting that they watch while the child engages in some type of performance, and fussing or crying until attention is received are all expressions of dependency well known to those who have children. Parents who are accepting of these needs, who are not unduly irritated or impatient when these needs are expressed, usually establish a close relationship with the child and thereby lay the foundation for the identification process in which the child incorporates within the self parental attitudes and expectations for behavior. Accepting parents tend to be warm and loving and are quite happy to have the child nearby, to talk with the child, to watch his antics, and to respond to his needs. This does not mean that the parents meet the dependency needs of the child at all times for this would by physically impossible and emotionally exhausting. Furthermore, one would be hard pressed to argue that it would be would be healthy for the child to receive such attention constantly. But it does mean that parents who enjoy being with their children and who accept them as children establish a bond that gives them more influence over the child than would be the case if they were cold and disinterested. By spending time with the child, parents can monitor the child's actions and convey their reactions to the child's behavior.

Reasoning with children regarding the consequences of behavior enables them to see cause-effect relationships between what they do and what happens as a result. Sometimes called consequence-oriented discipline, it involves talking with children about what they have done or plan to do and the effect of their behavior on others as well as on themselves. This technique is an effective means of getting children to feel a growing responsibility for the outcome of their actions and capitalizes on their capacity

for empathy. Saying "You will hurt his feelings if you say
that," "Don't run or you may drop it and it will break,"
"How would you feel if everyone in the family yelled 'shut
up' at you like you just did to your brother?" will help
children see that even as it matters to them what others
do, it matters to others what they do as well. The use of
reasoning enables children to think before they act, to
hold in check their impulses, and to take into consideration the rights of others.

Love-oriented techniques of discipline tend to make for
a strong superego whereas thing-oriented techniques of
discipline often result in inadequate conscience development. An explanation of terms is in order. Love-oriented
techniques involve the giving or withdrawing of either
physical or psychological manifestations of love. If the
child behaves in a way pleasing to the parent, reward may
come in the physical form of hugging the child or picking
the child up, or it may come in the psychological form of
letting the child know how proud you are of him, how
much he means to you, how glad you are to have him.
Parents who are warm and accepting of the child tend to
use the orientation of love to reward the child for behavior
deemed desirable. Children find this bond of warmth and
affection a most advantageous one and become quite unhappy whenever they feel they have done something to
cause a breach in this relationship. If they are disobedient
or act in some other unacceptable way, parents who use
love-oriented techniques temporarily withdraw their affection. The child is separated from the parent either physically or psychologically in such a way as to prevent the
child from getting the amount of attention and affection
to which he or she is accustomed. The parent expresses
disappointment with the child and conveys to the child
that the pleasant relationship they usually have cannot
continue under the circumstances. The child may be sent
to another room or the parent may "get tears in her eyes
and turn away" (Sears, 1960, p. 104), thus reducing or

eliminating for a time the conversation between them. This withdrawal of affection makes children miserable. They feel guilty and ashamed, and in an effort to get back into the good graces of the parent, they will be more willing than before to identify with the values, attitudes, and behaviors expected of them. Not wanting this gap to occur, they begin to resist the temptation of doing those things that are not acceptable. Love-oriented discipline arouses anxiety over losing the parent's love, and to reduce this anxiety the child learns to control unacceptable impulses. Withholding love intensifies the child's need for approval. This technique appears to work, however, only in homes where the parent is basically warm and loving and accepting of the child's dependency. Mothers and fathers who are cold, who normally do not give much love, cannot by lack of attention and affection produce a strong conscience in their children. Apparently one cannot withdraw what is not already there. And, like all forms of discipline, love-oriented techniques will lose effectiveness if used in excess.

Thing-oriented techniques of discipline involve the use of tangible rewards for desirable behavior and physical punishment or deprivation of privileges for undesirable behavior. If the child pleases the parents the reward comes in getting extra money or toys or permission to do something generally forbidden, such as staying up at night to watch the late show. If the child displeases the parents he or she is spanked or deprived in some way such as not getting an allowance or going to bed without supper.

All parents use some combination of love-oriented and thing-oriented techniques. To use one method or the other exclusively would be impossible. There probably are as many combinations of both kinds of discipline as there are homes in which children are being reared. Thus, the comparison is not between homes that are only love-oriented as opposed to homes that are only thing-oriented, but rather between homes in which the major controlling factor for keeping the child in line is the love relationship between parent and child as opposed to homes in which the major controlling factor is physical punishment, deprivation of privileges, and tangible rewards. Love-oriented parents will at times use thing-oriented techniques. They may spank or not let the child go out to play. They will find physical punishment effective *on occasion* and deprivation of privileges and tangible rewards productive of desirable results, but this will not be their usual method of discipline, and certainly not their preferred method. Children find it natural and easy to identify with love and will generally want to please the parent who is kind and warm. A child growing up in a thing-oriented household, however, will find identification with the parent a more difficult task. It is not natural to identify with someone who often brings pain and unhappiness or who, when pleased, gives money rather than time and favorable attention. Material objects cannot substitute for the companionship of parents.

The rationale for the effectiveness of love-oriented techniques as opposed to thing-oriented techniques includes such elements as the kind of model provided by the parent, the timing of the punishment, the emotion generated in the child, and the reaction of the child to the punishment. Love-oriented parents model socially desirable behaviors, whereas thing-oriented parents often display the very behaviors they find repugnant in the child. For example, love-oriented parents control their tempers and expect the child to do the same. Thing-oriented parents lash out when irritated and yell or hit, actions they do not wish to see in their children. The timing of the punishment also makes a difference. Love-oriented procedures take place over a longer time-span than do thing-oriented procedures. Love-withdrawal gives the child time to think about what he or she has done, to engage in a critical evaluation of oneself. A spanking, however, obviates the need for self-punitive thoughts, for the misdeed already has been paid for by suffering physical pain. Moreover, love-withdrawal is terminated when the child engages in the corrective act, such as confession, restitution, or reparation. Physical punishment, by contrast, is more likely to occur and terminate at the time of the deviant act and prior to any corrective act.

The emotion generated when the child in a love-oriented home has done something wrong is usually that of guilt, whereas the emotion generated in the child in a thing-oriented home is usually that of fear. Guilt brings the child to the parent to confess; fear sends the child the other direction to escape detection. Love-oriented procedures attempt to change the child's behavior by inducing internal forces toward compliance; thing-oriented procedures are more conducive to an orientation based on fear of punishment and less on changing the behavior from unacceptable to acceptable forms. Thing-oriented discipline also is an affront to the child's growing sense of autonomy and may leave the child frustrated and angry.

Observation, as well as research, tends to confirm that when parents accept the normal dependency needs of the child, reason with the child regarding the consequences of behavior, and use love-oriented techniques of discipline, the child is more apt to identify with the parents and with their values. Granted that these procedures are time-consuming and that they lose effectiveness as the child grows older, nevertheless, the development of internal controls must begin early, or they may never form at all. Having a strong conscience or superego is essential for a moral life and should not be left to develop by chance.

Sadly, some children never develop a superego. They relate only to what will bring pleasure (id) and to what they can get from a world of reality (ego). Not having the internal controls that monitor behavior when no one is present, they cannot be trusted. As adults, they continue to be opportunistic and unpredictable. They exhibit poor judgment and planning, project blame onto others when things go badly, and are unable to form deep and persistent attachments to other persons. If they display these characteristics in extreme form they are called psychopaths, sociopaths, or moral imbeciles. They are viewed as having a character disorder for they seem to lack anxiety or distress over their behavior and do not see why they are obligated to follow the rules of society. This attitude, coupled with the long-standing nature of the pathology (usually from early childhood), makes therapy virtually impossible. Interestingly, people with a character disorder often create a favorable first impression. They are intelligent, know how to glad-hand others, and have a salesman type personality. But they also are impulsive, feel no concern over the rights and privileges of others (although they act as if they do), and are masters at saying whatever is necessary to get others to satisfy their desires. We all know people like this for they are in every walk of life. In some cases it can be shown that as children they were neglected or mistreated, but in other cases no detectable reason can be found, leaving the possibility that constitutional factors may play a part in the pathology. If the problem is not environmentally based, it is most unfair to hold parents accountable for the child's lack of moral development, although since the advent of Freud, parents usually are the ones who are blamed if the child does not become an upstanding member of the community.

At the other end of the continuum are people who are so overcome by anxiety and feelings of guilt that they are unable to enjoy life. Rather than lacking a superego, as is the case with the sociopath, they seemingly have too much superego. They are miserable and afraid, and sometimes to alleviate their distress they will seek therapy.

> Trained to think rigidly about right and wrong, convinced of one's own imperfections and incompetence, fearful of failures or punishment, . . . these people are constantly plagued with guilt feelings. These guilt feelings come not

because of sorrow for sin or regret over law-breaking. They are signs that the person is preoccupied with a fear of punishment, isolation, or lowered self-esteem. To bolster oneself, such people often are rigid, critical of others, unforgiving, afraid of making moral decisions, domineering, and inclined to assert an attitude of moral superiority . . . they are angry, unhappy people who need help and understanding more than criticism. (Collins, 1980, p. 121)

For such individuals, the ego needs to be strengthened so that a healthy balance between a world of reality and a world of right and wrong will occur. The ego variables of intelligence, an adequate self-concept, and the ability to plan for the future play a role in moral decision-making, as do the superego variables of guilt, confession, and resistance to temptation. Parental standards should not be so high that the child can never succeed, nor should parents withhold love to the point where the child feels continuous blame.

There are times, of course, when guilt feelings are appropriate and even desirable. Guilt is healthy when it brings about a change in behavior from unacceptable to acceptable forms, but guilt is unhealthy when it renders the person anxious and afraid with no change in conduct taking place. Parents need to know when to praise and when to reprove, when to overlook and when to call attention to the child's actions. What parents do and say is crucial to the development of a conscience within the child. To become truly moral, the child's sense of well-being must be tied to the authority of the superego, an authority adopted as one's own from the restrictions and beliefs of the parents.

As we have seen, the psychoanalytic position is that morality develops within children as they internalize the expectations and normative demands of the culture as interpreted to them by the parents, and the critical time for this to occur is between the ages of two and six years.

Both ego and superego take shape at this early age, and both ego and superego must grow together, each in harmony with the other, if children are to someday take their place within the society as responsive and responsible adults.

Application to the School

Less is said in psychoanalytic literature about the influence of the school than about the influence of the home. This is understandable in the light of the fact that by the time the child enters school the most sensitive period for the formation of a superego has passed. Given this condition, it would seem there is little teachers can do to bring about the acquisition of internal controls within the child. The child already must have in place a superego that corresponds to the expectations of others, or the child will not be sufficiently motivated to learn. Furthermore, if the critical time for the development of a conscience is over before the child starts school, only the ego that continues to change as the child grows older could be affected by what takes place in the classroom. The ego is important in the development of morality, but an ego without the strictures of the superego will not produce a stable and mature disposition. An ego alone will result in opportunistic and selfish behavior rather than in trustworthy and altruistic conduct.

The question arises, then, whether educators should try to influence the child in matters of right and wrong as these relate to the adoption of self-accepted standards. Does it do any good for teachers to endeavor to get children to take responsibility for their own actions if they have not already learned to do so? The answer varies with one's interpretation of Freudian thought. Psychoanalysts concede, however, that although the conscience is formed during the early years, it may be strengthened or weakened by later experience. Obviously it does make a difference what teachers say and do, and the environment of the classroom does aid or hinder the moral development of children. We know that children will identify with the teacher, even as they do with the parent, adopting the ideas of the teacher and carefully observing both verbal and nonverbal behaviors. Parents are aware that if the one who instructs the child shares their attitudes and beliefs, it will help to confirm in the mind of the child what has already been taught in the home. Conversely, if the teacher has a value system contrary to their own, it may serve to impair their influence on the child. Freud wrote in the foreword of a book on delinquency that the purpose of education is "to guide the child on his way to maturity, to encourage him, and to protect him from taking the wrong path" (Aichhorn, 1925/1963, p. v). Teachers are expected to guide, to encourage, and to protect the student to keep the student from going in the wrong direction.

One of the first writers to address the issue of how a knowledge of psychoanalysis is beneficial to the educator was Freud's daughter, Anna, who applied her father's ideas both to the rearing of children in the home and to the teaching of children in school. Although Anna Freud does not deal specifically with the manifestations of the ego and the superego in school-age children, she does maintain that psychoanalysis does three things for "pedagogy":

> In the first place, it is well qualified to offer a criticism of existing educational methods. In the second place, the teacher's knowledge of human beings is extended, and his understanding of the complicated relations between the child and the educator is sharpened by psychoanalysis, which gives us a scientific theory of the instincts, of the unconscious and of the libido. Finally, as a method of practical treatment, in the analysis of children, it endeavors to repair the injuries which are inflicted upon the child during the process of education. (A. Freud, 1935, p. 106)

Anna Freud's criticism of education is that there is too much "decorum and convention" in the schools. Pressure is put upon children to conform, and when they do conform it is considered an educational success. But the price children pay may be too high. "These educational successes are too dearly bought. They are paid for by the failures with those children who are not fortunate enough to reveal symptoms of suffering" (A. Freud, 1935, p. 109). Anna Freud believed that educators should show more interest in the child who is suffering and less interest in what society considers to be proper. Meeting the emotional needs of students takes precedence over getting students to act in conventional ways.

With regard to the second point that a knowledge of psychoanalysis will help teachers understand the student and their relationship to the student, Anna Freud's opinion was that teachers need to understand themselves first, and then they are in a better position to understand the student and the nature of the relationship between them. She held that being psychoanalyzed is a necessary prerequisite to understanding oneself, and therefore she recommended that the educator go through psychoanalysis before beginning a teaching career.

She tells the story of a young woman who had an unhappy childhood and left home to become the governess of three boys, the second of whom was not as favored as the other two in either appearance or ability. This young woman gave the second child extra attention and tutoring until he was able to do as well as his brothers and was accepted and appreciated by his parents as were the others. Then a strange thing happened. The feeling of love she had for this child turned to hate, and although she was greatly desired by the family, the animosity between herself and the boy became so great she was forced to leave. It was not until she had undergone psychoanalysis some fifteen years later that she discovered the reason for what had occurred. Being an unloved child herself she unconsciously had identified with the boy and had given him the love and attention she felt she should have had as a child. When he became successful and won the favor of his parents she no longer could identify with him but rather became jealous and hostile. Had she been aware at the time of why she felt as she did she could have dealt with her emotions in a rational way thereby alleviating the strain that came between them.

Other writers who apply psychoanalysis to the school also stress Anna Freud's second point of the relationship between teacher and student. Few teachers though have either the money or the time to be psychoanalyzed, so less is said about psychoanalysis as a form of self-understanding for teachers, and more is said about psychoanalysis as knowledge to be applied to an interpretation of students' behavior in the classroom. By knowing how the id, the ego, and the superego combine to effect actions and attitudes, the teacher can appreciate the use of defense mechanisms in the child. The teacher needs to be aware that there is an underlying reason for the student's fantasies, that slips of the tongue and witty comments have psychic meaning, that instinctive forces play a part in one's emotions, that each person is a sexual being interested in exploring his or her own body and in finding his or her role as male or female. Although teachers are not trained as analysts or therapists, they should know how to bring about a positive transference between themselves and the students and how to encourage students to adopt a value system that will satisfy all three components of the personality—the id, the ego, and the superego. Children with deep-seated problems need to be encouraged to communicate their feelings and thus be aided in bringing into consciousness unconscious fears and anxieties so that these emotions can be dealt with in a rational, issue-oriented way.

The third way, according to Anna Freud, that psychoanalysis may be applied to pedagogy is in the area of repairing the damage done to the child during the process of being educated. Teachers today are concerned not only with problems the child may have incurred while going to school but also with problems that stem from the home and that subsequently affect performance in the class-room. School phobia and test anxiety are two such problems.

School phobia (not to be confused with truancy, espe-cially when observed in younger pupils at the elementary grade level), is not so much a fear of what may happen at school as it is a fear that something terrible will happen to mother when the child is not with her. The psychoan-alytic explanation (Kelly, 1973) is that the school phobic child has an overprotective mother who has not resolved her own need for dependency and consequently looks to her child to meet this need. She may say that she wants her child to go to school and she believes that this is so, but unconsciously she wants the child to stay with her. This is the mother who takes great pleasure in doing things for her child, distrusts the ability of anyone else to care for the child, feels uncomfortable whenever the child is out of her sight, and is quick to accept the child's com-plaint of not feeling well as an excuse to keep the child home. The result is a symbiotic relationship that feeds on itself, making the mother increasingly solicitous and the child increasingly dependent. The problem may not be evident until a specific incident such as the mother's not being home when the child returns from school or a rob-bery occurring in the neighborhood or the child's becom-ing ill at school, triggers the phobic reaction within the child. From then on, the thought of going to school makes the child sick, and recovery occurs only when it becomes obvious that he or she has won another day of reprieve. School phobic children are not faking, they are truly ill. Obviously they need help, but if therapy is to be successful it must include the parents, and especially the mother.

Without getting to the source of the difficulty, little will be accomplished.

Test anxiety is another problem some children face. The way the term is used in the literature, text anxiety refers not so much to the uneasy feeling all of us have experienced at one time or another in a testing situation, but rather to the crippling fear some people sustain whenever they are called upon to take a test. In the test-anxious person, the magnitude of the response is out of all proportion to what would be expected in that situation. Test-anxious students may become so frightened that they are unable to answer even the simplest questions or so perturbed at the thought of taking a test that they are incapacitated. They complain of feeling nauseous and are too sick to remain in the classroom. The solution is not to stop giving tests in school, for tests have always been used to evaluate the performance of students. Rather, it is imperative that children learn to live with tests and to overcome this handicap so they can function in a normal way.

A psychoanalytic interpretation of text anxiety has been given by Sarason, Davidson, Lighthall, Waite, and Ruebush in a book entitled *Anxiety in Elementary School Children: A Report of Research*. These scholars, all from Yale University at the time the book was written, wrote that test anxiety stems from a conflict between the unconscious internal world of the child and the conscious external reality that the child faces. Internally, test-anxious children feel hostility toward their parents for demanding more of them than they feel they can deliver. Externally, they have a high positive regard for their parents and want to please them. The test is a tangible reminder that they cannot meet parental expectations, thus signaling the conflict within, a conflict between hate and love, between anger and wanting to make parents happy. These children feel guilty, and in order to keep their feelings of hostility at the unconscious level, they derogate their own worth and lessen the turmoil within themselves by becoming too ill to take the test. This withdrawal from emotional involvement and retreat from situations that are psychologically threatening allow them to cope in the only way they know how. As Sarason and the others put it, "The most obvious manner in which our thinking has been influenced by psychoanalysis will be seen in our conception of the anxious response as a conscious danger signal associated not only with an external danger but also with unconscious contents and motivations the conscious elaboration of which is inhibited or defended against because such elaboration would place the individual in an even more dangerous relation to the external world" (Sarason et al., 1960, p. 6).

Children with test anxiety can be helped if they have an understanding teacher. The Yale scholars suggest that the teacher take a low-key approach to testing situations so as not to be perceived by these children as being like their parents. The teacher should convey the message that a test is a natural event, not a momentous occasion that marks one for life or portrays one's worth in the world. The less said about tests, the better. The atmosphere of the class and of the school should be sufficiently relaxed that the anxiety felt by these children while in a testing situation will not generalize to other situations. The problem only becomes worse if children become anxious about their role in playing games at recess time or if they begin to dislike their classmates who do well on tests. The teacher should give test-anxious children a lot of external support, thus easing their fears that they are not doing what is expected of them. Test anxiety may be overcome, but only when the conflict within the child is lessened by an understanding adult.

The well-known psychoanalyst, Bruno Bettelheim (1970), links the desire to study and to learn in school with superego development. In a lecture at Harvard University, Bettelheim said that children from lower-class homes often do poorly academically because they have not learned to postpone gratification, a superego characteristic. What brings pleasure at the moment (id) and what seems to work best for them in the world of reality (ego) takes precedence over the conviction that learning in school is a good thing to do and will be of benefit at some future time. Studying is not nearly as exciting for these children as many other things they could be doing, so unless they have within themselves a conscience that says that doing their best in school is right and not doing their best in school is wrong, they will not be sufficiently motivated to learn. "Fortunately for education as it now exists, most middle-class children still enter school with a very strong superego and . . . with the ability to postpone pleasure over long stretches of time well established . . . but . . . their number is constantly declining" (p. 96).

Bettelheim saw the reason for the decline in motivation among middle-class children as being due in large measure to the emphasis today on material possessions rather than on teaching the child to act in ways that would guarantee eternal salvation. "The image of the affluent society plays havoc with the puritanical virtues." Furthermore, parents believe they must assure the child of their love regardless of the child's behavior. Taken together, the stress on money and what money can buy, plus the promise of unconditional love, provide the reason for why today's child does not have a strong conscience. If the child has all that is needed now, and if the child has nothing to fear from either God or the parents, then from the child's perspective there is no reason to engage in the difficult task of studying as a way of gaining respect or of being assured of a better life to come. Bettelheim believes that middle-class children today are too comfortable and fear nothing. "My contention is that for education to proceed children must have learned to fear something before they come to school. If it is not the once crippling fear of damnation and the woodshed, then in our more enlightened days it is at least the fear of losing parental love (or later, by proxy, the teacher's) and eventually the fear of losing self-respect" (Bettelheim, 1970, pp. 97-98).

Bruno Bettelheim's explanation of why children are not motivated to learn may seem a bit harsh, even as Anna Freud's application of psychoanalysis to an understanding of the child may seem too permissive. Nevertheless, we must admit that children who are desirous of doing well in school and who consistently try to do their best often have strong internal controls that make them feel guilty when their homework is not done or when they are late for school or when they do something that displeases the teacher. Unless there is guilt and a sense of apprehension stemming from a religious conviction that one has not pleased God or from the feeling that the bond of love with the parent has been broken and will not be mended until confession is made and behavior changed, it may well be that the motivation to learn and to do well in school is impaired.

Joseph and Joseph (1977) have applied Bettelheim's ideas to children with learning and behavioral deficits. Using the case-study approach, they tell of Larry who could not learn because he was interested only in immediate pleasure, of Paul who also was an academic failure and had been involved in incidents of vandalism and smoking marijuana, of Kathy who was a clever shoplifter and was often truant, and of Bob who was so undisciplined and disruptive that the teacher was relieved when he did not come to school. By describing each child and his or her background, the authors gave a clear picture of what the child was like. Suggestions were given as to how each child could be helped in the context of the school and how psychoanalysis explained the difficulties each child faced. Larry needed help in developing an ego so he could feel better about himself and could learn to postpone gratification; Paul should receive positive attention whenever he did his work at school so that he would be less apt to seek attention in socially unacceptable ways; Kathy "needs the teacher to function as a superego for her" (p. 118) help-ing her sort out what is right and what is wrong; and Bob, who seldom got enough to eat, could be worked with by meeting his basic id needs for survival so that he, like Larry, might begin to develop an ego. By using case stud-ies, Joseph and Joseph (1977) showed how psychoanalysis may be applied to the school both as a theory to account for behaviors and as a form of therapy to enable teachers to assist those children with moral and motivational problems.

Application to the Church

Sigmund Freud likened the church to the army, both being highly organized groups protected from dissolution by the strength of the leader, the camaraderie of the mem-bers, and the threat of a foe. In both the church and the army the leader is charged with the welfare of the mem-bers, offering protection from forces that would war against the group, and providing direction for the organization as a whole. In the church the leader is Christ; in the army it is the commander-in-chief. "Each individual is bound by libidinal ties on the one hand to the leader (Christ, the Commander-in-Chief) and on the other hand to the other members of the group." (Freud, 1923/1970b, p. 444). The stronger the emotional ties of members to the leader and to each other, the stronger the group's chances for sur-vival. The loss of the leader constitutes one of the gravest dangers any organization may face. Freud gave as examples a general being killed in battle and the soldiers fleeing, and Christ being portrayed as less than divine ("Joseph of Arimathaea confesses that for reasons of piety he secretly removed the body of Christ from its grave") and therefore unfit to be the head of the church (p. 446). The loss of the leader creates panic because the relationship of members to each other is based on the relationship of each member to the leader. "There is no doubt that the tie which unites each individual with Christ is also the cause of the tie which unites them with one another" (p. 443).

Although the group offers both protection and companionship it also subjects its members to a common ideology and to a set pattern of behavior. Individuality is not encouraged, nor can it be condoned. Freud saw both the church and the army as authoritarian, each pressuring its members to conform to a standard of conduct determined by the leader. Members cannot have their own ideas of right and wrong and act upon them as this would weaken the structure, bringing diversity and making the organization less effective in fighting a common enemy. Nor are members free to leave the group at will. If they do try to leave, they will be scorned and ridiculed and cast in the role of the adversary, for nothing is more threatening to a group than for its own members to defect. "A religion, even if it calls itself the religion of love, must be hard and unloving to those who do not belong to it." (Freud, 1923/1970b, p. 445). Religious groups that are tolerant were seen by Freud not as showing "a softening of human manners," but as indicating "the undeniable weakening of religious feelings and the libidinal ties which depend upon them" (p. 447).

Freud by his own confession was not a believer in Christ. Consequently, he viewed the church differently than do those of us who are a part of that great company of believers called the Christian church. Freud saw religious worship as a compulsive act engaged in to relieve one's feelings of guilt. To him, God was nothing more than a glorified father complex stemming from childhood. Furthermore, he believed that science one day would replace religion, for as people come to know more about the world and are better able to control the forces of nature they no longer will be terrified of the elements and seek a deity to provide protection from the unknown. Such a view, of course, is incompatible with the Christian faith. Those of us who are followers of Christ believe that religious worship is a chosen act not a compulsive act. We confess our *guilt* to God not our *feelings* of guilt. God is the great I AM, the One who always was and is and always will be. We did not create him through the wish for a father figure, but he created us in his own image. Nor can we know him except as he chooses to reveal himself to us. Moreover, science never will take the place of faith for only God can control the forces of nature, and we would know nothing about the world and the forces within it apart from an intellect which he has given us.

Freud's likening the church to the army provides an interesting analogy, however, for we read in Scripture that Christians are to be like soldiers ready for battle. We are to put on the full armor of God: the belt of truth, the breastplate of righteousness, the shield of faith, the helmet of salvation, and "the sword of the Spirit, which is the word of God" (Eph. 6:17). And for what purpose? "So that you can take your stand against the devil's schemes" (v. 11). A good soldier is willing to endure hardship, wants to please his commanding officer, and will not allow himself to be distracted by civilian affairs (2 Tm. 2:3,4). We are told to be good soldiers of Jesus Christ.

We also are told to honor those who are placed in a leadership role over us. These lesser leaders when compared to Christ bear his name, are chosen for their qualities, and are ordained by God to care for the local church (1 Tm. 3:1-10). They serve in many ways—as preachers and teachers, as models of good behavior, and as holding "the deep truths of the faith with a clear conscience" (v. 9). They are deserving of respect for they have chosen "a noble task" (v. 1).

The work of the minister today is much the same as it was in the time of the apostle Paul. The one who leads the congregation is to preach the Word, visit the sick, and encourage the faithful in the things of the Lord. Ministers are to help those who are troubled, strengthen those who are weak, and bring aid to those in need. Yet ministers today often are assigned another task, namely that of counselor or therapist. In many churches they are expected to function in the role of a psychologist in addition to all the other duties of the clergy. It is thought that "the man of God" should advise on all matters, not just those pertaining to the religious. But what is not so readily understood is that it takes training to operate in this capacity. One must be educated to recognize the difference between anxiety and conviction, depression and guilt, abreaction and conversion, sickness and sin. If ministers consider all problems brought to them as being spiritual in nature and are unable to sort out the psychic ramifications of a parishioner's disturbance, they may advise in ways that will aggravate the condition, causing irrefutable harm. On the other hand, if they see only the psychological manifestations of the turmoil but do not recognize the spiritual needs of the parishioner, they may prostitute their calling as ministers of the gospel by glossing over sin and by saying little about the redemption provided for the one who has sinned.

The pastor or church leader who takes on the role of therapist should be prepared to handle any situation that may arise. This includes knowing what to do if the church member "falls in love" during therapy sessions. Even as it is not uncommon for a client to develop strong feelings of love or hate for the therapist, it is not uncommon for the parishioner to develop strong feelings of love or hate for the minister. Psychoanalysts are trained in such matters. They consider the transference between themselves and the patient a normal phase of the therapeutic process and are prepared to resolve any conflicts that may arise before sessions are terminated. But the clergy is not trained in this way, and some ministers have become so traumatized by a parishioner's feelings of intense love that they have behaved indiscreetly or have refused to see the person again. In some cases scandal has ensued, and the minister has had to leave the church.

The desire on the part of the clergy to know more about the field of psychology in an effort to help those within the church who are suffering from emotional stress is to be commended. Other things being equal, the pastor who is knowledgeable in psychotherapy will be in a better position to counsel those who have emotional needs than the pastor without this knowledge. Nevertheless, the Christian minister should remember that the principal calling of the clergy is to faithfully preach the Word of God, not to perform the duties of a psychotherapist. Karl Menninger (1973), has made a case for the preaching of repentance as being more therapeutic than the practice of counseling. He says this is so because preaching reaches a larger number of people and also serves to inhibit the kind of life that contributes to mental illness. As he puts it in *Whatever Became of Sin?:*

> Some clergymen prefer pastoral counseling of individuals to the pulpit function. But the latter is a greater opportunity to both heal *and prevent.* An ounce of prevention is worth a pound of cure, indeed, and there is much prevention to be done for large numbers of people who hunger and thirst after direction toward righteousness. Clergymen have a golden opportunity to prevent some of the accumulated misapprehensions, guilt, aggressive action, and other roots of later mental suffering and mental disease.
>
> How? Preach! Tell it like it is. Say it from the pulpit. Cry it from the housetops.
>
> What shall we cry?
>
> Cry comfort, cry repentance, cry hope. Because recognition of our part in the world transgression is the only remaining hope. (p. 228)

For those within the church, Karl Menninger's comments surely are valid. But what about those who are not members of the church and do not feel at home within the church? What if they hear the preaching of the gospel, feel convicted, and confess their sins, but no one in the church befriends them and the pastor never follows up to see if they are growing in the Lord? What if there are no hands to sustain, no hearts to love, no prayers to uphold them before the throne of grace? Will they be able to change their ways and live Christian lives because they have heard the minister preach? Will the feelings of guilt and the overt expressions of confession be enough to make them new persons, moral persons before God?

For some the answer may be in the affirmative, but for others it is not. Psychologist Joseph Hunt (1938) gives an account of several young men for whom more than preaching was needed. He writes of talking with an adult patient on the psychiatric ward of St. Elizabeth's Hospital in Washington, D.C., who informed him that five of his neighborhood gang of fifteen were confined to that institution. When hospital records confirmed this high percentage, Hunt became interested. He asked the informant, identified as Ww, to tell as much as he could remember about each of the boys. Ww described the neighborhood as poor, alcoholism was common, and the boys received little or no parental guidance. By the time most of the gang were in their teens they were introduced to homosexuality by the laborers at a slaughterhouse and to bestiality by the men who kept the barns where race horses were wintered. The boys often visited these places and regularly engaged in the perversions. In the same community was a church where frequent revival services were held. Some of this group attended the services and experienced intense feelings of guilt over their perversions. Ww mentioned that one evening he went forward four times, crying each time, and was informed that once each evening was sufficient. After these times of guilt and confession, the boys who went forward would tell each other that they were not going to return to the perversions. But when sexual tensions mounted and they were teased by other members of the gang who did not attend the revival services, they would break their resolves and return to their former behavior. Ww reported that by the time they were in late adolescence, they were almost continuously miserable. They quit school, did odd jobs, and drank heavily. There was seemingly no way to escape the conflict between the sexual perversions and the religious values. The guilt not only did not deter them from immoral behavior but also served to intensify their unhappiness. Hunt noted that of the seven who frequented both the slaughterhouse and the church, five were committed to the hospital. Those who indulged in the perversions but did not attend the revival services and those who went to the revival services but did not frequent the slaughterhouse or barns were not hospitalized.

In the case of these young men, the church had preached the consequences of sin and the need to confess, but this message had not sustained them in the hour of temptation. As boys growing up they needed to be with Christians, to see how Christians live, to be befriended by the young people of the church who had values different than their own. But this did not take place, and, although they repented of their sins, they did not have the power to follow through on their resolves. In *psychoanalytic* terms, Ww and the others who went to the revival services fluctuated between a superego that condemned and an id that demanded gratification. At no time was the ego, that component of the personality that makes rational decisions and carries them through, operating on their behalf. In *theological* terms, these young men had strong feelings of guilt, but the guilt did not bring them to salvation. They experienced a "worldly sorrow" rather than a "godly sorrow" and so were unable to change their behavior (2 Cor. 7:10).

Theology and the Psychoanalytic Approach

Freudian psychology and Christian theology both begin with the premise that the condition of the human race is

one of depravity. Each person comes into the world im-
perfect and in need of salvation. Freud saw the newborn
as having irrational passions and instincts and being oriented to pleasure, but as children grow older they learn to
adjust to the world, adopting the mores and restrictions
of the society, and in this way they become better persons.
Older children are easier to live with because they have
learned to consider the wants and needs of others as well
as their own, and their behavior is in line with what will
benefit the social order. Freud believed, though, that un-
derneath the surface of propriety the depraved portion of
the personality remains, and throughout one's life it waits
like a volcano ready to erupt whenever the opportunity is
given. Anxiety is one's lot when sexual and aggressive
urges are denied expression, and punishment becomes
one's lot when these urges are released in socially unacceptable ways, so that whether people repress their desires
or allow them demonstration they are anxious and fearful.
Violence and war occur when the molten lava of instinctive desires finds a crack in the surface of the unconscious
and breaks through to gratification spewing out hatred
and vengeance and destroying everything in its path. Freud
recognized that it is not only the will to transgress that
gets us into trouble but also the failure of the will to control the universal impulse to transgress.

The concept of sin in Christian theology resembles the
psychoanalytic view of irrational passions and instincts
insofar as sin is wanting one's way and caring for self more
than for others. But the Christian understanding of sin
goes beyond the psychoanalytic understanding of depravity. Sin is alienation from God as well as alienation from
others. Sin is missing God's standard of perfection as well
as failing to meet society's expectation of good conduct.
The Christian knows that the purpose of life is more than
coping with a real world, for one can gain the whole world
and lose his own soul (Mt. 16:26). The purpose of life is
to have a meaningful relationship with the Creator and

Redeemer, and this is possible only by salvation in Christ Jesus. Nevertheless, the sinful portion of the personality remains even though we want to please God. "If we claim to be without sin, we deceive ourselves and the truth is not in us" (1 Jn. 1:8). The inclination to transgress the law of God persists so that we must depend on him who is "faithful and just and will forgive us our sins" (v. 9).

The psychoanalytic concept of depravity and the Christian doctrine of sin is offensive to those who adopt the philosophy of learning psychology that people start out neither good nor bad but become whatever they are made to be by the environment. It also is offensive to those who adhere to the philosophy of humanistic psychology that people are naturally good and have within themselves the ability to become self-actualized. To both the behaviorist and the humanist it is an affront to the influence of the society (as in the case of the learning theorist) or to the dignity and worth of humankind (as in the case of the humanist) to say that the environment cannot make people what they should be or that people cannot make themselves what they should be. If this is true, what hope is there, then, for the human race? Is it not pessimistic and even morose to see people in need of alteration when neither the world around them nor the world within them can bring about the needed changes?

Freud's response would be that even though people start out with little to commend them to others, a combination of social mandates and their own adjustment to these mandates enables them to become better persons. It is not one but both forces at work—a force without and a force within. The society demands compliance, and the person demands satisfaction of individual needs. Together they struggle while the ego makes compromises between them. At first the compromises take the form of defense mechanisms, but later as the person matures the ego will shed its defenses and will find ways to cope that are more rational and less apt to produce neurotic consequences. In this way, even though children are born depraved, they become more goodly persons. But the balance between id, ego, and superego remains a delicate one. If the scales are tipped too far in the direction of the id, the result is sociopathy; if the scales are tipped too far in the direction of the superego, the result is neuroses. In Freudian psychology the ego must remain strong, keeping both id and superego in their proper places. And because the balance is delicate and because the ego often falters in its mission or may never be strong in the first place, Freud did not hold much hope for the human race. The charge that psychoanalysis is pessimistic is probably warranted.

The Christian message, in contradistinction, is one of hope and promise. We learn from the Bible that an all-powerful, all-loving God has chosen to free us from the bondage of sin. We cannot save ourselves, for we have neither the ability nor the inclination to do so, so that without him we can do nothing (Jn. 15:5). Nor can the society save us for it, too, is evil (1 Jn. 5:19). A Force greater than ourselves and greater than the social order has brought us salvation. Only in Christ can deliverance be found.

Both analytic therapy and Christian conversion would redeem from evil, and both would help the anxious person enter into a state of well-being. But the procedures differ, evil is not defined in the same way, and what constitutes well-being also is at variance. Psychoanalysis brings unconscious processes into consciousness where they can be dealt with by the ego. Christian conversion brings both the unconscious and the conscious into the light of God's Word where they can be dealt with by an omniscient God. Psychoanalysis uses the method of free-association; Christian conversion uses the method of confession. One deals with guilt feelings, the other with guilt. One provides a release from emotional tension enabling the person to come to terms with himself and with the society; the other provides a release from the power of sin enabling the person to come to terms with a holy and righteous God.

One brings a cathartic release, the other brings atonement. One puts the ego in charge; the other puts Christ in charge.

This does not mean that a person may not benefit from psychoanalytic therapy, but it does mean that the limitations of psychoanalysis should be recognized, and one should not confuse its methods or results with Christian salvation. Psychoanalysis saves people from the evil of neuroses; Christianity saves people from the evil of enmity against God. Well-being in psychoanalysis is a state of normalcy in which id, ego, and superego are all in the right relationship to each other. Well-being in Christianity is more than a regrouping of forces already present within the personality. It is being made a new creation in Christ Jesus (2 Cor. 5:17). "God is not satisfied with 'the given' in man. He demands something new and creates the new. The creative spiritual aptitudes which are released are not a given quantum of energy doled out to everyone and reserved in the subconscious. There are inexhaustible resources in the love of the living God, and his encounter with man is not a matter of bringing antithetical drives into harmony, but the recreating of a new life" (Runestam, 1958, p. 123).

In psychoanalysis the person comes to know the self better, and through the process of transference with the analyst is aided in the search for better mental health. In Christian conversion the person also comes to know the self better, and through the process of transference with Christ comes to see the self as God would see it and is aided in the quest for spiritual well-being. Both mental health and spiritual health are preceded by anguish of the soul. Conflict occurs when people see what they are really like in comparison with what they should be and would like to be. It is conflict that brings one to the psychoanalytic couch, and it is conflict that brings one to Christ. But in psychoanalysis the conflict is between the natural desires one is heir to and the cultural restrictions needed to assure the survival of the society. In Christian theology

the conflict is between the old nature that is sinful and
the new nature that is righteous. Both neuroses and sin
produce inner turmoil, and both neuroses and sin render
the person an unfinished product crying out for comple-
tion. But in psychoanalytic therapy the benefits extend
only to this life, whereas in the redemption that is in
Christ Jesus the benefits extend throughout eternity. An
important ingredient of the Christian hope is knowing
that our salvation will last forever (1 Cor. 15:19).

Freudian psychoanalysis condemns more than it for-
gives; it restricts more than it liberates. Catholic theologian, Albert Ple (1976), speaks to this point. "Morality
according to Freud appears . . . to be a morality of law,
composed of prohibitions, restraints of the instincts, and
source of obsessive guilt. . . . The morality of the Gospel
. . . requires that one should be animated by love . . . that
liberates from sin" (p. 103). Psychoanalyst Erich Fromm
(1980) puts it succinctly when he says, "Freud's therapeutic aim was control of instinctual drives through the
strengthening of the ego . . . *there is no place for grace*"
[italics added] (p. 7).

Without grace, where would we be? Without grace the
apostle Paul could not have said after his moral and spiritual struggle recorded in Rom. 7:7-25, "There is now no
condemnation for those who are in Christ Jesus, because
through Christ Jesus the law of the Spirit of life set me
free from the law of sin and death (Rom. 8:1-2). The Christian message is one of forgiveness, of life, and of liberty.
And most assuredly, the Christian message is one of grace.
"For it is by grace you have been saved, through faith—
and this not from yourselves, it is the gift of God" (Eph.
2:8).

In comparing psychoanalysis with Christian doctrine,
one is inclined initially to equate the id with the baser
desires of the flesh, the ego with the will or mind of man,
and the superego with the nobler virtues of the spirit. But
the analogies do not hold. There are commonalities, to be

sure—the id being self-serving and impulsive, the ego making decisions and coping with the challenges of the day, and the superego feeling guilt and the need to confess—but there are differences as well. Within the id is love as well as hate, self-preservation and procreation of the species (which are not condemned in Scripture) as well as selfishness and aggression. And, some of the desires of the flesh could be better relegated to the ego than to the id. Clinical psychologist Paul Meehl (1958) speaks to this point:

> Some pastoral counselors, overeager to make the Freudian lion lie down with the Christian lamb, have made an incautious identification of the two. . . . An example would be Freud's concept of the id and the Christian concept of original sin. . . . Now insofar as the imperious demand for impulse gratification is a property of the id, the id is like "the flesh" in New Testament language . . . but a complete identification of the concepts can certainly not be defended. For one thing . . . avarice, pride, and envy are works of the flesh, theologically speaking. From the Freudian point of view none of these could possibly be found in the id. Pride, for example, is a manifestation of the "ego's narcissism" in Freud's system and is therefore relegated to . . . the ego, which is contrasted with the id. (p. 168)

By the same token, the Freudian ego cannot be equated with "the will of man" (Jn. 1:13 KJV) as given in Scripture. Both ego and will involve decision-making, but in analytic theory a strong ego that weighs the demands of the id and the restrictions of the superego and makes a decision as to the best course of action is the mark of the psychologically healthy person, whereas in Christian theology a strong will is not the mark of a person committed to Christ. Rather, the spiritually healthy person knows that people are not capable on their own of making the right decisions and that they must turn to God for direction (Jas. 1:5). Although there need be no quarrel with the

Freudian concept of the ego when taken on the human level, the ego being recognized as important by psychoanalysts who are Christians as well as by psychoanalysts who are not Christians; nevertheless, the ego will not bring one into the Kingdom. The ego is restricted to the social order, whereas the will or volition given to people by God taps the very Source of Wisdom that is from above.

Likewise, the superego is not the same as the fruits of the Spirit nor should the superego be confused with the conscience of the Bible. The superego is heir of the Oedipus complex and remains a part of the personality throughout life, yet it becomes less important as the person matures and the ego is substituted in its place. The conscience, however, is not a product of human development but is given by God as a natural property and becomes more sensitive as the person matures in the Christian life (Acts 24:16). The believer does not outgrow the need for a conscience but rather uses it as a basis for decision-making.

> According to the NT man has in the depths of his personality a moral monitor which sin has affected but not destroyed, placing him in touch with the objective moral order of the universe. That order is translated into human awareness by means of the conscience. That it does not arise from the cultural mores can be seen when men press for moral reforms that directly challenge the existing social patterns. (Pinnock, 1973, p. 127)

Another way of comparing the superego with the conscience is to see the effect each has on the personality. Gregory Zilboorg (1962), a student of Freud and a psychoanalyst, writes:

> The origin of the superego lies in the child's ambivalence and fear. And conscience is not made up of fear, but of regret for having done something wrong. The superego

is by its nature unforgiving; it is the epitome of aggression and hatred. The superego cannot be quieted; it can only be pacified. . . . Conscience *regrets*, where the superego is *angry*. Conscience glows with hope when its owner repents and makes amends. (p. 187)

William May (1975) compared the superego and the conscience by describing the superego as "past-oriented: primarily concerned with cleaning up the record with regard to past acts" and the conscience as "future oriented: creative; sees the past as having a future." The superego "commands that an act be performed for approval, in order to make oneself lovable"; the conscience "invites to action, to love." The superego has the "urge to be punished"; the conscience "sees the need to repair" (pp. 56-57).

The superego, then, is blind, dictatorial, internalized during the first few years of the child's life, and yet essential for the continuance of a civilized world. But once internalized it produces anxiety and feelings of guilt that in some people become chronic. The superego is sensitive to the social order but insensitive to the psychological health of the person. Needed is what the apostle Paul calls "a pure heart, a good conscience, and a sincere faith" (1 Tm. 1:5). A good conscience combined with a heart that is pure and a faith that is sincere makes for good relationships with others (Rom. 14:1-23) and contributes to both psychological and spiritual well-being.

Sigmund Freud dealt with the great issues of all time, issues of life and death, of good and evil, and of the human struggle to satisfy personal desires while living in a world replete with restrictions and taboos. Conflict is inevitable, and although essential for social and moral development, nevertheless brings misery and neuroses. Conflict begins in the cradle and continues to the grave when life is no more. The Christian also knows conflict and struggles with the issues of life and death, good and evil, self and others. But the Christian has the Spirit of God within that

enables one to emerge victorious. We learn that it is only
as we lose our life for Christ's sake that we will find it
(Mk. 8:35), that the battle is not against flesh and blood
but against the spiritual forces of evil (Eph. 6:12), and that
life does not end with the grave but lasts forever (Jn. 3:15).
And so we count it as joy when the conflict comes, knowing that the "present sufferings are not worth comparing
with the glory that will be revealed" (Rom. 8:18). The
whole creation waits in eager anticipation for the time
when it will be liberated and brought into "the glorious
freedom of the children of God" (v. 21).

Notes

1. The role of the ego in moral development is being given increased attention by psychoanalysts as well as by social learning psychologists. Ego psychologists stress moral understanding and the
changes that occur during middle and late childhood, believing that
ego variables play as great a part in determining the moral behavior
and attitudes of adults as does the formation of the superego during
the early years. For a closer look at ego morality in psychoanalysis,
see S. Lorand (1972), Historical aspects and changing trends in therapy, *The Psychoanalytic Review*, 59, 497-525; and E. M. Pattison (1968),
Ego morality: An emerging psychotherapeutic concept, *The Psychoanalytic Review*, 55, 187-222.

2. The following true account was related to the author by a medical missionary from Nigeria and illustrates the damaging consequences of an inflexible superego. In the fall of 1966, soldiers were
coming in and slaughtering the Biafran people. Another missionary
working in Kano, Nigeria, was asked by a soldier if a certain man was
an Ibo. Feeling that he could not tell a lie, the missionary responded
in such a way that the man was killed by the soldier. The next morning when several of the missionaries got together to discuss the incident, some said that the missionary had done the right thing because,
after all, the murdered man was only a native, not one of their fellow
Christians.

3. Freud believed that male homosexuality occurs when the Oedipus complex continues until after puberty, at which time "mother
as object" becomes "mother as subject," and the teenager begins looking for a new object to love. Because he still identifies with mother

rather than with father, the object of his affection will be male rather than female. Freud (1937/1957) put it this way: "The genesis of male homosexuality in a large class of cases is as follows. A young man has been unusually long and intensely fixated upon his mother in the sense of the Oedipus complex. But at last, after the end of his puberty, the time comes for exchanging his mother for some other sexual object. Things take a sudden turn: the young man does not abandon his mother, but identifies himself with her; he transforms himself into her, and now looks about for objects which can replace his ego for him, and on which he can bestow such love and care as he experienced from his mother" (p. 186). In J. Rickman (1957), (Ed.), *A general selection from the works of Sigmund Freud,* Garden City, New York: Doubleday.

4. Scholars disagree as to the number and designation of Freud's defense mechanisms. For an in-depth discussion on this topic, see Sjöbäck, M. (1973), *The Psychoanalytic theory of defensive processes,* New York: John Wiley & Sons.

5. *The Diagnostic and statistical manual of mental disorders* (3rd ed—better known as DSM-III), (1980), Washington, DC: American Psychiatric Association, states that though Freud used the term *psychoneurosis* "both *descriptively* (to indicate a painful symptom in an individual with intact reality testing) and to indicate the *etiological process* (unconscious conflict arousing anxiety and leading to the maladaptive use of defensive mechanisms that result in symptom formation)" (p. 9), there is no consensus at the present time as to how neurosis should be defined. To avoid ambiguity, the Task Force on Nomenclature and Statistics of the American Psychiatric Association decided that "the term *neurotic disorder* should be used only descriptively" whereas "the term *neurotic process* . . . should be used when the clinician wishes to indicate the concept of a specific etiological process" (p. 9). The latter includes the use of defense mechanisms.

6. The sociopath is described as having a "personality disorder characterized by disregard for social obligations, lack of feeling for others, and impetuous violence or callous unconcern. There is a gross disparity between behaviour and the prevailing social norms. Behaviour is not readily modifiable by experience, including punishment. People with this personality are often affectively cold and may be abnormally aggressive or irresponsible. Their tolerance to frustration is low; they blame others or offer plausible rationalizations for the behaviour which brings them into conflict with society." DSM-III (1980), Washington, DC: American Psychiatric Association, (pp. 428-29).

7. This is not to imply that every psychoanalyst accepts all of

Freud's ideas or conducts the therapy session in precisely the same way as Freud. Neo-analysts, or neo-Freudians as they are sometimes called, however, do hold to many of the basic teachings of Freud, and therapy sessions are conducted in a way that is commensurate with those teachings. Among the more prominent psychoanalysts are Erik Erikson, Carl Jung, Alfred Adler, Karen Horney, Erich Fromm, and Bruno Bettelheim.

8. For information on the extent to which psychoanalytic therapy is used in the United States, see L. deMause (1979), New developments in applied psychoanalysis, *Journal of Psychohistory, 7*, 163-73.

References

Aichhorn, A. (1963). *Wayward youth.* New York: Viking. (Originally published, 1925)

Aries, P. (1962). *Centuries of childhood: A social history of family life.* (R. Baldick, Trans.). New York: Alfred A. Knopf.

Avstreih, A. K., & Brown, J. J. (1979). Some aspects of movement and art therapy as related to the analytic situation. *The Psychoanalytic Review, 66,* 49-68.

Bettelheim, B. (1970). Moral education. In N. F. Sizer, & T. R. Sizer (Eds.), *Moral education: Five lectures* (pp. 84-107). Cambridge, MA: Harvard University Press.

Collins, G. R. (1980). *Christian counseling: A comprehensive guide.* Waco, TX: Word Books.

Eysenck, H. J., & Wilson, G. D. (1973). *The experimental study of Freudian theories.* London: Methuen & Co.

Fisher, S., & Greenberg, R. P. (1977). *The scientific credibility of Freud's theories and therapy.* New York: Basic Books.

Freud, A. (1935). *Psychoanalysis for teachers and parents* (B. Low, Trans.). New York: Emerson Books.

Freud, S. (1949). *A general introduction to psychoanalysis* (J. Riviere, Trans.). New York: Perma Giants. (Originally published, 1920)

————. (1952). *Totem and taboo* (J. Strachey, Trans.). New York: W. W. Norton. (Originally published, 1913)

————. (1957). Group psychology and the analysis of the ego. In J. Rickman (Ed.), *A general selection from the works of Sigmund Freud* (pp. 169-209). Garden City, NY: Doubleday (Originally published, 1937)

————. (1961). *Civilization and its discontents* (J. Strachey, Ed. and Trans.). New York: W. W. Norton. (Originally published, 1930)

_____. (1963). The letters of Sigmund Freud to Oskar Pfister. In H. Meng & E. L. Freud (Eds.), *Psychoanalysis and faith: The letters of Sigmund Freud and Oskar Pfister*. (E. Mosbacher, Trans.). New York: Basic Books.

_____. (1968). The claims of psycho-analysis to scientific interest. In J. Strachey (Ed. and Trans.), *The standard edition of the complete psychological works of Sigmund Freud* (Vol. 13, pp. 163-90). London: Hogarth. (Original work published 1913)

_____. (1970a). The technique of psychoanalysis. In V. Comerchero (Ed.), *Values in conflict* (pp. 429-38). New York: Appleton-Century-Crofts. (Formerly published in *An outline of psychoanalysis*, 1949, New York: W. W. Norton.)

_____. (1970b). Two artificial groups: The church and the army. In V. Comerchero (Ed.), *Values in conflict* (pp. 442-47). New York: Appleton-Century-Crofts. (Originally published, 1923)

Fromm, E. (1980). *Greatness and limitations of Freud's thought*. New York: Harper & Row.

Hook, S. (1959). *Psychoanalysis, scientific method, and philosophy*. New York: New York University Press.

Hunt, J. McV. (1938). An instance of the social origin of conflict resulting in psychoses. *American Journal of Orthopsychiatry, 8*, 158-64.

Joseph, D. A., & Joseph P. B. (1977). Teaching children with deficient value systems. In L. J. Stiles, & B. D. Johnson (Eds.), *Morality examined: Guidelines for teachers* (pp. 105-19). Princeton, NJ: Princeton Book.

Kelly, E. W., Jr. (1973). School phobia: A review of theory and treatment. *Psychology in the Schools, 10*, 33-42.

Lee, R. S. (1948). *Freud and Christianity*. London: James Clarke & Co.

Lorand, S. (1972). Historical aspects and changing trends in psychoanalytic therapy. *The Psychoanalytic Review, 59*, 497-525.

May, W. E. (1975). *Becoming human: An invitation to Christian ethics*. Dayton, OH: Pflaum.

Meehl, P. E. (1958). *What, then, is man? A symposium of theology, psychology, and psychiatry*. St. Louis: Concordia.

Menninger, K. (1973). *Whatever became of sin?* New York: Hawthorn Books.

Messer, S. B., & Winokur, M. (1980). Some limits to the integration of psychoanalytic and behavior therapy. *American Psychologist, 35*, 818-27.

Pattison, E. M. (1968). Ego morality: An emerging psychotherapeutic concept. *The Psychoanalytic Review, 55*, 187-222.

Pearson, G. H. J. (1954). *Psychoanalysis and the education of the child.* New York: W. W. Norton.

Pinnock, C. H. (1973). Conscience. In C. F. H. Henry (Ed.), *Baker's dictionary of Christian ethics* (pp. 126-27). Grand Rapids: Baker.

Ple, A. (1976). Christian morality and Freudian morality. In B. B. Wolman (Ed.), *Psychoanalysis and Catholicism* (pp. 97-109). New York: Gardner.

Pumpian-Mindlin, E. (1952). *Psychoanalysis as science.* Stanford, CA: Stanford University Press.

Runestam, A. (1958). *Psychoanalysis and Christianity* (O. Winfield, Trans.). Rock Island, IL: Augustana.

Sarason, S. B., Davidson, K. S., Lighthall, F. F., Waite, R. R., & Ruebush, B. K. (1960). *Anxiety in elementary school children: A report of research.* New York: John Wiley & Sons.

Sarnoff, I. (1971). *Testing Freudian concepts: An experimental approach.* New York: Springer.

Sears, R. (1943). *Survey of objective studies in psychoanalytic concepts.* New York: Social Science Research Council.

————. (1960). The growth of conscience. In I. Iscoe, & H. W. Stevenson (Eds.), *Personality development in children* (pp. 92-111). Austin: University of Texas Press.

Sjöbäck, M. (1973). *The psychoanalytic theory of defensive processes.* New York: John Wiley & Sons.

Tice, T. N. (1980). A psychoanalytic perspective. In M. Windmiller, N. Lambert, & E. Turiel (Eds.), *Moral development and socialization* (pp. 161-99). Boston: Allyn & Bacon.

Wright, D. (1971). *The psychology of moral behavior.* Harmondworth, Middlesex, England: Penguin Books.

Zilboorg, G. (1962). *Psychoanalysis and religion.* New York: Farrar, Straus, and Cudahy.

6

A Theological Approach
Morality as Godliness

For the Lord watches over the way of the righteous,
but the way of the wicked will perish. (Ps. 1:6)

Morality or goodness is inseparably linked in the Scriptures with God. We read in Mark's Gospel that one came running to Jesus and asked him, "Good teacher, what must I do to inherit eternal life?" Jesus' response was, "Why do you call me good? No one is good—except God alone" (10:17-18). Did the young man asking the question recognize who Jesus truly is or was he using the adjective "good" as many people do today?

Goodness, then, means godliness, and godliness means perfection. No one is perfect but God, for only God is holy. Holiness is so inherently a quality of God as to belong to the definition of deity. Holiness refers both to the majesty of God and to his perfection. It is the majesty of what God is in himself that is awesome and hard for our finite minds to grasp. It is the perfection of God that relates to all that is moral and sets a standard of purity unequaled by any philosophical or psychological system. It is God's holiness that commands our worship as we,

299

like Isaiah, become painfully aware of our need for cleansing (Is. 6:5). Both the majesty of God and the perfection of God must be included in a definition of holiness. J. I. Packer (1981) writes:

> "Holy" is the word which the Bible uses to express all that is distinctive and transcendent in the revealed nature and character of the Creator, all that brings home to us the infinite distance and difference that there is between him and ourselves. Holiness in this sense means, quite comprehensively, the "God-ness" of God, everything about him which sets him apart from man. (p. 171)

The word "holy" is used not only of deity, but of those who are chosen by God. We read that God speaking through Moses told the children of Israel, "Consecrate yourselves and be holy, because I am the Lord your God" (Lv. 20:7). As a part of Christ's church today, we are called "a holy temple in the Lord" (Eph. 2:21). We have this status because "he chose us in him before the creation of the world to be holy and blameless in his sight" (1:4). Holiness is ascribed—never earned, never deserved.

For people in a fallen, sinful state to be thus elevated requires an act performed by an all-loving and all-powerful God. The epitomy of morality can be accomplished only by the redemptive work of Jesus Christ. We do not have within ourselves the propensity or the ability to be holy. Such is possible only as "his divine power has given us everything we need for life and godliness" (2 Pt. 1:3).

Basic Assumptions

The child is born with the potential for both evil and good. The potential for evil is a natural consequence of being a member of the human race corrupted in Adam's fall. The potential for good is also a result of being human as man is the only species made in the image of God (Gn. 1:26). Although marred by sin, the image may be seen in numerous acts of kindness and selflessness. It becomes clearer as the saving work of the "second Adam," Jesus Christ, enables the believer to utilize the divine power to live a life characterized as truly good, or godly. We are assured that some day the image will again be clear, reflected in perfect form, for "we shall be like him: for we shall see him as he is" (1 Jn. 3:2).

> The Bible clearly affirms the grandeur as well as the misery of man. He has been made a little lower than the angels and has been given dominion over the animals (Ps. 8:5-8κJν). He is created in the image of God and endowed with freedom for service and fellowship. . . . We must not close our eyes to man's original goodness, but we must also acknowledge that his whole being is now marred by a deeprooted perversity. Every part of his being is now corrupted by an insatiable desire for a place in the sun. . . . But herein lies his hope: God in his holy love will not let go of the prodigal son. . . . God can come to him, and God has done so in Jesus Christ. (Bloesch, 1978, pp. 88-90)

Whether children turn toward evil or good will depend on a number of factors all interrelated in ways we do not fully comprehend: their temperament at birth, the way they are punished and rewarded, the example of parents, relationships with peers, experiences at school, and the religious orientation of others they come in contact with. All these play a part. Add to this the fact that no two children will react in exactly the same way to the same set of circumstances, and that one child will be affected by some events, another child by others. Often the credit or the blame is given to the parents without taking account of all the other forces at work, leaving the parents with undue pride or crippling guilt. Sometimes the school may be said to make all the difference, the church blamed for being doctrinally sound or deficient, or the friends and associates of the child commended or faulted. Those who praise or denounce the home, the school, the church, or peers should be aware that they, too, are part of the society that affects the child. Their attitudes become a portion of the total social milieu in which the child develops and to which the child reacts. Impose upon all this the theological truths of determinism and free will and the possible ramifications of these doctrines, and the answer to the question of why one child is drawn to God while another turns away becomes an even greater mystery, a part of the human puzzle with no definitive answer. As David Meyer (1978) puts it: "Just as divine sovereignty and human responsibility are warp and woof in the fabric of Christian doctrine, so also a simultaneous awareness of environmental control and of personal control are warp and woof to a personal existence" (p. 270). And Robinson (1962) writes:

> For Christian faith, predestination . . . proclaims the freeness of God's saving grace in Christ, without making of His will an arbitrary fatalism. The ways of Him who predestines are past our tracing out, and the mystery thereof bids us worship where we cannot fathom. . . . Indeed, the thought of God who personally wills, decides, and acts is close to the heart of the Gospel. It rings in the finite verbs in the Creed. It shines in the great passives by which John Wesley describes the strange warming of his own heart. It is a genuine part of the study of the *kerygma*, which is blessing the Church today. (pp. 49, 51)

Morality as godliness is the only complete definition of morality. As was mentioned, morality cannot be separated from goodness, and goodness cannot be separated from God. Jesus told the young man who came running to him that only God is good and that more than an obedience to Old Testament commandments is required of the one who will live forever with God (Mk. 10:17-21). A God who is

good demands goodness of his followers, and this includes
sharing with those who are in need and a willingness to
become a disciple of Jesus Christ.

Morality as godliness also is a complete expression of
what it means to be moral in that it includes within its
scope all four psychological expressions of the moral state:
moral behavior, moral reasoning, moral potential, and
moral conflict. No other definition of morality is so broad
or so encompassing. We will look in turn at each of these
psychological expressions of morality in the context of the
Word of God.

Moral Behavior as a Function of Godliness

The Scriptures place great stress on the behavior of those
who belong to God, and what one does is an indication of
one's relationship to the Lord. Israel, as a covenant nation,
was constantly reminded of this, and worshipers presenting themselves at the gate of the temple would hear the
question:

> Lord, who may dwell in your sanctuary?
> Who may live on your holy hill?

And the answer:

> He whose walk is blameless
>   and who does what is righteous
> who speaks the truth from his heart . . .
> who does his neighbor no wrong . . .
> who despises a vile man
>   but honors those who fear the Lord. (Ps. 15:1-4)

Time and again, God told the Israelites that if they would
follow his commandments, he would do great things for
them. But if they disobeyed, destruction would be their
lot. These words of promise and warning were followed

by the admonition, "Be holy because I, the Lord your God, am Holy" (Lv. 19:2). Often the Israelites turned from God and followed the customs of their heathen neighbors, and sometimes before the promised destruction occurred they would continue the ritual of worship, thinking that this was all that was necessary to please God. Then God through his prophets would remind them that he had no delight in either them or their sacrifices. Unless their personal lives reflected the obedience that comes from an understanding of who God is in all his holiness, they were not to come to the house of the Lord (Is. 1:13-17). Roland Murphy (1978) stresses this thought:

> It was characteristic of them [the prophets] that they would not tolerate a divorce between liturgy and morality, between sacrifice and obedience. They had harsh words for sacrifices, and even for the ark (Jer. 3:16) and the Temple itself (Jer. 7:4), when these were mistakenly interpreted as divine guarantees of national well-being. The honesty and integrity of worship dominates the prophetic approach. There can be no possibility of trading in divine favour; worship must be ethically responsible. (p. 32)

God was concerned with both personal morality and social responsibility. Speaking through the prophet Amos, the Lord chided the people for such affluent behaviors as lounging on couches, dining on choice lambs, drinking by the bowlful, and using the finest lotions (Am. 6:4-6). He also condemned them for sexual immorality, "Father and son use the same girl and so profane my holy name" (2:7). But the main thrust of the message of Amos was the lack of concern for those less fortunate:

> You trample on the poor
> and force him to give you grain . . .
> You oppress the righteous and take bribes
> and you deprive the poor of justice in the courts.
> (5:11-12)

Because of this God tells them:

> I hate, I despise your religious feasts;
> I cannot stand your assemblies.
> Even though you bring me burnt offerings and grain offerings,
> I will not accept them. (vv. 21-22)

Then the people were asked to change their ways and were admonished to "seek good, not evil" (v. 14) and to "let justice roll on like a river, righteousness like a never-failing stream!" (v. 24) It is who God is in himself that demands moral action. For the child of God, moral behavior is inseparably related to godliness—to the "holiness" of a "Sovereign Lord" (4:2)

> The Old Testament prophets called for ordinary justice on a common human scale. They wanted poor people to get their rights. Yet they had a still larger vision for them than mere justice. True justice is fulfilled, they believed, in righteousness. Justice and righteousness come in tandem. . . . Justice exists where people's rights are respected. Righteousness exists where people care for their neighbors and befriend them, concerned not merely that they get their due, but that their deepest personal needs are satisfied. (Smedes, 1983, pp. 29-30)

Moral behavior as a function of godliness is stressed in the New Testament as well. Throughout the Gospels and the Epistles there is a continuous reiteration of the link between what one does and who one is in relationship to God. Jesus told his disciples in the Sermon on the Mount: "You are like salt for all mankind. . . . Do not swear. . . . Do not take revenge. . . . Love your enemies (Mt. 5:13-14, 33-34, 39, 44 TEV). Why were the disciples to do these things? Jesus gave the answer: "You must be perfect—just as your Father in heaven is perfect" (v. 48 TEV). "The Sermon on the Mount shows that additional dimensions must be added to moral behavior. Keeping the 'letter' of the law is not enough, nor is 'external' conformity to law sufficient. The inward motivation must be as right as the external deed" (Ramm, 1971, pp. 42-43).

The apostle Paul made it clear that one is saved by faith and not by works, but he exhorted his fellow believers to a careful accounting of their behavior. He tells the "faithful brothers in Christ at Colosse" (Col. 1:2) that whatever they do "in word or deed, do it all in the name of the Lord Jesus" (3:17). Timothy is instructed to "do the work of an evangelist" (2 Tm. 4:5), and "to all in Rome who are loved by God and called to be saints" (Rom. 1:7), Paul wrote, "There will be trouble and distress for every human being who does evil . . . but glory, honor and peace for everyone who does good. . . . For it is not those who hear the law who are righteous in God's sight, but it is those who obey the law who will be declared righteous" (2:9-10, 13). James, writing to the "brothers," asked for such personal virtues as patience, stability, thankfulness to God for his gifts, humility, and a dependence on God's will (Jas. 1). This request is coupled with the social mandate of visiting the fatherless and the widows and converting sinners from the error of their ways.

Personal morality and social morality (what John Stott, 1975, calls "micro-ethics" and "macro-ethics" in *Balanced Christianity*) are thus seen to be integrated in the Scriptures. An emphasis on one to the exclusion of the other does not do justice to the holiness of God. Some Christians show far more concern with personal habits that reflect right behavior than they do with the evils of racism, poverty, pollution, and child abuse. They seem to be caught in their own little world and reflect the narcissism of many who do not profess to know Christ. Other believers become so involved in social issues such as abortion, war, welfare programs, politics, or penal reform that they ignore God's commands for sexual purity, control of temper, and a life of prayer.

Both aspects of moral behavior are important. When the young man who wondered what he could do to inherit eternal life told Jesus that he had kept the commandments: do not murder, do not commit adultery, do not steal, do not give false testimony, do not defraud, honor your father and mother; Jesus recognized that the social aspect of moral behavior had been neglected in his life and said, "One thing you lack. Go, sell everything you have and give to the poor" (Mk. 10:19-20, 21). However, when Judas objected to Mary's act of pouring expensive perfume on Jesus' feet and said that the perfume could have been sold and the money given to the poor, Jesus responded that Mary's act of worship was of greater significance. "You will always have the poor among you, but you will not always have me" (Jn. 12:8).

The apostle Matthew records a time when Jesus and his disciples were together on the Mount of Olives, and Jesus was asked what would happen at the end of the age. He answered:

> When the Son of man comes in his glory, and all the angels with him, he will sit on his throne in heavenly glory. All the nations will be gathered before him, and he will separate the people one from another as a shepherd separates the sheep from the goats. He will put the sheep on his right and the goats on his left.
>
> Then the King will say to those on his right, "Come, you who are blessed by my Father; take your inheritance, the kindgom prepared for you since the creation of the world. For I was hungry and you gave me something to eat, I was thirsty and you gave me something to drink, I was a stranger and you invited me in, I needed clothes and you clothed me, I was sick and you looked after me, I was in prison and you came to visit me."
>
> Then the righteous will answer him, "Lord, when did we see you hungry and feed you, or thirsty and give you something to drink? When did we see you a stranger and

invite you in, or needing clothes and clothe you? When did
we see you sick or in prison and go to visit you?"

The King will reply, "I tell you the truth, whatever you
did for one of the least of these brothers of mine, you did
for me." (Mt. 25:31-40)

> It is interesting to note that the separation of the "sheep"
> and the "goats" depends on numerous small acts of kind-
> ness—the social aspects or "macroethics" of Christian
> behavior. Those chosen by the King are those who are
> sensitive to the needs of others and act to relieve human
> suffering. Being a part of God's family means morality not
> only in our personal lives but also in our everyday dealings
> with others. Moral behavior, both personal and public, is
> a function of our relationship to a holy God.

Moral Reasoning as a Function of Godliness

"The Supreme Reason makes human reason possible.
Christian theology therefore connects the human faculty
of reason not merely with our sense experience of the
outer world, or with our subjective knowledge of an inner
psychological world. Rather, it correlates man's reason
also and above all else with the Divine intelligence. The
Logos of God has endowed man with the logical forms of
the mind" (Henry, 1982, p. 383). God is the great I AM
and did not originate in our thinking. As such he is over
and above the intellectual processes that are characteristic
of the human race. To be godly means to be like God in
cognition, to know what he knows, to think as he thinks.
But the Scriptures make it plain that there is a wide gap
between the Creator and the creation.

> For my thoughts are not your thoughts,
>   neither are your ways my ways. . . .
> As the heavens are higher than the earth,
>   so are my ways higher than your ways
>   and my thoughts than your thoughts. (Is. 55:8-9)

The image of God consists of knowledge and rationality as well as of righteousness and holiness. But in its present muted form the image as borne by man is unclear, for the thought processes are blunted, the senses dulled, the understanding limited. As Rigali (1978) puts it: "To the extent . . . that human nature is wounded by sin, the human person is subject to a sin-generated darkness of intellect—that is not simply a natural absence of perfect knowledge, but a darkness participating in absurdity—which impedes self-understanding and an understanding of the norm of self-fulfillment" (p. 18).

Carter and Narramore (1979) write:

> The assumption that humanity is fallen leads to a cautious attitude about all methodologies and "facts" since we realize that human reason is less than perfect. It influences our view of psychopathology since it carries with it a concept of both personal and corporate sin and consequently of both personal and corporate responsibility. It leads to certain assumptions about the resolution of guilt feelings. And it limits our acceptance of the optimistic predictions of some humanistic thinkers. (p. 108)

One might despair at such a state. If sin has interfered with thinking abilities; if the mind has been "darkened" by disobedience; if the way that "seems right to a man . . . leads to death" (Pr. 14:12), it would appear that one could not even begin to approach godliness through the avenue of the intellect. But the Scriptures tell us that even though sin has interfered with the image, it has not eradicated it. People remain in the image of God and are asked by God to use their minds—to reason, to think, to judge. "Come now, let us reason together" (Is. 1:18) was the invitation given to Israel. "Incline thine ear unto wisdom, and apply thine heart to understanding" (Pr. 2:2 KJV) is the advice given to youth. We read that Moses chose capable men, and "they served as judges for the people at all times"

(Ex. 18:26). God expects us to use our intellect. Without rationality there can be no fellowship with God. Without a knowledge of him there would be no theology, no understanding of those things that pertain to godliness. Without a mind we would not differ from the rest of God's creatures that know neither good nor evil. Gordon Clark (1973) put it succinctly when he said: "Reason makes possible both sin and fellowship with God. Sin has caused a malfunctioning of man's mind, but redemption will renew men in knowledge, righteousness, and holiness" (p. 313).

After David died and Solomon had been crowned king, the Lord appeared to Solomon in a dream and asked him to state the one thing that he wanted the most (1 Kg. 3:5). Solomon's response was given in humility. He said that he was God's servant, that he was as a little child in understanding compared to the magnitude of the task of ruling a large nation. He asked that God give him discernment so he could govern fairly, so he could distinguish between right and wrong. God was pleased with Solomon's answer and said: "Since you have asked for this and not for long life or wealth for yourself, nor have asked for the death of your enemies but for discernment in administering justice, I will do what you have asked. I will give you a wise and discerning heart" (vv. 11-12). The fulfillment of the promise came in large measure.

> God gave Solomon wisdom and very great insight, and a breadth of understanding as measureless as the sand on the seashore. ... He spoke three thousand proverbs and his songs numbered a thousand and five. He described plant life, from the cedar of Lebanon to the hyssop that grows out of walls. He also taught about animals and birds, reptiles and fish. (1 Kg. 4:29-33)

It is the creation by God, a creation that Solomon understood in a way that no one else did, that gave human beings their intellect and set them apart from other forms of life. Only people are able to name animals, study plants, write proverbs, and compose songs. God made us as rational beings, and this rationality is to be used not only to obtain information about nature but to guide us in determining the way to truth. The Scriptures are replete with verses that link knowledge with practice, wisdom with conduct. David asked God for understanding, "and I will keep your law and obey it with all my heart" (Ps. 119:34), and Solomon advised the young men to turn their ears to wisdom and apply their hearts to understanding. "Then you will understand what is right and just and fair—every good path" (Pr. 2:9). Jesus told the disciples after he had washed their feet and explained the spiritual significance of this ordinance that if they understood the things he was telling them, they would be blessed if they would do them (Jn. 13:17). Paul told the Philippians that what they had "learned or received or heard," they were to put into practice (Phil. 4:9); and James wrote that "the wisdom that comes from heaven is . . . peace loving, considerate, submissive, full of mercy and good fruit, impartial and sincere" (Jas. 3:17). John Stott (1972) in *Your Mind Matters* says it this way:

> Knowledge is indispensable to Christian life and service. If we do not use the mind which God has given us, we condemn ourselves to spiritual superficiality and cut ourselves off from many of the riches of God's grace. At the same time, knowledge is given us to be used, to lead us to a higher worship, greater faith, deeper holiness, better service. What we need is not less knowledge but more knowledge, so long as we act upon it. (p. 60)

The link between knowing and doing finds its greatest expression in the life of Jesus. The mind of God was revealed not only in the natural world of creation but in the spiritual world of revelation through Jesus Christ. Jesus came to do his Father's will, and this will was the fulfillment of a plan in the mind of God to regenerate mankind, to bring people again into fellowship with God. Both the revelation in nature and the revelation in Christ speak to our minds. Without intelligence neither would be known. Without the Bible to explain to us the significance of the Creator, without whom the creation would not be, and the attributes of the Redeemer, without whom there would be no salvation, we would be like those who are "without hope and without God" (Eph. 2:12).

Wisdom in the Bible always has a moral component. Wisdom means moral reasoning and moral behavior. Inasmuch as wisdom is related to godliness, moral reasoning and moral behavior also are related to godliness. The Scriptures tell us that there is a battle between the forces of good and the forces of evil, and the ammunition needed is not physical but mental. "For though we live in the world, we do not wage war as the world does. The weapons we fight with are not the weapons of the world. On the contrary, they have divine power to demolish strongholds. We demolish arguments and every pretension that sets itself up against the knowledge of God, and we take captive every thought to make it obedient to Christ" (2 Cor. 10:3-5).

Moral Potential as a Function of Godliness

The human race as created by God and made in the image of God takes precedence over all other forms of life. Adam and Eve emerged as the culmination of the creative will of God and provided for the Creator a fellowship not shared with any other being. And God was pleased with what he had made, "and it was very good" (Gn. 1:31). William Counts (1973) writes:

> Man is a special creature of God and as such is exalted and significant above all other created beings. The opening

pages of Genesis presents him in all his grandeur. Adam is a sin-free, corruption-free, death-free being. He is the capstone of creation. He alone of all living things is created "in the image of God" (Gen. 1:26-27). He alone is given dominion over all the earth (Gen. 1:28), and has aptly been called "The King of the Earth." (p. 40)

The uniqueness of this species "man" came not only from the ability to communicate with God and to govern the earth but from a potential to be "like God, knowing good and evil" (Gn. 3:5). Moral potential is a function of godliness, of knowing the difference between what is right and what is wrong. God created Adam and Eve with this potential, and the serpent who tempted Eve was aware that it was this characteristic that set humans above animals, that made them like unto God. When Eve was told of this possibility she understandably found it most attractive. But rather than becoming godly by continuous fellowship with God, she was deceived into thinking that moral knowledge could come quickly and that obedience to God's commands was not a prerequisite. The "fall" that resulted is a theme running through both the Old and the New Testaments, and it adversely affects each of us in all aspects of our lives. But it does not mean that in our sinful condition we no longer have worth. Sin did not make man into nonman. The very essence of being human means that the image of God remains and sets people in a higher position than any other creature.

The distinction of being human is most meaningfully represented in the life of Jesus Christ. God, in his infinite love, chose to become one of us, to take on human form, to be truly man even as he is truly God. That the Creator of the universe, the one in whom all things consist (Col. 1:17), should clothe himself in the form of mankind is an amazing fact. But it is precisely because of this that the human race has a dignity and a potential that far exceeds all imagination. The capacity to accept our humanity and the humanity of others is related to God's love for us in that Christ came "in human likeness" (Phil. 2:7).

The enormous worth and importance given to humankind and the moral potential that humans share with no other creature is a consequence not only of the creative will of God and the fact that God chose to be clothed in human form, but also of what is sometimes referred to as the saving will of God or the process of redemption. Counts (1973) emphasizes this point: "But man's importance because he is at the center of God's plan of creation is almost overshadowed because he is also at the center of God's plan of redemption. Man's value is now also calculated in terms of his status as one for whom Christ died" (p. 41).

The Creator is also the Redeemer. The fellowship between God and man that was lost due to disobedience is possible once more. God made the human race for a special reason, and the reason as revealed through the written Word and the Incarnate Word is that we should become more like him. The potential for godliness is through Jesus Christ, and lest anyone think that it is possible to be like God without divine alliance, Jesus set the matter straight in the illustration of the vine and the branches.

> I am the true vine and my Father is the gardener. He cuts off every branch in me that bears no fruit, while every branch that does bear fruit he trims clean so that it will be more fruitful. . . . Remain in me, and I will remain in you. No branch can bear fruit by itself; it must remain in the vine. Neither can you bear fruit unless you remain in me. (Jn. 15:1-4)

Godliness comes to fruition only through unity with Jesus Christ and is not to be confused with the self-deification of the secular humanist. Moral potential is a function of our relationship with God; a God who created us, a God who redeems us. "Those who put themselves in His hands will become perfect, as He is perfect—perfect in love, wisdom, joy, beauty, and immortality" (Lewis, 1960, p. 175).

Even as all the capabilities of the fully functioning adult are wrapped up within the newborn child, all that the Christian can be as an heir of God and a co-heir with Christ (Rom. 8:17) is potentially within him or her upon arrival into God's family. But the process of development takes time. "As newborn babies, crave pure spiritual milk, so that by it you may grow up in your salvation" (1 Pt. 2:2). Peter also admonished those "who through the righteousness of our God and Savior Jesus Christ have received a faith" (2 Pt. 1:1) to "grow in the grace and knowledge of our Lord and Savior Jesus Christ" (3:18). Paul wrote that "we . . . are being transformed into his likeness with ever-increasing glory, which comes from the Lord, who is the Spirit" (2 Cor. 3:18). "Glory" is a term used to set forth the perfection of God. Being in Christ means that we can say with the psalmist, "The Lord will perfect that which concerneth me" (Ps. 138:8 KJV). We are given this ever-increasing glory by virtue of God's purpose for us as part of his church.

Perfection is the ultimate in morality, and this potential for perfection is imputed to us as members of the family of God. Moral potential as a function of godliness has greater meaning than the moral potential postulated by the non-Christian humanist. Terms such as "becoming" and "fulfillment" may be used by both believers and unbelievers, but an understanding of "glory" and "godliness" is reserved for those who are a part of God's adopted family.

Moral Conflict as a Function of Godliness

The Christian is portrayed in Scripture as having two natures: a sinful nature inherited from Adam, and a spiritual nature inherited from Christ. "For if, by the trespass of the one man, death reigned through that one man, how much more will those who receive God's abundant provision of grace and of the gift of righteousness reign in life through the one man, Jesus Christ?" (Rom. 5:17). A conflict is set up between the two natures, a conflict which is made more acute in the light of God's standard of perfection. The apostle Paul struggled with this problem and revealed his anguish in a letter to the Romans. "When I want to do good, evil is right there with me. For in my inner being I delight in God's law; but I see another law at work in the members of my body, waging war against the law of my mind and making me a prisoner of the law of sin at work within my members. What a wretched man I am!" (7:21-24).

Those who do not take the claims of Christ seriously or desire the attributes of godliness would not face such a conflict for they possess only the nature acquired from Adam. Their time and energies are spent doing such natural tasks as making a living, seeking friends and entertainment, and taking each day as it comes along. Because there is little interest in spiritual things, there is no conflict between a nature that desires the world and a nature that desires to be godly. C. S. Lewis (1960) says it this way:

> Christianity tells people to repent and promises them forgiveness. It therefore has nothing (as far as I know) to say to people who do not know they have done anything to repent of and who do not feel that they need any forgiveness. It is after you have realised that there is a real Moral law, and a Power behind the law, and that you have broken that law and put yourself wrong with that Power— it is after all this, and not a moment sooner, that Christianity begins to talk. (pp. 38-39)

The Bible tells us that the human race did not come to its present evil state without help. The serpent who deceived Eve is still busy blinding the eyes of unbelievers (2 Cor. 4:4) and "looking for someone to devour" (1 Pt. 5:8).

It is the art of a superior power to make the evil appear of little consequence, even as good, and so ensnare man in hell's larger revolt against heaven. Because of this demonic dimension of moral evil, man cannot simply undo what he has done; moral evil is beyond him. Neither reformation nor resolution, neither psychiatric adjustment nor social uplift, but only the sovereign promise of a Deliverer, the Seed of the woman who shall bruise the serpent's head (Gen. 3:15), can ever redeem man from his sinful alienation. (Jewett, 1973, p. 236)

Given this truth, it is understandable why Paul and other devout Christians through the ages have had such a spiritual struggle. The closer one is to God, the greater the realization of the forces that would keep one from being godly. Moral conflict comes not to those who are "wicked" but to those who would "live in the Spirit" (Gal. 5:16). Moral conflict is a function of godliness.

In the Old Testament, the children of Israel often faced a decision as to which god they would serve. Jehovah said he would not accept their worship if any other god was included.

Before me no god was formed,
   nor will there be one after me.
I, even I, am the Lord,
   and apart from me there is no savior.
I have revealed and saved and proclaimed—
   I, and not some foreign god among you." (Is. 43:10-12)

Gleason Archer (1973) emphasizes this point.

From the standpoint of Biblical revelation, all deities other than Yahweh Elohim are imaginative products of fallen man's mind, so corrupted by sin as to be unable to see that mere artifacts of metal, wood or stone are utterly devoid of life, reality, or power. They were to be despised as "the work of men's hands," unable to see or hear (Deut. 4:28), and utterly helpless to deliver those who called upon them, since they were devoid of real existence. (p. 265)

Conflict comes when a choice must be made. The children of Israel wanted both the true God, Yahweh, and the false gods of their heathen neighbors. This way they could cover all bases, so to speak. They would have Jehovah's help when necessary, and they would not offend their neighbors. But Joshua, whom God appointed to lead the people after the death of Moses, reminded the Israelites that this proliferation of deities was not acceptable. They would have to decide which way they would go and to whom they would give their allegiance. "Now fear the Lord and serve him with all faithfulness. Throw away the gods your forefathers worshiped beyond the River and in Egypt, and serve the Lord" (Jos. 24:14). Then the people answered, "Far be it from us to forsake the Lord to serve other gods! . . . The Lord drove out before us all the nations, including the Amorites, who lived in the land. We too will serve the Lord, because he is our God" (vv. 16-18). The Amorites did not have a conflict. How they would live and what they would worship was predetermined. They were not called upon to decide between their idols and Jehovah. It was only those whom God called his people, those whom God was dealing with and whom he asked to be "holy" (Dt. 7:6) who experienced the inner turmoil that comes with making such a decision. C. S. Lewis (1960) used the term "dismay" to describe this turmoil.

> Of course, I quite agree that the Christian religion is, in the long run, a thing of unspeakable comfort. But it does not begin in comfort; it begins in the dismay I have been describing, and it is no use at all trying to go on to that comfort without first going through that dismay. In religion, as in war and everything else, comfort is the one thing you cannot get by looking for it. If you look for truth, you may find comfort in the end: If you look for comfort you will not get either comfort or truth—only soft soap and wishful thinking to begin with and, in the end, despair. (p. 39)

And so it has been for generations. Those who know and follow their natural inclinations or subscribe to the lifestyle of those around them do not have to face a decision as to how they will act or who they will be. They know no other way than that which they already adhere to. They can be no one other than who they already are. There may be no Joshua to tell them there is more than one option and that a choice should be made. Or, if a Joshua does appear, the subsequent conflict is often short-lived for they do not understand the true destiny of the human race or the purpose for which it was created. Not experiencing the anguish of the apostle Paul in his struggle between the two natures and not perceiving a righteousness other than their own, they miss the best of what life has to offer. They miss God's plan with all the accompanying benefits. William May (1975) states it this way:

> The Christian knows in a more explicit and formal way what man is meant to be than does the non-Christian, because the incarnation of God's Word . . . illumines the meaning of human existence. But we also know that in order for us to become the kind of being we are meant to be we need help, we need a supportive context. We need what theologians call grace. (pp. 137-138)

Paul found this help—this grace through Jesus Christ. He wrote to the believers in Rome:

> Therefore, there is now no condemnation for those who are in Christ Jesus, because through Christ Jesus the law of the Spirit of life set me free from the law of sin and death. For what the law was powerless to do in that it was weakened by the sinful nature, God did by sending his own Son in the likeness of sinful man to be a sin offering. And so he condemned sin in sinful man, in order that the righteous requirements of the law might be fully met in us, who do not live according to the sinful nature but according to the Spirit. (Rom. 8:1-4)

The sinful nature of the human race is not a popular theme. It seems more kindly to think of others as being affected either by their environment and hence not responsible for their actions, or to look only at the good they display and ignore those actions and statements that would be injurious to them and to others. Some have said that a religion that emphasizes the sinful condition of humanity is pessimistic and morose. But such a charge is a misunderstanding of the Christian message, for the end result is glorious. The contrast of the acts of the sinful nature and the fruits of the Spirit (Gal. 5:13-26) shows the change that can come when a person is willing to go through the conflict necessary to live a life that is pleasing to God.

There are many verses to encourage one to live such a life. Paul wrote that it puts believers in a filial relationship with the Father and entitles them to certain privileges (Rom. 8:14-17). Jude promised that God is able to keep us from falling and will present us "without fault" (Jude 24); and James asked us to *enjoy* the struggle because the end result is well worth it: "Consider it pure joy, my brothers, whenever you face trials of many kinds, because you know that the testing of your faith develops perseverance. Perseverance must finish its work so that you may be mature and complete, not lacking anything" (Jas. 1:2-4).

For the Christian, the major moral conflicts are those between the sinful nature inherited from Adam and the spiritual nature given us as a member of God's family. Without these conflicts we would miss the purpose and meaning of our existence. "And just as we have borne the likeness of the earthly man, so shall we bear the likeness of the man from heaven" (1 Cor. 15:49). For the child of God, moral conflict becomes a function of godliness, a desire to be more like the one who redeemed us.

The Theological Answer

We have seen that morality as godliness includes within its meaning all the emphases of the major psychological

approaches. Rather than centering on only one aspect o
morality, as do the psychological theories, the theological
approach encompasses within its definition all four ways
of looking at morality and consequently provides a more
complete picture. Moral behavior as observed by the learning theorist, the reasoning and judgmental processes of
morality studied by the cognitive psychologist, the moral
potential postulated by the humanist, and the moral conflicts hypothesized by the psychoanalyst are all incorporated into one view—a view that reckons with the fact
that people as created by God are understood, not only by
observing overt actions or measuring intellectual processes or inferring potential or listening to their problems,
but rather by seeing the person as a whole being composed
of all these elements. As a complete creation "fearfully
and wonderfully made" (Ps. 139:14), the totality of what
it means to be moral can be understood only in the context of Christian theology.

As we observed in earlier chapters, studies show inter-
relationships between different expressions of morality;
and correlations have been found between the behavioral,
the judgmental, and the affective. As research studies pro-
liferate and theoretical statements become more sophisticated, we will understand better these relationships.
However, closure is not possible due to the seemingly infinite number of possible combinations of behaviors, stages
of moral reasoning, varying emotions, and types of conflicts. Also, given the diversity of philosophical orientations of the major psychological groups, any final statement
would differ, not only in emphases and terminology but
in conclusions as well. The nature of the intellectual quest
makes the understandable and not necessarily undesirable.
Nevertheless, it is noteworthy that the only view of morality that easily encompasses all the ways of looking at
morality—the behaviorial, the reasoning processes, the potential, and the conflicts—is the one that comes from
Scripture. It is a view of morality as a function of godliness.

If we ask How does the amoral infant become capable

of morality? the theological answer would be: *The amoral infant becomes capable of morality as he or she becomes a more goodly, or godly, individual. Godliness is the culmination of a long process of development of which a birth in God's family, made possible by a relationship with Jesus Christ, is the necessary first step. What one does and thinks, what one can potentially be, and the conflicts that arise in meeting the potential are all part of the journey.* Morality as godliness is the ultimate and most complete definition possible.

Not only does theology, unlike the separate psychologies, present humanity as a totality and emphasize all functions that relate to morality, it also has an adequate basis for determining what is right and what is wrong. As we have seen, the learning approach lacks theoretical roots, humanism means many things to many people, and psychoanalysis often engages in circular reasoning. Cognitive psychology appears to have a philosophical base for its theory of morality, but even this has been questioned by some. Although these psychological views help us to understand what people are like and merit our attention, they do not have as firm a foundation of morality as one based on the Word of God. As J. N. D. Anderson (1972) expresses it:

> The Christian's contention ... is based on the whole body of historical and experimental evidence which has led him to the firm conclusion that Jesus Christ was not merely a supremely wise religious and moral teacher, but the incarnate Son of God—and that the moral teaching which he gave is therefore of unique authority. And he will also point to what are to him, at least, convincing reasons for believing that that teaching has come down to us in a reliable form; that it was, in part, authoritatively explained and applied by the apostles; and that Christ himself bore testimony to the validity of the moral teaching enshrined in the Old Testament. (p. 58)

Problems

Although the scriptural view of morality includes all the functions or ways that morality is expressed, and although it provides a firm basis for a doctrine of morality, this does not mean there are no problems in theology relevant to moral development.

One problem already alluded to is why one person comes to Christ desiring a morality of godliness and another has no interest in spiritual matters. Christian authors have produced numerous books and articles explaining various passages of Scripture and endeavoring to bring together seemingly conflicting views. The age-old controversy between determinism and indeterminism, or what is often referred to as the sovereignty of God and the free will of man, is an issue which if resolved would bring us closer to a solution. Both predestination and freedom of choice are themes running through the Bible, and as such, both must be accepted into one's belief system. According to Richard Bube (1971)

> It is difficult to maintain the balance between these two apparently contradictory biblical affirmations. Historically the pendulum has swung from those who emphasized the sovereign predestination of God at the apparent expense of human responsibility and freedom of choice to those who emphasized the human prerogative at the apparent expense of the trustworthiness and reliability of God's purpose. This concept-pair—sovereignty of God and responsibility of man—has many of the attributes of a complimentary pair. It is not unique in interpretations of the biblical revelation, and such pairs are commonly cited in theological circles as examples of *paradox*. Each of these pairs seems to involve two apparently contradictory concepts to describe reality fully, the cause of the contradictory appearance lying in our inability to pictorialize to an extent required by reality. (pp. 174-175)

This concept-pair, to use Bube's term, is closely related to our discussion of morality and to the basic question of how the amoral infant becomes capable of morality. Does the child turn to God because God has foreordained that he or she will be a part of the family of God, whereas another child who has not been chosen will have no part in the Kingdom? Does each person have an opportunity to accept or reject Christ and therefore have responsibility for the decision made? Could the answer to both of these questions be in the affirmative?

God asked for an offering from Cain and Abel. Each man brought what he had produced, Abel a lamb and Cain some vegetables. The Scriptures tell us that God was pleased with Abel's offering but was not pleased with Cain's offering. Cain was furious, and even though God explained that he could still bring an acceptable offering, the thought of bringing the fruit of his brother's labor rather than of his own was so revolting that he was unwilling to do so.

The theme of this story, that God is pleased with some individuals but not with others, occurs time and again throughout Scripture. Although the details vary with each incidence, the message remains the same. Some are inclined to follow the Lord, to obey his will, to live in a way pleasing to him, to receive his blessing. Others, by temperament, inclination, or choice turn from the way of truth and follow the path that leads to destruction. The question that has been asked for centuries is *why*. Why do some people go one direction and others go another? Does God foreordain whom he will love and whom he will hate? Was Abel's death by the hand of his brother programmed in the mind of God before either boy was born? Did Cain's parents raise him incorrectly by not saying enough about the results of disobedience to God? Did they play favorites as the parents of Esau and Jacob did and thus escalate Cain's jealousy? Or did Cain's angry and jealous behavior stem from a difficult temperament present at birth, which

remained with him for a lifetime? Could it have been
Cain's own volition that made him turn from God? And
if Cain, and Cain alone, was responsible, why did he decide against God rather than coming to him to be blessed
in the same way as was his brother?

The story of Cain and Abel, albeit in modified form, is
repeated in homes today—even in Christian homes. Parents may see some of their children grow in grace and in
the knowledge of God, while other children eating from
the same table and given the same discipline and direction
and love turn from those values that have made the home
secure and in contempt adopt attitudes and behaviors detrimental both to themselves and to others.

If we could answer the question of why there are the
Cains and the Abels even within the same family we would
be closer to an understanding of such basic theological
issues as the origin of evil, the relationship of determinism
and free will, and the interplay of the forces of good and
of evil. We could give a more definite answer as to why
some infants become capable of morality and desire godliness, while other children show no interest in spiritual
matters and refuse to take even the first step in becoming
a member of God's family.

A second problem in viewing morality as godliness is
that the culmination of the desired state will not take
place as long as we are in our mortal bodies. "Neither the
individual Christian character, nor the Christian church
as a whole, attains its destined perfection in this life (Rom.
8:24). This perfection is reached in the world to come
(1 Cor. 13:10)" (Strong, 1953, p. 981). This realization
should bring both hope and humility. Bruce Larson (1978)
speaks of hope.

> Each of us is still an unfinished product, incomplete in
> this world. No one can be taken for granted. To me, this
> view of man is infinitely hopeful and the implications are
> unlimited and dynamic. If I believe that I "have it all"

spiritually and I am still restless, unfulfilled and unhappy, then despair is natural and inevitable. But, if I know that my spiritual life, however radical and sudden its inception, is only a beginning of all that God has in store for me, I live with hope and expect growth. (p. 177)

In Paul's letters we read that "hope that is seen is no hope at all" (Rom. 8:24) and that it is "by faith we eagerly await through the Spirit the righteousness for which we hope" (Gal. 5:5). Much has been written about the Christian's hope in contrast to those who have no hope. Hope serves as a source of comfort (2 Cor. 1:7) and stability (Heb. 6:19) and has a purifying effect on those who claim it (1 Jn. 3:3). Herbert Dymale (1973) draws the following conclusion:

> For evangelical Christians, hope will continue to denote the fulfillment and completion of history when we together with creation will be freed for a glorious new life. This hope is the secret of strength even under the most adverse conditions and is nurtured by God's steadfast love, as promised in the Scriptures, demonstrated in the resurrection of his Son, and experienced by Christians in the past and present. (p. 298)

Even as there is hope, there also must be humility. As we have not yet acquired a morality of godliness, we are not in a position to know the details of what such a life would entail. To date we have only a glimpse of what living a godly life means. A certain reservation is therefore in order when we make up our mental list of dos and don'ts or when we say what one's attitude should be on a certain matter. This humility, this tempering of opinion and withholding of judgment often is difficult to practice. We feel more important, more secure if we speak without hesitation; if we declare that a certain passage of Scripture should be interpreted in a certain way; if we infer that those who would know the will of the Lord will agree with our views.

Teachers and ministers appear to be especially vulnerable to speaking with authority on any topic related to belief or behavior. Perhaps the forceful proclamation of the Word of God on those doctrines clearly revealed in Scripture, such as the divinity of Christ and the inspiration of the Scripture, brings about a behavior pattern that generalizes in everything said or done. One's whole manner of speaking may become a communication to others that the mind of God is known on every matter. That the Scriptures do not speak specifically to some issues is not of great concern to the person who feels increasingly confident that the Bible may be applied directly to every situation. Parishioners also encourage this attitude by asking the minister or evangelist for advice and assuming that one who has been to seminary and educated in the Word is in a position to answer any question. If, rather than speaking with authority, the minister responds to questions with reservation or suggests a variety of options, this may be mistaken by the laity as ignorance of the Bible or as spiritual weakness. The sheep want a shepherd who will lead them, who will tell them what is right and what is wrong. They find it easier to look to someone for advice than to search the Scriptures and spend time in prayer asking for the guidance of the Spirit.

This is not to say that ministers should not be advisers or counselors or that many pastors and Sunday school teachers are not aware of their own shortcomings and in humility ask God for strength and wisdom. But there are those who say they are true to God's Word and in the name of Christ will proclaim on any subject without the slightest hesitation. They may warn their listeners that other ideologies are trying to control people's minds, and even as they speak they seem oblivious to the fact that they are doing precisely the same thing.

Where is the humility, the tempering of judgment, the

willingness to say, "The Bible doesn't answer that question. We must pray and ask God for wisdom"? Those with positions in the church as teachers or ministers must constantly keep in mind that their duty is not to speak authoritatively on every issue but rather to serve the people of God. We must constantly remind ourselves that we do not have all knowledge. As Gary Collins (1977) states:

> The Bible is the Christian's guidebook, but no one individual or group is likely to have a corner on all truth. We are finite, imperfect creatures, whose interpretations are sometimes wrong. So we continue to study the Bible, searching for a clearer view of the written truth, just as we explore the universe scientifically in order better to understand the truths found in nature. (p. 160)

In the devotional book *With Heart and Mind*, Kenneth Pike (1962) says that just as "it is wrong when a tyrant calls himself a benefactor . . . it is wrong when a Christian tries to lord it over the flock." Jesus told his disciples that those who are first shall be last, and the last shall be first (Mt. 19:30). He also told them they were not to judge, or they too would be judged (7:1). "He who has chosen for rewards a status at the top of the Peck Order will be at the bottom of the Christian order" (Pike, 1962, p. 116).

Both hope and humility are in order for the believer until that day when "the righteousness for which we hope" (Gal. 5:5) will be realized and the humility in which we are clothed will give place to exaltation (1 Pt. 5:5-6).

Still a third problem in looking at morality as godliness is knowing to what extent our lives should correspond to the life of Jesus Christ as he walked this earth. Jesus is the only one who was without sin. As no fault was found in him it would seem that those who hold to the historic Christian position would look to Jesus as the ultimate example of moral conduct and to his words as recorded in Scripture as a guide to the most advanced thinking possible in the realm of moral discernment.

It has been argued, however, that Jesus lived in another era and in another culture, and there is little virtue in living life as he did. To dress as he did, speak the language he spoke, to abide by the customs of first-century Palestine would not profit anyone today. Nor would it even be possible to do many of the deeds that Jesus did; everyone cannot be an itinerant preacher or heal the sick or raise the dead. But even if we agree that walking in his steps does not mean a literal execution of his actions or saying the same words to our acquaintances that he said to his, this does not negate the fact that Jesus' life and teachings are just as relevant to problems today as they were almost two thousand years ago. If we are to be used by him we must be aware of what he did and what he said to meet those problems. As John Stott (1970) expresses it:

> Christianity is Christ Himself, together with the prophetic and apostolic witness to Christ. It depends on a historical event (the birth, life, death, resurrection, ascension and Spirit-gift of Jesus) and on a historical testimony by eyewitnesses. In the nature of the case neither the event nor the witness can be changed or superseded. We live in the twentieth century, but we are tethered to the first. What Jesus Christ said and did was unique and final. (p. 37)

In 1896, Charles Sheldon began writing a story entitled *In His Steps*, which he read a chapter at a time to the young people in his congregation in Topeka, Kansas. By 1935 it had been printed in twenty-one languages and by sixty-six different publishers. A single printer sold over three million copies of one edition in the streets of London. This highly readable book is a fictional account of what happened in one congregation when the pastor and members pledged not to do anything for a year without first asking the question, "What would Jesus do?" and then endeavoring to follow Jesus as closely as each one knew how no matter what the result might be.

They soon discovered that doing what Jesus would do made them distinctly unpopular with employers, family, and friends. Opportunities for career and advancement were adversely affected and loss of employment and property resulted. Yet, even with the reverses, each one who was willing to follow "in his steps" found that God's grace was sufficient. Together they had the joy of relieving human suffering, winning souls to Christ, and encouraging other Christians to new discipleships. A miraculous change came into their own lives and to the congregation as a whole.

Few Christians have ever tried to do what Sheldon's characters did. Is this because the cost would be too great; one's lifestyle would have to change; and friends would question stability and judgment? Perhaps so. But if we call ourselves Christians, that is, followers of Christ, we must accept the invitation to go with him, to learn his teachings, to let him lead us, if not literally, at least in spirit and in truth. Even as he humbled himself (Phil. 2:8), we are to humble ourselves (Jas. 4:10). As he became a servant (Phil. 2:7), we, too, must serve (Gal. 5:13). As he cared for the poor and helpless (Lk. 4:18), we also must seek to help those who can do nothing for us in return (14:13-14). As he confronted the religious leaders who reinterpreted the Scripture to their own advantage (11:46), we may be called upon to confront religious leaders today who seize upon certain biblical passages that put them in positions of authority. Jesus judged those who were not used to being judged (11:43) and did not condemn those whom society said should be condemned (Jn. 8:11). He scorned those at the top of the social ladder but was kind and gentle to those at the bottom. He turned the world upside down, reversed the normal way of thinking, and was a constant enigma even to those who knew him best. "I have come down from heaven not to do my will but to do the will of him who sent me" (6:38), he told the people. Those in power came to hate him and tried to have him killed, and those who were powerless and without status grew to love him and with changed lives worshiped him. He said this is the way it would be—that in the Kingdom the last would be first and the first would be last (Mt. 19:30).

As we have seen, morality as godliness poses several problems. One is why one person is drawn to Christ while another person is not. The theological concept of determinism and free-will provides a basis for discussion of this question. Another concern is that even though we are to be holy and blameless, such a desired state will not be attained until we see him and are made in his likeness. Both hope and humility must sustain us until that time when we will be made perfect. A third problem is that of knowing in what ways our lives should correspond to the life of Jesus Christ. We are so much a part of the present world that it is difficult to determine how our lives should differ from Jesus' life because our culture today is different and how our lives should be the same as his because some behaviors should never change. Should we follow him in any kind of literal sense, or should we be like him only in applying the principles he taught? The mandates of discipleship and evangelism are inexorably linked to the answer.

Although we continue to search for the answers, the problems need not overwhelm us. God in his graciousness has provided for us until that time when the revelation will be forthcoming. There need be no loss of fellowship as we join God's creation waiting to be "liberated from its bondage . . . and brought into the glorious freedom . . . of God" (Rom. 8:21). The gap between where we *are* and where we *should be*—and one day *will be*—is bridged by a declaration of God, a statement that we have been justified. By faith in Christ's sacrificial death we are declared righteous and treated as such. Acquitted of any transgression, we can come freely into his presence knowing that we have found acceptance. Although lacking the morality of godliness, we are given the same status as though we were indeed godly. The doctrine of justification speaks of imputed righteousness so that rather than being crippled by guilt we can relate to God and to others openly and with confidence, doing the work he would have us do.

Practical Applications

Application to the Home

The morality of godliness is a foreign concept in the homes of many people. Time is taken up with a myriad of responsibilities, with places to go and things to do—all of which crowd out a concern to be holy. Observation might bring one to the conclusion that Christian homes are not very different than the homes of unbelievers. The world in which we and our children live is a world of television, stereos, radios, and movies; a world of scouts, basketball games, music lessons, and school; a world of bicycles, mopeds, motorcycles, and cars; a world of clothes, food, parties, and the constant display of sex in advertised products. It is also a world of work and responsibility, of caring for our homes and our families. And if we take our jobs seriously, more and more demands are placed upon us, leaving less and less time to consider the things of the Lord. Unless we as Christians make a concerted effort to plan our lives so that God is at the center of all we do, and unless there is active consideration as to how to break into the routine of each day so that we will not forget God, morality as related to godliness will remain foreign to us.

Jehovah explained to the Israelites how they were to remember the Lord, and although these directions came many centuries ago, they are as appropriate today as they were then.

> Love the Lord your God with all your heart and with all your soul and with all your strength. These commandments that I give you today are to be upon your hearts. Impress them on your children. Talk about them when you sit at home and when you walk along the road, when you lie down and when you get up. Tie them as symbols on your hands and bind them on your foreheads. Write them on the doorframes of your houses and on your gates. (Dt. 6:5-9)

These were not mere suggestions given to Jewish parents at that time. Rather they were commandments to be enacted. One *must* love the Lord with one's whole being and observe the "decrees and laws." Parents *must* impress upon their children the importance of knowing the law and obeying that law in order that they, too, would serve God. This was to be done as naturally and regularly as getting up in the morning, sitting in one's house, walking from place to place, or lying down at night. And the tangible reminders were to be all around them—on the gates and on the doorframes, and even on their hands and their foreheads.

Parents also were instructed to give personal testimony to their children, recounting God's goodness in the past and reiterating his promises for the future.

> When your son asks you, "What is the meaning of the stipulations, decrees and laws the Lord our God has commanded you?" tell him: "We were slaves of Pharaoh in Egypt, but the Lord brought us out of Egypt with a mighty hand . . . brought us out from there to bring us in and give us the land that he promised to our forefathers. The Lord commanded us to obey all these decrees and to fear the Lord our God, so that we might always prosper and be kept alive, as is the case today. And if we are careful to obey all this law before the Lord our God, as he has commanded us, that will be our righteousness." (Dt. 6:20-25)

These directions involve far more than bringing young children to the church to be baptized or dedicated, or taking them to Sunday school so they can be taught the Word. Although giving public testimony that one desires to rear the child in the nurture and admonition of the Lord (Eph. 6:4 KJV) and getting the child accustomed to meeting with other believers on a regular basis (Heb. 10:25) are important, these acts constitute only a small part of responsible Christian parenting.[1] Parents have a greater influence on the young child than those outside the family, so it is understandable that the charge is given to them to instruct the child in the things of the Lord.

> The Judaeo-Christian perspective sees the circle of covenanted care as the right setting for the nurture of children into commitment to what is right and true about life. Parents are parents mainly to take care of the child's initiation into faith and morals. And the two go together. Morality has to do with what is truly important and right about life, and what is important about life depends on what is true about God. So, the heart of family is the parents' calling to pass on the moral and spiritual reality of life to their children. (Smedes, 1983, p. 80)

Because of the dependence of children on their parents, children come to identify with their parents and to imitate their actions, attitudes, and beliefs. They try to be like them because this makes them feel more grown up, and growing up is something every child wants to do, as we have noted. The child learns by observation and identification, by copying parental behavior, and by incorporating parental values. This means that parents who believe in Jesus Christ and in the Scriptures and who communicate this by their actions and speech often will have the satisfaction of seeing the young child adopt similar actions and speech, and may even have the joy of leading the child to faith in Christ.

Although the dependency - identification - conformity

pattern is typical, there are some children who do not adhere to this progression. The cause has sometimes been attributed to bad blood or bad seed, especially if there appears to be no noticeable environmental deficit. Or the term *black sheep of the family* is used, indicating that the child has gone in a very different direction than that considered appropriate by the family. Studies reveal, however, that children are born with different temperaments (Chess, Thomas, & Birch, 1965). Babies with difficult temperaments usually have a high activity level, are irregular in biological functions, dislike any new situation, and are negative in mood. They may fuss or cry for the first two years, have temper tantrums the next two years, and resist any attempts thereafter to become acculturated. The high activity level may translate into hyperactivity, a major reason for children doing poorly in school.

> Of all the children who are a challenge to raise, few are more exasperating and demanding than the hyperactive child. Unfortunately, not only are the parents struggling, so is the child.
>
> This particular child may span the extremes between being easily distracted because of a short attention span to being totally uncontrollable. He may not complete his work. He may not remember what you said to him three minutes ago. He may not follow rules and regulations. He may fail to manifest certain kinds of affectionate behavior. He may be impulsive, easily upset, loud, disorderly, and disorganized (untucked shirts, unzipped zippers). . . . It's amazing to me how tolerant and understanding people can be of parents of the handicapped, yet unbelievably intolerant of parents of the hyperactive. (Swindoll, 1977, pp. 136-137)

Whether hyperactivity results from inherited characteristics, congenital problems, or birth trauma is not known. But we do know that neither the parent nor the child should be blamed. Hyperactivity is no respecter of families, and Christian parents may have a hyperactive child.

Such a child may not respond to directions or adopt the values of the parents or see the importance of becoming a Christian, not because the parents have been negligent, but because the child finds it difficult to respond to directions from anyone or to adopt the values of the larger society or to see the importance of accepting any ideology that would bring his or her life into a conformity that cannot be appreciated or understood.

This is not to say there is no hope for this child, but it does mean that the amount of effort put forth by the parents will be far greater than for the other children in the family, and the end result may not be all that is desired. Both patience and firmness are required as well as medical and psychological help for the more extreme cases. Parents also may have to turn a deaf ear to well-meaning friends and relatives who advocate a back-to-the-woodshed approach to keep the child in line or imply that something must be very wrong with those who raise such a child.

Another deficit that appears to be linked to inadequate moral development, at least in some children, is dyslexia. As with hyperactivity, more males are affected than females. The literal meaning of the term *dyslexia* is "word blindness." This does not mean that the child cannot see words, for his vision appears to be normal, but he cannot retain an image of words or other patterns in his mind or recall them when appropriate to do so. The neurological dysfunctioning, which is probably present at birth, may manifest itself in poor coordination, learning to talk late, not understanding directions, and not remembering how to get from one place to another unless the same route is taken each time. When the child starts school the problem becomes more noticeable because each time the child sees a word it may look different to him, and he therefore cannot remember it to read it the next time he sees it or to spell it if he is asked to put it in writing. Although care is taken not to label children who have learning disorders, a term such as *dyslexia* is reserved for those who have average or above average intelligence, have an adequate home life, do not have visual or auditory impairments that would keep them from seeing or hearing, and are not diagnosed as emotionally disturbed. Yet, they are unable to learn in school commensurate with their abilities and backgrounds.

Some of the most noted figures in history such as Leonardo da Vinci (Aaron & Clouse, 1982), Hans Christian Anderson, Thomas Edison, Woodrow Wilson, and Nelson Rockefeller are said to have been dyslexic. But the usual pattern is not fame; it is more apt to be delinquency (Berman & Siegal, 1976; Rubenstein, 1982). It is difficult to say whether this propensity toward wrongdoing is because the problems of patterning may be manifested, not only in the printed word, but in social and interpersonal relationships as well, and the young person is not able to understand the consequences of certain behaviors before he has acted (Johnson & Myklebust, 1967); or whether it is a reaction to the frustration and anger he has experienced in a futile attempt to do what others can do so easily.

Although some dyslexic children do not manifest these behavioral problems, many do. The Christian parent needs to understand that having such a child should not arouse feelings of guilt. Neither the parent nor the child is responsible for anomalies present at birth. Although remediation is obviously desirable, neither the hard approach of punishing the child for not doing better nor the soft approach of trying to protect the child seems to be helpful. Meeting with other parents who have children with the same problems, lobbying for educational programs within the schools to help the learning disabled child, and becoming familiar with research methods that are used in controlled situations and can be duplicated in the home may provide some relief.[2]

The concern we face here is that both parent and child need help and understanding from the Christian community so that this child in time will identify with other Christians and will accept as his or her own the values and morality that come from being a part of God's adopted family. This is less apt to occur if the people of God that the child knows within the church are judgmental because he or she does not fit their stereotype of what a child should be or are quick to state what they would do if they were the parents to get the child "straightened out."

Both Cain and Esau showed some of the traits we now link with hyperactivity, and had they been expected to perform in the type of social and educational setting that children are in today, they might have displayed other forms of learning difficulties as well. When we as Christian parents dedicate a child to the Lord we want to have some assurance that, even though by temperament that child may have great difficulty in following the normal dependency-identification-conformity pattern and by disposition could easily be a Cain or an Esau, he or she will, with special help and understanding and prayer, come to know the Lord and the morality of godliness, and in turn will rear the next generation in the "training and instruction of the Lord" (Eph. 6:4).

A problem in many Christian families is not knowing how to handle the growing independence of the teenager. As a son or daughter approaches adolescence, the parents may develop an uncomfortable feeling, realizing that their influence is decreasing while the influence of peers is increasing. Careful scrutiny of the child's friends and regulation of the child's time and activities become more difficult and may be met with hostile reactions. If the child does get into trouble, the first thing parents usually do is to blame his or her friends.

> Parents are apt to blame their adolescent privately, but in public they place the blame on unfortunate group associations. They explain their failure by the fact that the son or daughter got into bad company, but it is probably

> more correct to say that something within the personality—impulsiveness, antisocial conduct, defective control or judgment ability, lack of foresight, shallow self-centeredness, failure to respect the rights of others, failure to profit by experience—is at the basis, and these characteristics cause the delinquent adolescent to seek out his own level. He invites the bad companions by that within himself which attracts them. Like a magnet he draws them out of the atmosphere. (Cramer, 1959, p. 167)

Whether the child has delinquent tendencies or not, the desire of Christian parents is that the son or daughter will become an adult who is moral, not only in the societal meaning of the term, but in the Christian sense of being what God would have him or her to be. But we may ask: What can we do? Are there any guidelines that will help us as parents in this endeavor? Is the only answer to commit our children to the Lord, to hope and pray that God will take care of the matter in his own way? Some may feel this is the way of faith, but most of us are unwilling to adopt this approach exclusively. We feel strongly that our children are a charge to keep and that we must plan carefully to help them remain in the faith.

One alternative is to guard our children against environmental situations that would lead them from the truth. In this approach, children while still young are surrounded by others who share the parents' beliefs. This means that the social life of the child is kept within the church or church-related groups. It also means that the child will attend a Christian day school where teachers reinforce the views taught in the home. There is little reason under these circumstances for children to question the truths of Scripture. Those who care for them physically and emotionally and those who teach them, all hold similar religious convictions. All information they acquire adds to their faith. Truth is built upon truth year after year until, it is hoped, the whole structure stands firm and solid, and the parent feels confident that the child has been well grounded in the faith.

Other parents feel that even as Jesus prayed for his disciples, saying to the Father, "My prayer is not that you take them out of the world but that you protect them from the evil one" (Jn. 17:15), children from Christian homes should not be taken out of the world with no opportunity to evaluate the Christian position within the total context of that world. Children should have friends who are not of the faith as well as those who are, and it is best that they attend the state-supported neighborhood school. They must, of course, be kept from the evil one, but this is better accomplished by giving them the opportunity and ammunition they need to recognize and attack evil as they meet it. The research of social psychologists (Lumsdaine & Janis, 1953; McGuire, 1962; McGuire & Papageorgis, 1961) on the effects of one-sided versus two-sided communications as these relate to attitude stability and attitude change lends credence to this alternative.

The method calls for giving small doses of an opposing view and then helping the receiver counteract this view. This has sometimes been referred to as inoculation. If arguments against a belief are presented in weakened form, resistance will be built to future attacks on that belief. Two essential aspects of this process are that children be aware that Christian beliefs may be subject to attack and that they be given the opportunity to develop defenses against the attack. Children raised in an environment in which they have not had the opportunity to build up these defenses may succumb when placed in a situation in which "disease" thrives.

This means that Christian parents must talk with their children about those views learned from unbelievers in a social or educational context that are not in accord with Christian doctrine and conviction. The presentation of opposing arguments in a context that rejects them weakens the future effectiveness of the arguments and gives children practice in weighing the issues so that they are in a position to do this more effectively in the years to come. Children cannot be protected forever, and they need to know how to cope when they are on their own.

It is difficult to say whether protection or inoculation is more effective. One cannot go back and try the other way with the same child to see which is better. Maybe one child thrives with one method, another child with the other. Probably some of both approaches is needed. Thus, we as Christian parents will commit our children to the Lord. We will protect them from much of the contaminating influence of the world, give them practice in recognizing and combatting opposing views, and provide a model of Christian behavior so that the dependency-identification-conformity pattern will take its desired course. Our prayer for our children parallels the prayer of our Savior for us as he spoke to the Father:

> I have revealed you to those whom you gave me. . . . They were yours, you gave them to me. . . . While I was with them, I protected them and kept them safe by that name you gave me. . . . Sanctify them by the truth; your word is truth. As you sent me into the world, I have sent them into the world. . . . I have made you known to them and will continue to make you known in order that the love you have for me may be in them. (Jn. 17:6, 12, 17, 18, 26)

Application to the School

If a morality of godliness is a foreign concept in many homes, it is even more alien in our schools. One cannot speak of godliness in the Judeo-Christian sense without theological dogma, and advocating adherence to a specific doctrine is not in keeping with the Supreme Court ruling of the separation of church and state. As public education is paid for by public funds, and taxpayers represent a wide range of religious beliefs, it is understood that the teaching of any particular faith cannot be allowed in a state-supported institution.

The first amendment stipulates that "Congress shall make no law . . . abridging the freedom of speech, or of the press; or the right of the people . . . to petition the Government for a redress of grievances." This provides the primary legal basis for pressure groups, for those wishing to change conditions within the schools. Such groups are important in America and often are motivated by racial, political, and religious concerns. Racial pressure from organizations such as the National Association for the Advancement of Colored People generally comes from those of a more liberal persuasion, whereas political pressures emanate from both the left and the right. Religious groups in the past have run the gamut from liberal to conservative, and in the 70s and early 80s the influence of the Moral Majority, an organization conservative in both politics and religion, became well known and was espoused by such preachers as Jerry Falwell, James Robison, and Tim LaHaye. Often referred to as the Christian Right in newspapers and magazines, the group was strongly pro-defense, anti-communist, anti–Equal Rights Amendment, pro-family, pro–school prayer, and anti-homosexual. To their way of thinking, a conservative theological position mandated a conservative political stance. They said that parents rather than the government should be in control of the schools, and they voiced their opposition to the creation of the new Department of Education on the grounds that the department might result in increased legislation.

Groups such as the Moral Majority have gained in power and influence understandably in light of the fact that most decisions of the courts have supported the liberal position, leaving those who take a conservative view to feel they are not fairly represented. Some say that the establishment of Christian schools is a necessary consequence of leaving

God out of the educational process. Since public schools do not include Bible reading, prayer, and the teaching of Christian principles, and since lobbying for such changes has had a limited effect, another alternative must be found. Our children are our most precious possession; they are our contribution to the future, and we must give them the best. If we want them to become godly men and women, a morality based on godliness must be stressed in the educational program as well as in the home.

The concept of Christian schools is not a new idea. Such schools have had a long and noble tradition, and those associated with them have often kept them operating at great personal sacrifice. But the number and nature of these schools appear to change from time to time. In 1980 the *Phi Delta Kappan* reported that the "most rapidly growing segment of American elementary and secondary education is that of private Protestant fundamentalist schools." This is in contrast to a 22.7 percent overall decline in nonpublic schools between 1965 and 1975, a decline "due almost entirely to a decrease in enrollment of Roman Catholic schools" (Nordin and Turner, 1980, p. 391). More recently, *USA Today* in a cover story on Christian schools stated that "enrollment at schools affiliated with religious denominations other than Catholic rose 22 percent between 1980 and 1983." In 1985 there were "about 12,000 fundamentalist and evangelical Christian schools enrolling about one million children" (Zigli, 1985, p. 1-2).

Some Christian schools are academically poor, substituting programmed instructional materials for well-trained teachers and hindering the creative abilities of students by establishing a strict authoritarian atmosphere. Other Christian schools are well administered. Teachers with strong credentials are employed; there is sufficient funding for a broad-based program, and a knowledge of children's needs and developmental stages is taken into consideration. But whether the Christian school is weak or strong, deficient or adequate, the reasons for enrolling the child are often the same. Parents want the child to be taught according to biblical principles and to learn that the beginning of wisdom is "the fear of the Lord" (Pr. 1:7), that creation rather than evolution gives understanding to our origin, that salvation comes through Jesus Christ and not by a deification of humankind, that morality is more than getting along with others but relates to the nature of who God is in himself. Although for some parents the more immediate reason may be to conform to the prevailing attitudes of others within the local church or to remove their children from racially integrated classes, spare them long bus rides, or keep them from courses in sex education, for other parents it is far more. The decision is made only after carefully looking at the alternative, prayerfully asking for divine guidance, and then coming to the conclusion that their child is better off in a Christian atmosphere at school as well as at home.

There are other Christians, just as devout and just as concerned for the spiritual well-being of their children, who do not advocate the establishment of church-related schools. Not only do they feel it is not best for their own children, but they take the position that any weakening of the public schools will be damaging to the whole society, and Christians are obligated to be "salt," using their influence to bring about needed changes within the state supported system. "What kind of society will we have if all Christians abandon the public schools?" is the question asked by William Willimon (1978) in an article in *Christianity Today*. Willimon also expressed other concerns about the establishment of private education, such as the drain on the family budget and less money given to the church; the lack of regard for children other than our own as though our only obligation is to ourselves and our immediate families; the seeming fear that "immorality, scientism, and materialism are stronger than our Gospel" (p. 966) which places little faith in the power of God; and the abandonment of our obligation as Christian parents to teach our children the things of the Lord by having them taught at school instead.

Good people disagree. What seems so right to one parent seems so wrong to another. And the children of both kinds of parents, the ones who believe in the Christian school and the ones who do not, turn out to be fine Christian men and women—even as other children from both kinds of homes reject the faith and turn from their Christian heritage. And yet, both kinds of parents would agree on the importance of the teacher in the classroom. The values expressed, the vocabulary used, the actions displayed by the teacher are as important as anything the child is specifically taught. The establishment of parochial schools, both Catholic and Protestant, has not only been for the purpose of religious instruction but also to provide for the child a learning environment where teachers exemplify the attitudes and the behaviors condoned by the supporting group. Parents feel more comfortable if the child's teacher shares their Christian convictions. If they cannot afford to send the child to a church-related school or if one is not available or if they feel it best to place the child in the public school; knowing that the child's teacher is of the same faith gives a measure of encouragement even though this faith cannot be specifically taught in the classroom.

There is little specific information on the religious beliefs of teachers, but for the most part they represent the more conservative element of our society. Paul Kurtz (1976) observes that, "The majority of the more than two million school teachers identify with the Judeo-Christian tradition" (p. 4). In a study conducted at a midwestern state university (Clouse, 1974), approximately six out of ten prospective elementary and secondary teachers either agreed or strongly agreed with statements concerning the divinity of Christ (59 percent), the inspiration of the Bible in its first writing (58 percent), and the eternal life of the believer (57 percent). Although further studies would need to be conducted to determine if similar responses would be obtained from prospective teachers in private colleges or in other geographical areas, there is reason to question Tim LaHaye's (1980) statement that, "If a survey were made of atheists in this country, it is probable that a large percentage of them are employed in education, where they have access to the minds of our young" (p. 182). One would not expect teachers to differ greatly from respondents to a 1982 Gallup poll in which it was found that 60 percent believed in "the divinity of Jesus Christ" and 79 percent believed that the Bible is "the actual word of God" or "the inspired word of God" (Gallup, 1982).

This is not to say that large numbers of teachers live holy lives or understand a morality based on godliness. They, like us, do not always live up to the light within. But it does mean that many of those who "have access to the minds of our young" share our Christian faith. Even though at times we may feel as did Elijah, that we are the only ones who have not bowed the knee to Baal (Rom. 11:4), God shows us, even as he did Elijah, that this is far from the truth. With us are a host who also follow that greatest of all teachers, our Lord Jesus Christ, and some of this number are themselves teachers—teachers in both the private and the public sectors who join us in our efforts for a moral society. God has not left himself without a witness, and the witness is in the schools as well as in other segments of the society.

Application to the Church

The church was established by God for the communion of saints and is bonded together by the relationship of each saint with the Lord. We are members of this great family by adoption, a process made possible through a relationship with the only begotten Son, Jesus Christ. Becoming an heir of God and a co-heir with Christ puts us in union with all other believers, and this large body composed of all the faithful, both past and present, constitutes a cohesive group or community sealed by the Spirit of God, upon which the image of God is conferred. To be called a saint or member of this family makes a statement as to our standing and rights before God as a consequence of adoption and is in no way related to any worth or merit apart from this kinship.

Jesus is the focal point of the church, and a number of analogies are used in Scripture to show the special relationship of Christ to the believer. He is the bridegroom, and the church is the bride. He told his disciples that he was going to prepare a home and would come again so that one day they would live with him forever. He is the Good Shepherd who cares for the sheep and will look for the one who has gone astray. He is the Door by which no entrance can be made except through him. He is the Vine, and believers are the branches that can bear no fruit unless they remain in him. He is the Bread of Life that gives nourishment to all who will eat. He is the Cornerstone of the house of God built upon a foundation laid by the prophets and the apostles. He is the Judge who will determine at the last day who, among all who claim to be his followers, are really a part of the great body of believers called the church.

As all matters within the church relate to Jesus Christ, any discussion of morality as applied to the church must of necessity show morality as a function of godliness. Believers are to deal with each other even as Christ dealt with those who followed him. He is our example, and we are admonished to follow in his steps. Even as Jesus loved those he met and healed those who needed his touch, the church must show itself to be a loving, healing community. Love is the basis of fellowship. It is greater than faith, it is greater than hope. It is patient and kind, not self-seeking or easily angered. Nor does it keep a record of wrongs. Love protects, perseveres, and lasts forever (1 Cor.

13). Differences in faith or doctrine have divided many congregations, and varying interpretations of hope or eschatology have produced uncharitable attitudes, but love covers over a multitude of sins, and for this reason the people of God are admonished to "love each other deeply" (1 Pt. 4:8).

Love does not exist in a vacuum like some pleasant thought we have when we think of others. Rather, it is expressed in ways that contribute to the well-being of those we come in contact with. Love means offering hospitality, sharing our gifts and competencies, and serving with the strength God has given us. The principal reason for showing this love is to glorify God (1 Pt. 4:9-11). The apostle John records a time when Jesus prayed to the Father and asked that the love God had for him be given to the church so that believers could share the same unity that Christ had with the Father. "May they be brought to complete unity to let the world know that you sent me and have loved them even as you have loved me" (Jn. 17:23). Love produces unity because it does not let differences in perception and interpretation destroy the communion the saints enjoy with one another and with their Lord. Love brings us closer together and glorifies the Father. A morality of godliness must have love as its basis, for God is love (I Jn. 4:16).

A special mandate was given to care for those no one else cared for, to love those no one else loved, to understand the worth of every living soul regardless of appearance or competencies. Those members of society who had the least to offer politically or economically were the very ones Jesus attended to. The demoniac, the lepers, the blind, the "publicans and sinners," the woman at the well, and the children—all were beneficiaries of his love. He was gracious and kind when others would have scorned or ignored. He talked, touched, healed, and promised the Kingdom. Everyone who met him was changed in some way by the encounter. He told those who wanted to follow him and be his disciples that they, too, must do those things he had done. They were to touch the infirm and heal the sick and provide for the poor and welcome the company of small children.

Luke, the physician, records an encounter Jesus had with "an expert in the law" (Lk. 10:25) who asked what he must do to inherit eternal life. Jesus, in turn, asked the lawyer how he interpreted the law, and the man replied, "Love the Lord your God . . . and love your neighbor as yourself." Then the lawyer asked Jesus for his interpretation of the meaning of the term "neighbor," and Jesus answered with a story about a man who was robbed and beaten as he traveled from Jerusalem to Jericho. The story included a priest who saw the man half-dead along the road but did not bother to help, a Levite who also passed by on the other side and did not offer aid, and a Samaritan who stopped, bound the man's wounds, placed him on his donkey, and paid for his care in the next town. The good Samaritan had become a neighbor to someone he had never seen before. Jesus told the lawyer to go and do likewise.

We know the Jews despised the Samaritans, calling them half-breeds and saying they did not worship in the proper place, and so it is doubtful that the priest, the Levite, or the man who had been robbed and beaten would have associated with the Samaritan; and living near him as a neighbor would have been out of the question. But Jesus was saying that a neighbor is anyone we come in contact with at any time and at any place; and the one who shares love, time, and sustenance, even with those who would despise him, is the one who is truly a neighbor and has God's promise of eternal life.

This expression of concern is what God wants of his church. Those who are disliked may love and help those who are favored, just as those who are more fortunate may love and share with those who have little. Each one is a member of the body and has much to contribute to the rest. In this way there is mutual caring and healing. Paternalism has no place in this setting, and a condescending attitude is unacceptable. "The eye cannot say to the hand, 'I don't need you!' And the head cannot say to the feet, 'I don't need you!' . . . God has combined the members of the body . . . so that there should be no division in the body, but that its parts should have equal concern for each other. If one part suffers, every part suffers with it; if one part is honored, every part rejoices with it" (1 Cor. 12:21, 24-26). Morality within the church is a function of godliness, and to be godly is to suffer and rejoice with one another even as Jesus did, to stop and take the time to bind the wounds, to offer aid, to pay the price for the healing of others.

Not only is the church to follow Jesus' example by being a loving, healing community, it is also to obey his command to witness to others. "Therefore go and make disciples of all nations, baptizing them in the name of the Father and of the Son and of the Holy Spirit, and teaching them to obey everything I have commanded you. And surely I will be with you always, to the very end of the age" (Mt. 28:19-20). As Jesus bore witness of the Father who had sent him, the church must bear witness of Jesus Christ and of his saving power. Those who are not yet believers are to be treated as potential brothers and sisters in Christ.

> The primary purpose of the church in relation to the world is evangelization. The confusion of the present church concerning her purpose is difficult to understand in light of the unequivocal command of the Lord to the church. . . . According to the instruction of the Scriptures and the example of the early church in Acts, the witness of the church is accomplished through the total life of the members of the church, both in word and act, as a community and as individuals. (Saucy, 1972, p. 91)

If witnessing "is accomplished through the total life of the members of the church, both in word and act, as a community and as individuals," it behooves us to make witnessing as natural as anything else that we do. In the enjoyable and readable book *Out of the Salt-Shaker*, Rebecca Pippert (1979) speaks of evangelism as a way of life. Christians are the salt of the earth, but we must get out of the salt-shaker and into the world where the salt will do some good.

> Our problem in evangelism is not that we don't have enough information—it is that we don't know how to be ourselves. We forget we are called to be witnesses to what we have seen and known, not to what we don't know. The key is authenticity and obedience, not a doctorate in theology. We haven't grasped that it really is okay for us to be who we are, when we are with non-Christians, even if we don't have all the answers to their questions or if our knowledge of Scripture is limited. (p. 24)

Pippert recounts the characteristics of our Lord as he walked this earth and shows that we, too, must develop the same qualities to be effective witnesses. Jesus was a remarkably open man who did not think it unspiritual to share his physical needs or ask for support during emotional stress. He was a delightful person to be with for he enjoyed people and liked to go to parties and weddings. He was approachable and established rapport with all types of people. He was compassionate, caring deeply for others. He was perceptive, having an extraordinary ability to sense the unspoken need or question. And at times he was quite exasperating to the religious leaders who were offended by his lifestyle and to the disciples who expected him to bring in the Kingdom.

The Scriptures tell us that many of the early Christians obeyed the command to be witnesses. "The Lord added to their number daily those who were being saved" (Acts 2:47). As persecution came and the faithful were scattered to other towns and cities to avoid imprisonment or death, they continued to obey the command, and in this way the message of Jesus Christ was proclaimed "in Jerusalem, and in all Judea and Samaria, and to the ends of the earth" (1:8).

The mandate to witness, to tell others of Jesus Christ, to fulfill the Great Commission of adding others to that great body we call the church, is given to us just as surely as it was given to those who saw and heard Jesus almost two thousand years ago. Realizing that God is not willing that any should perish, that he would have all come to repentance, and that he has chosen us as his instruments in proclaiming the good news, we are awed by the task before us. It changes the whole perspective of our relations to others, of how we are to follow Christ, and of what it means to be obedient to his will.

The church, then, is a healing, caring community and a witness to those without the fold. Furthermore, it is a worshiping body of believers looking forward to the coming of the Lord, to that day when "we shall be like him, for we shall see him as he is" (1 Jn. 3:2). "The creation waits in eager expectation for the sons of God to be revealed. . . . We ourselves . . . wait eagerly for our adoption as sons" (Rom. 8:19, 23). And as we wait for that glorious day, we "worship by the spirit of God" and "glory in Christ Jesus" (Phil. 3:3).

> Worship is the submission of all our nature to God. It is the quickening of conscience by his holiness; the nourishment of mind with his truth; the purifying of imagination by his beauty; the opening of the heart to his love; the surrender of will to his purpose—and all of this gathered up in adoration, the most selfless emotion of which our nature is capable and therefore the chief remedy for that self-centredness which is our original sin and the source of all actual sin. (Temple, 1939, p. 68)

Thus we have seen that morality as godliness, when applied to the church, is demonstrated in loving and caring for one another, witnessing to those who are still outside the family of God, and worshiping the Creator and Redeemer who will come again and make us like unto himself. Morality for the Christian includes all aspects of moral development: our behavior, our thoughts and the words that express the thoughts, the potential that we have in Christ Jesus, and the promise of victory over the conflicts that we experience in our walk with God. As we "grow up into him" (Eph. 4:15), we learn the meaning of godliness, and godliness is the ultimate and complete expression of what it means to be moral.

Notes

1. It is not the purpose of this book to go into detail on the subject of child rearing, so the reader is referred to the following excellent sources: Collins, G. R. (1980). *Christian counseling: A comprehensive guide.* Part 4, Developmental family issues. Waco, TX: Word Books. Narramore, B. (1979). *Parenting with love and limits.* Grand Rapids: Zondervan.

2. Parental tutoring of the dyslexic child is generally not recommended. The result may be "harmful in that it leads to anger, frustration, friction, negativism, loss of motivation and considerable family disorganization and conflict" (p. 482 of "Parental Tutoring in Childhood Dyslexia" by D. K. Worden and R. D. Snyder, 1969, in *Journal of Learning Disabilities*). Yet, parents feel they should do something to help the child who is facing learning difficulties. Typical problems faced by the dyslexic and suggestions for parents are given in the following sources: Brown, G. W. (1969). Suggestions for parents. *Journal of Learning Disabilities, 2,* 97-106. Golick, M. (1968). A parents' guide to learning problems. *Journal of Learning Disabilities, 1,* 366-77. Johnson, D. J., & Myklebust, H. R. (1967). *Learning disabilities: Educational principles and practices.* New York: Grune & Stratton.

References

Aaron, P. G., & Clouse, R. G. (1982). Freud's psychohistory of Leonardo da Vinci: A matter of being right or left. *The Journal of Interdisciplinary History, 13*(1), 1-16.

Anderson, J. N. D. (1972). *Morality, law and grace.* London: Tyndale.

Archer, G. L. (1973). Gods, false. In C. F. H. Henry (Ed.), *Baker's dictionary of Christian ethics* (pp. 265-66). Grand Rapids: Baker.

Berman, A., & Siegal, A. W. (1976). Adaptive and learning skills in juvenile delinquents: A neuropsychological analysis. *Journal of Learning Disabilities, 9,* 583-90.

Bloesch, D. G. (1978). *Essentials of evangelical theology: Vol. 1. God, authority, & salvation.* San Francisco: Harper & Row.

Bube, R. H. (1971). *The human quest: A new look at science and Christian faith.* Waco, TX: Word Books.

Carter, J. D., & Narramore, B. (1979). *The integration of psychology and theology.* Grand Rapids: Zondervan.

Chess, S., Thomas, A., & Birch, H. G. (1965). *Your child is a person: A psychological approach to parenthood without guilt.* New York: Viking.

Clark, G. H. (1973). Image of God. In C. F. H. Henry (Ed.), *Baker's dictionary of Christian ethics* (pp. 312-13). Grand Rapids: Baker.

Clouse, B. (1974, Summer). Religious beliefs of prospective teachers at a midwestern state university. *Midwest Education Review, 6,* 19-25.

Collins, G. R. (1977). *The rebuilding of psychology.* Wheaton: Tyndale House.

Counts, W. M. (1973). The nature of man and the Christian's self-esteem. *Journal of Psychology and Theology, 1*(1), 38-44.

Cramer, R. L. (1959). *The psychology of Jesus and mental health.* Grand Rapids: Zondervan.

Dymale, H. R. (1973). Hope. In C. F. H. Henry (Ed.), *Baker's dictionary of Christian ethics* (p. 298). Grand Rapids: Baker.

Henry, C. F. H. (1982). *God, revelation, and authority: Vol. 5. God who stands and stays,* Part 1. Waco, TX: Word Books.

Jewett, P. K. (1973). Fall of man. In C. F. H. Henry (Ed.), *Baker's dictionary of Christian ethics* (pp. 235-37). Grand Rapids: Baker.

Johnson, D. J., & Myklebust, H. R. (1967). *Learning disabilities: Educational principles and practices.* New York: Grune & Stratton.

Kurtz, P. (1976). The attack on secular humanism. *The Humanist, 36*(4), 4-5.

LaHaye, T. F. (1980). *The battle for the mind.* Old Tappan, NJ: Fleming H. Revell.

Larson, B. (1978). *The meaning and mystery of being human*. Waco, TX: Word Books.

Lewis, C. S. (1960). *Mere Christianity*. New York: Macmillan.

Lumsdaine, A. A., & Janis, I. L. (1953). Resistance to "counterpropaganda" produced by one-sided and two-sided "propaganda" presentations. *Public Opinion Quarterly, 17*, 311-18.

May W. E. (1975). *Becoming human: An invitation to Christian ethics*. Dayton, OH: Pflaum.

McGuire, W. J. (1962). Persistence of the resistance to persuasion induced by various types of prior belief defenses. *Journal of Abnormal and Social Psychology, 64*, 241-48.

McGuire, W. J., & Papageorgis, D. (1961). The relative efficacy of various types of prior belief-defense in producing immunity against persuasion. *Journal of Abnormal and Social Psychology, 62*, 327-37.

Meyer, D. G. (1978). *The human puzzle*. New York: Harper & Row.

Murphy, R. (1978). Moral formation. In F. Bockle & J. M. Pohier (Eds.), *Moral formation and Christianity* (pp. 29-36). New York: Seabury.

Nordin, V. D., & Turner, W. L. (1980). More than segregation academies: The growing Protestant fundamentalist schools. *Phi Delta Kappan, 61*, 391-94.

Packer, J. I. (1981). *God's words: Studies of key Bible themes*. Downers Grove,IL: Inter-Varsity.

Pike, K. L. (1962). *With heart and mind: A personal synthesis of scholarship and devotion*. Grand Rapids: Wm. B. Eerdmans.

Pippert, R. M. (1979). *Out of the salt-shaker & into the world: Evangelism as a way of life*. Downers Grove, IL: Inter-Varsity.

Ramm, B. L. (1971). *The right, the good and the happy*. Waco, TX: Word Books.

Religion in America. (1982, June-July). *The Gallup Report*, pp. 1-185, (Nos. 201-2).

Rigali, N. (1978). Christ and morality. In F. Bockle & J. M. Pohier (Eds.), *Moral formation and Christianity* (pp. 12-20). New York: Seabury.

Robinson, W. C. (1962). Predestination. In C. F. H. Henry (Ed.), *Basic Christian Doctrines* (pp. 49-55). New York: Holt, Rinehart, and Winston.

Rubenstein, C. (1982). Oops—learning disabilities do get boys in trouble. *Psychology Today, 16*(5), 74-5.

Saucy, R. L. (1972). *The church in God's program*. Chicago: Moody.

Sheldon, C. M. (1896). *In his steps.* New York: Grosset & Dunlap.

Smedes, L. B. (1983). *Mere morality: What God expects from ordinary people.* Grand Rapids: Wm. B. Eerdmans.

Stott, J. R. W. (1970). *Christ the controversialist.* London: Billing & Sons.

————. (1972). *Your mind matters.* London: Inter-Varsity.

————. (1975). *Balanced Christianity.* Downers Grove, IL: Inter-Varsity.

Strong, A. H. (1953). *Systematic theology.* Philadelphia: Judson.

Swindoll, C. R. (1977). *You and your child.* Nashville: Thomas Nelson.

Temple, W. (1939). *Readings in St. John's gospel.* London: St. Martin's.

Willimon, W. H. (1978). Should churches buy into the education business? *Christianity Today, 22,* 964-67.

Zigli, B. (1985, January 22). The boom in born-again education. *USA Today,* Sec. D, pp. 1-2.

Index

application of, 200–204; theological application of, 218
Values education, 203–4
Values & Faith: Activities for Family and Church Groups (Larson and Larson), 196, 206
Valuing programs, 203–4. *See also* Values clarification
Verbal habit-families, 40
Vicarious learning, 88–89. *See also* Social learning
Vitz, Paul: on humanistic selfism, 185
Vos, A.: on behaviorism, 92

Waite, R. R., 275
Ward, Ted: on family and development of moral reasoning, 132
Watson, John B., 38, 39, 46, 62
Welch, I. D.: on scientific method of humanism, 186
Wertheimer, Max: on humanism, 182; on psychotherapy, 219 n. 3
Whatever Became of Sin? (Menninger), 283
Whelan, M.: on cognitive conflicts among church members, 146; on parenting, 133
Wiggin, E. E.: on Accelerated Christian Education (ACE) programs, 83

Willimon, William: on Christian versus public schools, 344
Wilson, Bill, 86
Wilson, G. D.: on psychoanalysis as science, 253
Wilson, J.: on justice, 124
Windmiller, M.: on punishment, 129
Winokur, M.: on psychoanalysis, 247
Wisdom, 312
With Heart and Mind (Pike), 328
Witness, command to, 350–52
Woodward, K. L.: on parenting, 131
Woodward, W. R., 94 n
Worship: meaning of, 352; moral behavior and, 304, 317–18
Wright, Derek: on Freud, 257–58
Wundt, Wilhelm, 31
Wynn, J. C.: on moral action versus judgment, 121; on morality as calling, 154

Yablonsky, L., 198
Your Mind Matters (Stott), 311

Zigli, B.: on Christian schools, 343
Zilboorg, Gregory: on Christian conscience versus superego, 292–93
Ziv, A., 134–35; on guilt, 124